DATE DUE

OC 2 0 '99			
NO 1 0 '99			
DE 1 '99			
~~MY 25 '00~~			
~~AP 16 '01~~			
~~MY 22 '01~~			
~~JY 6 '01~~			
~~DE 21 02~~			
~~FE 13 03~~			
AP 21 04			
JE 1 0			

DEMCO 38-296

RECONSTRUCTING GENDER IN THE MIDDLE EAST

Tradition, Identity, and Power

Fatma Müge Göçek and
Shiva Balaghi, Editors

COLUMBIA UNIVERSITY PRESS
NEW YORK

Columbia University Press
New York   Chichester, West Sussex
Copyright © 1994 Columbia University Press

Data

adition, identity, and

ghi, editors.

0–231–10123–6 (pa) :

1. Women–Middle East–Social conditions. 2. Sex role–Middle
East. 3. Power (Social sciences) 4. Middle East–Social life and
customs. I. Göçek, Fatma Müge. II. Balaghi, Shiva
HQ1726.5.R43 1995
305.42'0956–dc20   94-3733
                                                              CIP

Farzaneh Milani, "Neotraditionalism in the Poetry of Simin Behbahani" is a revised
version of a chapter in *Veils and Words: The Emerging Voices of Iranian Women Writers*
by Farzaneh Milani. Reprinted by permission of Syracuse University Press.

CHAPTER 12.
Anton Shammas, "Arab Male, Hebrew Female: The Lure of Metaphors" copyright
© 1994 Anton Shammas. This chapter is printed with his express approval and
permission. All requests to quote or reprint any portion of chapter 12 should be
directed to Mr. Shammas.

∞

Casebound editions of Columbia University Press books are printed on
permanent and durable acid-free paper.

Printed in the United States of America

c 10 9 8 7 6 5 4 3 2 1
p 10 9 8 7 6 5 4 3 2 1

for our mothers

CONTENTS

ABOUT THE CONTRIBUTORS   ix

ACKNOWLEDGMENTS   xi

INTRODUCTION
Reconstructing Gender in the Middle East Through Voice and Experience   *1*
Fatma Müge Göçek and Shiva Balaghi

Part one   The Reconstruction of Tradition

1. *Gender, Tradition, and History*   23
   Juan R. I. Cole

2. *Neotraditionalism in the Poetry of Simin Behbahani*   30
   Farzaneh Milani

3. *Wearing the Hijab in Contemporary Morocco: Choice and Identity*   40
   Leila Hessini

4. *Turkish Women and the Republican Reconstruction of Tradition*   57
   Zehra F. Arat

Part two   The Reconstruction of Identity

5. *Gender, Identity, and Anthropology*   81
   Ruth Behar

6. *Notes from the Village: On the Ethnographic Construction of Women in Iran*   85
   Erika Friedl

7. *Women's Movement of the 1980s in Turkey: Radical Outcome of Liberal Kemalism?*   100
   Yeşim Arat

8. *Growing up in Israel: A Personal Perspective*   113
   Rachel Persico

9. *Coming of Age in Occupied Palestine: Engendering the Intifada*   123
   Leila Hudson

Part three The Reconstruction of Power

10. *"Metaphors Can Kill": Gender, Power, and the Field of the Literary*   *139*
Anne Herrmann

11. *Arab Women Arab Wars*   *144*
Miriam Cooke

12. *Arab Male, Hebrew Female: The Lure of Metaphors*   *167*
Anton Shammas

13. *Where Has All the Power Gone? Women and Politics in Popular Quarters of Cairo*   *174*
Diane Singerman

14. *Keeping It in the Family: Gender and Conflict in Moroccan Arabic Proverbs*   *201*
Elizabeth M. Bergman

BIBLIOGRAPHY   219

About the Contributors

Yeşim Arat is Associate Professor of Political Science at Boğaziçi University in Turkey. Her publications include *The Patriarchal Paradox: Women Politicians in Turkey* (1989).

Zehra F. Arat is Associate Professor of Political Science at the State University of New York at Purchase. Her most recent publications include *Democracy and Human Rights in Developing Countries* (1991).

Shiva Balaghi completed her Ph.D. in Middle Eastern History at the University of Michigan in 1994. Her dissertation is entitled *Nationalism and Cultural Production in Iran, 1848–1906*. She is currently a Research Associate at the International Institute and a Visiting Assistant Professor in the Department of Near Eastern Studies at the University of Michigan.

Ruth Behar is Professor of Anthropology at the University of Michigan. A MacArthur Fellow, she has published *Translated Woman: Crossing the Border with Esperanza's Story* (1986), and *Santa Maria del Monte: The Presence of the Past in a Spanish Village* (1989).

Elizabeth M. Bergman teaches Arabic at Columbia University. Her dissertation at the University of Michigan focused on Arabic linguistics.

Juan R. I. Cole is Associate Professor of History at the University of Michigan. His publications include *Colonialism and Revolution in the Middle East: Social and Cultural Origins of Egypt's Urabi Movement* (1993), and *Roots of North Indian Shi'ism in Iran and Iraq: Religion and State in Awadh, 1722–1859* (1988).

Miriam Cooke is Associate Professor of Arabic Literature at Duke University. She has published numerous books, including *The Anatomy of an Egyptian Intellectual, Yahya Haqqi* (1984), *War's Other Voices: Women Writers on the Lebanese Civil War* (1987), and *Gendering War Talk* (1993).

Erika Friedl is Associate Professor of Anthropology at Western Michigan University. Her most recent works include *Women of Deh Koh: Stories from Iran* (1989).

Fatma Müge Göçek is Assistant Professor of Sociology at the University of Michigan. Her publications include *East Encounters West* (1987), and *The Rise of the Bourgeoisie, Demise of Empire: Ottoman Westernization and Social Change* (1995).

Anne Herrmann is Associate Professor of English Language and Literature and Women's Studies at the University of Michigan. She has published *The Dialogic and Difference: "an/other woman" in Virginia Woolf and Christa Wolf* (1989).

Leila Hessini works with the Ford Foundation in Egypt. A Former Fulbright Fellow in Morocco, she holds degrees from the School of Public Health and the Center for Middle East and North African Studies at the University of Michigan.

Leila Hudson is a Ph.D. candidate in the Anthropology-History Program at the University of Michigan. She is currently conducting research on her dissertation on public and private culture and politics in twentieth century Syria.

Farzaneh Milani is Associate Professor of Persian and Women's Studies at the University of Virginia. Her most recent book is *Veils and Words: The Emerging Voices of Iranian Women Writers* (1992).

Rachel Persico was born and raised on an Israeli kibbutz and had a long career in television and film. She holds an M.S. degree in Clinical Psychology and lives in Ann Arbor, Michigan.

Anton Shammas, a Palestinian novelist and essayist who writes in Hebrew and English, is affiliated with the Program in Comparative Literature at the University of Michigan.

Diane Singerman is Assistant Professor in the Department of Government's School of Public Affairs of the American University. Her forthcoming book is entitled *Avenues of Participation: Family, Politics and Networks in Urban Quarters in Cairo* (1995).

Acknowledgments

"Opening an inquiry from the standpoint of women means accepting our ineluctable embeddedness in the same world as is the object of our inquiry" Dorothy Smith (1987: 127) reminds us. Indeed, as this volume also attests, our work is always informed by our experiences. Our collaborative efforts in studying gender issues in the Middle East began in 1989 when one of us, Müge Göçek, was teaching a course at the University of Michigan called "Women and Islam: A Sociological Perspective" and the other, Shiva Balaghi, was a student in that class. The enrollment of the class was rather evenly divided between those who focused on gender issues and those who studied the Middle East. As the semester progressed, some of the basic problematics of studying women in the Middle Eastern context began to emerge. Issues such as the universality of women's rights versus cultural relativism were debated.

After the semester was over, the two of us decided to try to continue the debates among a larger audience. With a grant from the Women's Studies Program, we organized a biweekly discussion group. This interdisciplinary group of faculty and graduate students focused on a different discipline or genre each session. So a student specializing in Turkish and Arabic comparative literature discussed the images of prostitutes in Turkish novels. An anthropologist discussed the work of Lila Abu-Lughod within the context of feminist anthropology. Another student working on women and labor in Bangladesh talked about the importance of looking at gender and Islam from the perspective of South Asia as well. Hence we shared ideas, works in progress, and debated different approaches to studying gender and society in the Middle East.

Energized by the lively nature of the discussion group, we decided to edit a volume on the topic that would further explore the particular issues that kept surfacing in our debates. As part of that project, we organized the conference "Gender and Society in the Middle East" in September 1991 which was sponsored by several different departments and programs at the University of Michigan. Most of the papers of that conference appear in this volume. A few of the essays in the collection were commissioned after the conference took place.

We would like to acknowledge the immense support we received from various units of the University of Michigan. Specifically, we would like to thank the Departments of History and Sociology, the Comparative Study of Social Transformation Program, the Horace H. Rackham School of Graduate Studies, the Office of International Academic Affairs, the Center for Middle Eastern and North African Studies, and the Women's Studies Program of the University of Michigan for making the conference and the volume possible. Abigail Stewart, the Director of the Women's Studies Program, gave us her enthusiastic support for which we are grateful. Ernest McCarus gave excellent advice; this project benefitted greatly from his Directorship of the Center for Middle East and North African Studies. Kenneth W. Stein offered valuable suggestion for organizing the volume for which we are especially grateful. In organizing the discussion group, Michael Bonner was most helpful. Pat Preston's heroic efforts were crucial as we completed the manuscript, and we owe her much gratitude. We would also like to thank all our contributors for their enthusiastic support and diligence throughout the completion of the volume. We have learned from their scholarship and working with them made this experience memorable for both of us. Many of us have travelled throughout the preparation of this volume to such places as Turkey, Egypt, Iran, Syria, Germany, England, France, and Mexico. Shiva Balaghi would like to thank her dissertation committee, especially her advisors K. Allin Luther and Geoff Eley, who have patiently supported this distraction.

The Columbia University Press has been a pleasure to work with. The astute comments of their readers, the punctuality and care with which the press approached the volume has much improved it. We would like to thank, in particular, Kate Wittenberg, the editor we worked with at Columbia University Press, for her enthusiasm, encouragement and support.

INTRODUCTION

Reconstructing Gender in the Middle East Through Voice and Experience

Fatma Müge Göçek
and Shiva Balaghi

How can one study the relationship between gender and society without marginalizing the experience of women? How is such a study possible, particularly in the context of the Middle Eastern Studies, which has a long tradition of such marginalization embedded in its scholarship? These were the two main questions we asked when putting together this volume. Third-World discourse, particularly in its recent subaltern form, focuses on the colonial and neocolonial hegemony of the West over the translation and interpretation of the Third-World. Feminist discourse similarly emphasizes the patriarchal hegemony over our current explanations of gender relations. How can we liberate ourselves from this dual hegemony? We argue that voice and experience can be utilized as the two conceptual parameters to recapture the agency of the hegemonized. Voice advantages the text of the subject over that of the interpreter; experience assigns primacy to the way the subject and the interpreter actively and consciously give meaning and mediate their social realities.

Yet the current literature also alerts us to the ambiguities embedded within the concepts of voice and experience, especially in delineating their epistemological boundaries. We therefore selected three dimensions that have been most frequently used to convey "Middle Eastern" social realities: tradition, identity, and power. Explorations of the different aspects of tradition, identity, and power, we assumed, would bring us closer to the voices and experiences embedded within. We sought out authors who employed interdisciplinary perspectives in reconstructing the matrix of voices and experiences, both of their subjects and themselves. We are all keenly aware that the scholar always serves in a

mediating role; the processes of selecting, editing, translating, and collat-
ing texts are no longer assumed to be transparent. Each author inscribes
their own experiences onto those of the subjects.' That interchange is
further mediated by the paradigms of the author's discipline.

We also thought it important to create a dialogue between scholars
who study women in the Middle East and scholars in other disciplines.
Creating a dialogue is a necessary step toward more fully integrating the
field of Women's Studies. We therefore asked a historian, an anthropologist, and a literary scholar to comment on the essays in the volume.
These three scholars are uniquely equipped to examine the essays'
implications for the fields in which they are placed. The richly textured
articles and the commentaries fully convey the complex gender-society
relationship in the Middle East.

Drawing the Theoretical Framework Around Gender, Voice and Experience

We base our definition of gender on the one offered by Joan Scott as
"the social organization of sexual difference."[1] She argues that the
interpretive mechanism behind social organization is where sexual difference acquires a socially or culturally constructed meaning. While this
meaning situates itself in societal processes, it diffuses into power relations. In addition, it guides the identity formation of the subjective male
and female. We agree that the construction of gender contains within it
significant elements that, when juxtaposed against societal processes,
informs us about the nature of tradition, identity formation and power
relations inherent in the society. Within feminist theory, however, there
is still a debate over the mode in which to approach gender and society.
Joan Scott and other poststructuralist theorists tell us to study meaning-
laden texts and to then deconstruct them to arrive at the contours of the
power relations which inform and define the gender division.[2] The critics
of poststructuralism and feminist standpoint theorists, such as Dorothy
Smith, urge us to look beyond the textual surface at the social experience
of the real, not textually created, people.[3] After a brief review of the
main theoretical issues in this debate, to unfold the social construction
and reproduction of gender in the Middle East, we concur with Dorothy
Smith and Sandra Harding that we need to bring in the standpoint of
women by relying on their experience and everyday practice. At the
same time, we note the conceptual difficulties in defining the boundaries

of the term "gender" by focusing on tradition, identity, and power as the three main dimensions of experience.

Our theoretical emphasis on voice and experience is based on the feminist standpoint theorists' critiques of the social sciences and the theorists' attempts to "produce less partial, less distorted beliefs through acknowledging their historicity and social construction."[4] Dorothy Smith comments on the contemporary woman's "bifurcated consciousness between home and work"[5] to demonstrate the explanatory power of social relations over behavior or institutions. She differs from poststructuralists by going beyond "the textual surface of discourse"[6] to the actualities of women's lives. In doing so, she advocates the method of experience which "returns us always to the subject active in remembering, in finding out how to speak from the actualities of her life, bringing forward what was into a speaking for which she is the only authority."[7] We therefore embed our analysis in women's realities.

Dorothy Smith also does not overlook the coercive power contained in the "relations of ruling," specifically in bureaucracies, administration, management, professional organizations, and the media. This organization of power is known as "patriarchy," a term identifying both the personal and the public relations of power. But how to counter this patriarchy? Unlike the postructuralists, Smith presents an alternative: she proposes to focus on the everyday world as a problematic, "where the everyday world is taken to be the various and different matrices of experience—the place from within which the consciousness of the knower begins."[8] Such a stand addresses the issue of subjectivity and unifies the perspectives of the researcher and her subject; it also unites the experiences of all women, Western or Third World, without privileging one over the other. Yet the experiences of Western and Third World women assume different shapes because of large-scale social processes. Dorothy Smith's willingness to go back to these structures and institutions (yet this time from the standpoint of women's experience) unites the textual with the real. She quotes[9] Marx and Engels's description of social relations to justify this move; she notes how Marx and Engels argue in the *German Ideology* that "individuals always proceeded, and always proceed, from themselves. Their relations are the relations of their real life process. How does it happen that their relations assume an independent existence over them? And that the forces of their own life become superior to them? " Smith tells us that only by combining the personal with the societal can we understand how, and more importantly, *why* this happens. Only then we can free ourselves. By bringing together the everyday level (as feminist theory suggests) and the underlying relations (as Marx and Engels propose), Smith captures the allegedly elusive agency of the oppressed, the hegemonized.

Yet it is hard to capture this experience. The work that first alerts us to the problems embedded in the concept of experience is E. P. Thompson's account of the formation of the British working class.[10] Reacting to deductive and deterministic concepts of class formation, E.P. Thompson argued that the British working class emerged as a product of the complex and contradictory experience of the workers, and that the class could not be understood apart from that experience. At the same time, he encountered the problem of differentiating the actual events from the way people construed them.[11] The actual experience and its mediation through the narrative were hard to separate without references to the structures or dimensions (such as tradition, identity, and power) that constrained experience. Both Joan Scott and Kathleen Jones further criticize the concept of experience[12] in terms of gender analysis. Scott argues that the concept "weakens the critical thrust of histories of difference. . . [since it] takes as self-evident the identities of those whose experience is being documented and thus naturalizes their difference."[13] Rather than giving agency to women, experience can end up reproducing and legitimating the ideological systems that constrain women. Jones adds that "by privileging women's experiences as the unproblematic foundation of authoritative readings of women's lives, we do not automatically challenge the masterfulness of a discourse. Rather, we substitute one sovereign regime of truth for another."[14] Hence, experience does not automatically give agency to women. In addition, experience contains within it the experiences of both the scholar and his/her subject—a mix that is epistemologically hard to separate.

Even so, experience is very powerful as a concept. How then to use the concept of experience without suffering from its limitations? Joan Scott suggests that we bring "historicity" to experience.[15] In this volume, we argue that we need to contextualize experience spatially (in our case, to the Middle East) and epistemologically (to the dimensions of tradition, identity, and power). Why do we give prevalence to these three dimensions over others, however? We argue that these dimensions contain the epistemological tensions in the study of the Third-World. Tradition, identity, and power are either used hegemonically by the West, or critically by the Third-World; both positions stifle the agency of the actors involved. Hence we can only reconstruct gender and society in the

Middle East by problematizing these dimensions and reconceptualizing experience through them.

Tradition

Studies on the Third World often contain Orientalist elements that treat social processes in cultures and societies other than itself as static or, at best, as derivative. Such studies place a particularly strong emphasis on tradition to demonstrate this immutability.[16] Raymond Williams reveals the forces that necessitate tradition: tradition legitimates hegemony and reproduces power. Tradition, as an active, coopting agent, is the most powerful means of societal incorporation.[17] Hence we can conjecture that in order to justify its own hegemony, the Western gaze needed to portray tradition in the Middle East as an immutable force.

How can we detect and eradicate this negative portrayal of tradition embedded in the Western gaze? Gayatri Spivak explains that Western knowledge privileges the Western observer or the Western-trained native at the expense of her subject. She states that "the theoretical problems only relate to the person who knows. The person who *knows* has all of the problems of selfhood. The person who is *known* somehow seems not to have a problematic self."[18] Also, the West "reactively homogenizes the Third-World ... their literatures ... thus subalternizing Third-World material."[19] It is this untexturedness of the subject that reifies and legitimates the conceptualization of tradition as an immutable force. Only by conveying the complexities of Third-World women's subjectivities, and by problematizing the depiction of tradition as constricting can we start to reverse Western hegemony. Such an endeavor is not easy, however.

Even the well-meaning attempts of feminists to study Third-World women have reproduced Western hegemony. For example, the production of the "Third-World Woman" as a singular monolithic subject in some Western feminist texts has recreated the colonial discourse based on inequality.[20] In addition, Western feminist discourse assumes Third-World women as a coherent, already constituted group. This assumption defines Third-World women as subjects outside of social relations, instead of looking at the way women are constituted through them. Such an approach to Third-World women erases "all marginal and resistant modes of experiences."[21] By doing so, one runs the risk of reproducing male oppression, rather than eliminating it. Aihwa Ong concurs with Mohanty in her criticism as she points out that "when feminists look overseas, they frequently establish *their* authority on the backs of non-Western women, determining for them the meanings and goals of their lives. If from the feminist perspective there can be no shared experience with persons who stand for the Other, the claim to a common kinship with non-Western women is at best, tenuous, at worst, nonexistent." [22]

What is to be done? How can one escape the double-bind when one finds herself located between the First and Third Worlds, and between her own reality and that of her subject? Ong believes that feminists should keep their vigilance on behalf of their oppressed First and Third-World sisters "because of their privileged positions as members of hegemonic powers." [23] Therefore, she advocates that feminists exploit the hegemonic elements embedded in their Western position on behalf of the Third World. Mohanty is more explicit in her recommendations when she suggests context-specific differentiated analysis to overcome this double-bind in studying the Third World. [24] It is Gayatri Spivak who goes beyond identity politics of the Third World to advise that "let us at least situate [our practice] at the moment, let us be more vigilant about our own practice and use it as much as we can rather than make the totally counter-productive gesture if repudiating it." [25] Indeed, we can only assess how our position within society influences our perspective on gender. Such an assessment of "position" can only become analytically rigorous if we bring in the underlying social relations of material existence, however. These relations reveal the coercive power behind the gender categories, and we can reach them by analyzing women's experiences. Hence, this volume emphasizes experience, both of the researcher and her subject. Once the negative portrayal of tradition is eliminated within this experience (as our authors do in this volume), tradition in Middle Eastern gender relations emerges as a vibrant force that can be both constricting and liberating.

Identity

The dual experience of the researcher and her subject problematizes the dimension of identity. The tension within the concept of identity lies in its homogenization of the identity of the researcher with her subject, and of the subject with that of the community within which she is embedded. Carolyn Steedman notes, for example, how the contemporary assessments of women's self-worth are closely connected to the capacity to produce and retain an identity. She emphasizes that "a modern identity, constructed through the process of identification, is at once a claim for absolute sameness, a coincidence and matching with the desired object, group, or person (perhaps a historical identity located on the historical past) and, at the same time, in the enclosed circuit of meaning, it is a process of individuation, the modern making of individuality and a unique personality."[26] It is this tension between the social definition and the individual meaning of identity that makes its analysis so difficult. In addition, one can question the wisdom of assigning primacy to identity and to the politics that surround it. As Stuart Hall aptly notes "looking at new conceptions of identity requires us also to look at re-definitions of the forms of politics which follow from that: the politics of difference, the politics of self-reflexivity, a politics that is open to contingency but still able to act. The politics of infinite dispersal is the politics of no action at all; and one can get into that from [the] best of all possible motives."[27] Identity, like tradition, can thus be used to immobilize and stifle the agency of the oppressed—rather than to liberate them. We consequently need to problematize the concept of identity to reveal its liberating potential.

At the same time, how constructive is it for feminists to assign primacy to their gender identity? Many scholars concur that such boundaries are disadvantageous to the feminist cause in the long run. If one exclusively focuses on gender identity, one would stifle gender rather than liberate it. As with tradition, Mary Louise Adams suggests that in a system of oppression, the focus on identity can deflect political vision as it prevents one from forming an image of the self in relation to others.[28] Laura Downs agrees that emphasis on identity implies an "assertion of the inaccessibility of one's experience,"[29] and adds that this, at best, is a fragmenting approach. Chandra Mohanty points out that focusing solely on gender identity and "completely bypassing social class and ethnic identities"[30] reinforces the binary divisions between men and women. The problem becomes even more complicated in non-Western contexts, where gender identity contains a mosaic of indigenous elements as well as those imposed by Western ideas and institutions. Unlike the West, Third-World gender identity includes strong nationalist and anticolonial elements.[31] We therefore approach and problematize identity as a general concept, without limiting it to the gender experience.

Methodologically, then, how do we study identity that becomes an even more complex term in the non-Western context?[32] It is not sufficient to make excursions into the construction of discourses and social practices of identity; such an approach systematically avoids questions of causation and change. In using this approach, everything becomes a representation of itself; however, the origins, causes, and consequences of power disappear. As Laura Downs notes, "the fragmentation of both subject and knowledge, and the concomitant collapse of social relations into textual ones, diverts our attention from the operation of power in the social sphere, fixing our gaze upon its metaphorical manifestations in the text."[33] By focusing exclusively on discursive power, we fail to analyze the other component of power, the coercive. As David Scobey argues, we need to once more unite "that which constitutes with that which determines."[34] As poststructuralism blurs the distinction between textual and social relations, it leaves no room for change or for other paths to women's subjectivity. In studying the connection between gender and power, we therefore take care to emphasize the Middle Eastern women's presence and vibrancy in literature, metaphors, and wars, as they construct and alter their space within society.

Power

Simone de Beauvoir noted early in the women's movement that the personal was the political; the most intimate, the most private social relations—and ones therefore most hidden from public scrutiny—contained elements that subjugated women.[35] One could argue that it was this statement, potentially subjecting all social relations to criticism, that revolutionized the study of gender. The analyses of Michel Foucault and Pierre Bourdieu then mapped the undertheorized domain of the private, and, by implication, the feminine. Foucault's emphasis on the "technologies of power" revealed the knowledge and practice intimately associated in the creation of social relations based on domination.[36] His definition of power[37] captured the significance of relations, processes, supports, and strategies that obfuscate hegemony. Pierre Bourdieu underlined another source of power within which women's participation was much more readily visible. He went beyond the economic and political power to define "symbolic" power located within language, religion, education, art, and ideology. As a mode of analysis, symbolic power underlined relations and advocated a "relational mode of thinking,"[38] rather than a publicly defined institutional mode that disadvantaged women.

It is this problematization and redefinition of "social" power by Bourdieu and Foucault that opens a participatory space for the experiences of *all* the oppressed, including women. By redefining power we escape the immutability of tradition and the convolution of identity to arrive at a more "real" experience. Only then can we see patterns of resistance, vibrancy, activity in the domains of the long imagined immutability of the Middle East and its gender relations.

Situating the Volume among the Multiplicity of Voices in the Field

In developing our approach to the field, we have benefited from the rapidly increasing number of studies on gender in the Middle East. The origins of these studies can be traced to the 1970s and to the women's movement, which drew attention to the marginalization of women within most academic fields. The field of Middle Eastern studies was no exception. Until recently, many scholars considered a discussion of sexuality and morality within the context of Islam adequate to describe *and* explain women's lives in the Middle East. Time was frozen in such discussions; changes in women's circumstances over generations, through the decades, even over centuries, were often overlooked. According to these accounts, the situation of women in the Middle East remained immutable, even as their societies were beginning to be transformed. With the rise of the women's movement, scholars became increasingly aware of the importance of studying Middle Eastern women. In their attempts to present a more integrated view of Middle Eastern society, some scholars began to seek out the voices of the women and to acknowledge their role in constructing their own experiences. How did this transformation occur?

In 1977, Elizabeth Fernea and Basima Qattan Bezirgan published *Middle Eastern Women Speak,* a volume on women in the Middle East.[39] Fernea and Bezirgan underlined the absence of substantive studies on Middle Eastern women, pointing out that neither the ethnographers nor the Orientalists had offered adequate approaches. The problem of textuality was central to the study of Middle Eastern women, for one of the main claims for writing women out of major studies of the region's society and history was the paucity of textual sources. At this stage, then, the main task was to lay this myth to rest. In order to do so, Fernea and Bezirgan turned to Middle Eastern women. They presented the volume as a forum in which "Middle Eastern women speak for themselves . . . [through] autobiographical and biographical statements by and about Middle Eastern women."[40] In 1985, Elizabeth Fernea edited another collection which featured Middle Eastern women speaking for themselves. *Women and Family in the Middle East: New Voices of Change*[41] was a "progress report" about the status of women. Fernea emphasized the multiplicity of the voices she heard—the voices of "anxiety, optimism, fear, hope, bitterness" as women continued to "ask questions and conscientiously struggle to improve not only their situation but that of their societies as a whole." [42] Another pioneering study on Middle Eastern women was a collection of essays edited by Lois Beck and Nikki Keddie, *Women in the Muslim World* [43] which addressed another major issue. The study of women in the Third World, wrote Keddie and Beck, was "sparked largely, in the West at least, by movements here for the liberation of women." [44] The volume examined women's issues in a variety of contexts using a range of methodologies. Together, these early exploratory works legitimized the field of gender studies in the Middle East.

In 1990, Margot Badran and Miriam Cooke edited an anthology entitled *Opening the Gates: A Century of Arab Feminist Writing.* [45] This seminal work shows that Middle Eastern women have been debating issues of gender equality and the role of women in society for at least a century. In this regard, the volume helps to set aside the misconception that feminist thinking is a recent development in the Middle East. In their introduction, Badran and Cooke noted, "our everyday experience in the Arab world, our contacts and debates with Arab women, and with men, as well as our studies have informed our feminist thinking in ways that transcend purely academic interests. . . . These were voices that had shaped our own thinking and had often given us pause in debates on feminist theory going on in the West." [46] Like Beck and Keddie a decade earlier, Badran and Cooke openly acknowledged the influence of the feminist movement in the West on their study. Like Fernea and Bezirgan, they wanted their book to be a medium for the Middle Eastern women's voices. However, Badran and Cooke's efforts also reflected the influence of post-modernist criticism on women's studies. They openly acknowledged their own role in framing those voices. Furthermore, Badran and Cooke recognized the influence of their subjects on their thinking; that interaction had helped shape their scholarship.

The attempts to incorporate the voices of Middle Eastern women in the academic milieu have led to an interest in the genre of autobiography. Some of these women have chosen to write their autobiographies as a means of setting the record straight, of leaving behind traces of their personal history, and of empowering themselves through words. Sattareh Farman-Farmaian, the founder of the Tehran School of Social Work and the daughter of a prince of the Qajar dynasty, wrote in the introduction to her autobiography: "From the day I was born I have always loved action more than words. But now only words are left." [47] One of the most famous autobiographies by an Iranian woman, *Khatirat-i Taj os-Saltanah*, the memoirs of a daughter of Nasir al-Din Shah, has received the attention of scholars who are interested in its unique perspective of life inside the Qajar aristocracy. [48] Taj os-Saltanah's is a female voice, a voice from the *andarun*. [49] When her teacher encouraged her to read the history of other peoples rather than reflect on her own, Taj os-Saltanah replied, "Is it not the best preoccupation in the world to review one's personal history?" [50]

Harem Years: The Memoirs of an Egyptian Feminist also offers a rare glimpse into nineteenth century harem life. [51] Like Taj os-Saltanah, Huda Shaarawi received her education in the harem; in her youth, books became her connection to the world beyond. Living in a time of nationalist upheaval, Shaarawi became involved in political life, and worked for national and women's causes. Returning from an international feminist meeting in Rome in 1923, she disembarked from her train in the Cairo station and became the first Egyptian woman to unveil publicly. Margot Badran's English translation of Shaarawi's memoirs has become a basic text for the study of Middle Eastern women's history.

Autobiographies of Middle Eastern women are clearly an important source for studying the social fabric of the area. Still, for some women, a reticence to expose one's personal life for public consumption remains. For others, the powerful symbolism of breaking the silence, of blurring the lines between public and private, and of writing oneself into history serve as strong motivations for writing their autobiographies. [52] In the first novel published by an Iranian woman, *Savushun*, [53] the novelist Simin Daneshevar explored the cultural representation of women; through the character of Miss Fotuhi, she examined the process of self-representation through writing one's own story. Farzaneh Milani explains:

> Wanting voice and visiblity, she unveils herself publicly before the compulsory unveiling act of 1936 and writes her life story. This desire to give voice to her body and give body to her voice ultimately leads to her madness. Her nakedness, in both a literal and a literary sense—her appropriation of her body and her pen—becomes her crime. She is thrown into a mental asylum where both her body and her pen are kept under seal, censored and suppressed. Self-representation turns into self-destruction, gestation into decay, song into silence. [54]

Middle Eastern women have turned to writing as a means to participate in society when attempts have been made to mute their public voice.
Literary scholars have translated and studied some of these writings and
made them available to Western audiences. The short stories of as-
Saqqaf, ash-Shamlan, and at-Tuwayjiri appear in an anthology of Saudi
Arabian short stories, *Assassination of Light*.[55] These stories are a potent
means of self-expression from women living in a highly segregated
society; they offer scholars of the Middle East a unique opportunity to
incorporate a particular perspective on Saudi life. The stories of Alifa
Rifaat, an Egyptian writer who expresses her strength and identity within
the paradigms of her Arab culture and Islamic faith, offer another
perspective on Middle Eastern society.[56] Minoo Southgate's collection of
Persian short stories includes the works of two important writers, Simin
Daneshvar and Mahshid Amirshahi, women whose activism spans decades. Both women write of seemingly ordinary day-to-day events that
turn out to be anything but simple. Forugh Farrokhzad's poetry has been
widely translated, and studies of her work have been important in
showing the complexities of women's issues in prerevolutionary Iran.[57]
Some authors, like Nahid Rachlin and Shusha Guppy, have chosen to
write their novels in English; their fiction emerges from the experience
of exile. The exile needs to remember her past and examine her present
foreignness. The pen becomes her cure.[58]

At times of war too, Middle Eastern women have taken pen in hand.
The frontiers of suffering can change when we incorporate the female
voice into our studies of war. Sometimes, women are the voice of the
Mother, bold and defiant in the face of the enemy, offering up their sons
for the greater cause. Other times, they are the voice of Reason; they
poke a determined finger at the inflated chest of war and ask why killing
has become so easy. When all seems shattered (as during the Lebanese
Civil War), women offer their poems of hope, comfort, and endurance.[59]

While literary scholars have made great strides in the study of Middle
Eastern women, the field of history has been less able or willing to bring
gender in. For too long, the paucity of sources was used as an excuse.
Ground-breaking research, however, has begun to set the record straight.
Indeed, the archives have proven to be replete with texts for the study
of women. Financial records, divorce papers, inheritance registers, birth
certificates, and marriage documents have been used to reconstruct the
role of women in history. Some scholars have begun to incorporate the
place of women and gender relations into the social history of the Middle
East. Abraham Marcus's work on eighteenth century Aleppo is a notable

example.[60] Some scholars have turned to Islamic texts as a source for examining women's lives. John Esposito has examined the gendered implications of Islamic law. Recent works by Leila Ahmed and Fedwa Malti-Douglas have drawn from Arabo-Islamic texts to show the divergence in the discourses on women in the Islamic Middle East.[61] While enhancing our knowledge of women's history, such studies show the diversity in the Islamic experience. Works by Deniz Kandiyoti and Kumari Jayawardena have shown that the rise of nationalism and the state are intrinsically connected to issues of gender.[62] Indeed, Billie Melman reveals that the colonial enterprise looks quite different when examined through the female gaze.[63] Her study of English women travelers to the Middle East in the eighteenth and nineteenth centuries suggests that European women's writings on the Middle East often included self-examination and avoided the cultural smugness which marked the writings of mainstream male European Orientalists. Together, these historians have shown that "bringing gender in" is not only possible but essential. A growing interest in the history of women has encouraged some scholars to dig more deeply into the archives, to reexamine our definition of what constitutes a historical text and to redefine the boundaries of history.

Among the academic disciplines, anthropology has perhaps most fully addressed the concept of voice and the experience of women. The ethnographer lives among her subjects, intermingles with them without the barriers of text; she records and interprets the voices she has heard, the experiences she has witnessed. Some anthropologists have begun to look more closely at their mediatory role and at their own positions in the midst of the examined societies. As Lila Abu-Lughod wrote of her study of the Awlad Ali, "Being a female made it difficult for me to assume a non-situated perspective on the society, or rather to mistake a situated perspective for an 'objective' one." This self-awareness had an impact beyond the field of anthropology, however. For as Abu-Lughod contended, "since every member of a society experiences life from a particular vantage point, it could be argued that a picture of society that claims generality is a fiction. While my presentation of Bedouin society is partial, no presentation could be complete."[64]

Anthropologists have also helped to bring to the fore the question of the interrelationship of the known and the knower. For over twenty years, Erika Friedl has been visiting an Iranian village she calls Deh Koh. In her latest study of the village, she wrote a series of stories, "stories *of* village women, not *about* them."[65] In her book, Friedl talked of her five years living in Deh Koh, "I have not become a Deh Koh woman ... but at least I have ceased to be conspicuous there." Friedl also reflects upon the impact which Deh Koh may have made on her own approach to ethnography. The essays in this volume show that often there is an important interaction taking place between the researcher and the subject, between the knower and the known.

Organization of the Volume

This volume focuses on the ways in which gender is being reconstructed in the Middle Eastern context. We have used a tripartite organizational structure that moves from a reconsideration of tradition to identity formation and culminates in the renegotiation of power relations. We have examined gender issues, in order to reveal how Middle Eastern women attain voice and reconstruct their experiences. All the authors creatively employ multiple narratives to reach those experiences. Each section of the volume highlights one dimension of the contemporary experience and voice of Middle Eastern women is reconstructed. We refer to this process as "reconstruction," to give back to the women the agency for giving meaning to their environments. The Middle Eastern women themselves reinterpret their experiences within the parameters of their societies. Some of our essayists have long specialized on the study of women in the Middle East. Others are focusing on issues of gender for the first time. All of the essays demonstrate the importance of incorporating gender into our study of the Middle East. The collection is designed to create dialogue, within disciplines and across areas of study. To that end, we have asked three scholars to comment on the implications of the essays. Each commentator traces patterns among the works and discusses them from the perspectives of their own field.

Part One problematizes the relationship between tradition and gender. Women in the Middle East have often been portrayed as mute followers of tradition. Despite frequent criticism of such portrayals, alternate representations have not gone beyond descriptions—previous scholars have not studied the reasons and patterns of women's use of tradition. They also have not taken into account women's agency in the creation of tradition. The three authors of Part One examine the lives of women in Iran, Morocco, and Turkey. They show that aspects of "tradition" can be employed by women as a means of empowerment. In some cases, traditional mores can be reconstructed and reinterpreted to give voice to women. In this sense, the authors reexamine the assumption that tradition-bound societies leave little room for female participation in society.

Part Two centers on Middle Eastern women's reconstruction of "identity" in Iran, Turkey, Israel, and Palestine. Once more, the authors critique stereotypes of Middle Eastern women and propose new methods to challenge preconceptions. The authors debunk notions of the quiet, passive Middle Eastern woman. They examine the complex variables that contribute to the engendering of identities in various Middle Eastern contexts. In addition, the intersubjectivity of identity formation is discussed. Some of the authors reflect on their own perspectives, the gaze with which they view the societies they examine.

Part Three problematizes the relationship between gender and power in Lebanon, Israel, Egypt, and Morocco. The authors in this section look at the diffusion of this socially constructed, complex relationship. They pay close attention to the ways women and men contest the boundaries of their transformative capacities. Power lies at the core of gender inequality; in Middle Eastern society (as in any society), power is contested between family members, within members of a community, and between nations. Prisms of power reflect and deflect gender issues within society. In the Middle East, the boundaries of power are perpetually negotiated. This section examines the gendered implications of these pervasive renegotiation of power.

Together, the essays show that in all of the fields that comprise Middle Eastern Studies, whether history, anthropology, political science, literary studies, or linguistics, the examination of women and gender roles is feasible and significant. Our essayists use a variety of approaches, but all of them have found ways to integrate the voices and experiences of Middle Eastern women into their studies. They have done so with a keen awareness of their own place in framing and presenting those voices and experiences. Together, the essays reconsider the image of the passive Middle Eastern woman, bound to a static and powerless existence; at the same time, the authors suggest venues for future studies that better reflect the diversity of the human experience in the Middle East.

REFERENCES

1. Joan W. Scott, *Gender and the Politics of History* (New York: Columbia University Press, 1988), 2.

2. See Judith Butler, *Gender Trouble: Feminism and the Subversion of Identity* (New York: Routledge, 1990); Joan W. Scott, "Experience," in J. Butler and J. Scott, eds., *Feminists Theorize the Political* (New York: Routledge, 1992) 22–42; Joan W. Scott, "The Evidence of Experience," *Critical Inquiry* 17: 773–97; and Joan W. Scott, *Gender and the Politics of History* (New York: Columbia University Press).

3. See Sandra Harding, *Whose Science? Whose Knowledge? Thinking from Women's Lives* (New York: Basic Books, 1991); Dorothy Smith, *The Everyday World as Problematic: A Feminist Sociology* (Boston: Northeastern University Press, 1987); and Dorothy Smith, *Texts, Facts, and Femininity: Exploring the Relations of Ruling* (London and New York: Routledge, 1990).

4. Fatma Müge Göçek, "Subject's Experience, Social Action and Social Structure in Historical Materialism: Extending Feminist Standpoint Theory to the Oppressed" (Working Paper, 1993), 4.

5. Smith, *The Everyday World as Problematic*, 6–7.

6. Smith, *Texts, Facts, and Femininity*, 5.

7. Smith, *Texts, Facts, and Femininity*, 5

8. Smith, *The Everyday World as Problematic*, 88.

9. Smith, *The Everyday World as Problematic*, 104.

10. E. P. Thompson. *The Making of the English Working Class* (New York: Vintage, 1978).

11. Willaim H. Sewell. Jr., "How Classes Are Made: Critical Reflections on E. P. Thompson's Theory of Working Class Formation," in H. Kaye and K. McClelland, eds., *E. P. Thompson: Critical Perspectives* (London: Polity, 1990), 59–60.

12. See Scott, "Experience," 27, for a detailed analysis of the alternative ways in which the term has been used in the Western tradition.

13. Scott, "Experience," 24–25.

14. Kathleen Jones, "The Authoritativeness of Women's Experiences: The Politics of Interpretation," in *Compassionate Authority* (New York: Routledge, 1993), 202.

15. Scott, "Experience," 33, and Scott, "The Evidence of Experience," 780.

16. Yet recent work on tradition in the Western context itself disputes this claim. In *The Invention of Tradition* [Eric Hobsbawm and Terence Ranger, eds. (Cambridge: University Press, 1983), p. 2], Hobsbawm contends that tradition is malleable, often socially constructed according to differing social visions; he argues that "insofar as there is such a reference to the past, the peculiarity of 'invented' traditions is that the continuity with it is largely fictitious."

17. Raymond Williams, *Marxism and Literature* (Oxford: University Press, 1977), 111.

18. Gayatri C. Spivak, *The Postcolonial Critic: Interview, Strategies, Dialogues* (New York: Routledge, 1990) 66.

19. Gayatri C. Spivak, "A Literary Representation of the Subaltern: A Woman's Text from the Third World" in Gayatri Spivak, ed., *In Other Worlds: Essays in Cultural Politics* (New York: Methuen, 1987), 246, 253–54.

20. Chandra Talpade Mohanty, "Under Western Eyes: Feminist Scholarship and Colonial Discourses," *Boundary*, 12/13:333–34 (1982).

21. Mohanty, "Under Western Eyes," 351–352.

22. Aihwa Ong, "Colonialism and Modernity: Feminist Re-presentations of Women in Non-Western Societies," *Inscriptions*, 3/4:80 (1988).

23. Ong, "Colonialism and Modernity," 87.

24. Mohanty, "Under Western Eyes," 347.

25. Spivak, *The Postcolonial Critic*, 11.

26. Carolyn Steedman, "Living Historically Now?" *Arena* 97, 49 (1991).

27. Stuart Hall, "Minimal Selves," *Identity* (ICA Documents, volume 6, London: 1987), 45.

28. Mary Louise Adams, "There's no Place like Home: On the Place of Identity in Feminist Politics," *Feminist Review* 31, 22–33 (1989).

29. Laura Downs, "If 'Woman' Is Just an Empty Category, Then Why Am I afraid to Walk Alone at Night? Feminism, Post-structuralism, and the Problematics of Identity," *CSST Working Paper Series:* The University of Michigan, Ann Arbor, 1 (1992).

30. Mohanty, *Under Western Eyes*, 344.

31. Kumari Jayawardena, *Feminism and Nationalism in the Third World*, (London: Zed Books, 1986).

32. The concept of identity is particularly problematic in the post-colonial context, where "the problem of identity returns as a persistent questioning of the frame, the space of representation, where the image—missing person, invisible eye, Oriental stereotype—is confronted with its difference, its Other." Homi K. Bhabha, "Interrogating Identity," *Identity* (ICA Documents volume 6, London: 1987) 5.

33. Downs, *If 'Woman' is Just an Empty Category*, 4

34. David Scobey, "Exterminating Gestures: On Linking the Coercive and Discursive Moments of Power," *CSST Working Paper:* The University of Michigan, Ann Arbor, 12 (1992).

35. In *Feminist Sociology: An Overview of Contemporary Theories* (Itasca Ill.: F. E. Peacock, 1988), Janet S. Chafetz points out that all theories that could be utilized to dispute, offset or alter a social relation that disadvantaged or devalued women were then brought under the transdisciplinary umbrella of feminist theory. The analyses of language, subjectivity, and discourse provide feminists with useful ways of understanding gender and its relation to social power (see Chris Weedon, *Feminist Practice and Poststructuralist Theory*, Oxford: Basil Blackwell, 1987).

36. Mark Poster, "A New Kind of History," *Foucault, Marxism, and History*, (New York: Polity Press, 1984) 149–150.

37. In *The History of Sexuality* (New York: Pelican, 1981), Foucault defines power as "the multiplicity of force relations immanent in the sphere in which they operate and which constitute their own organization; as the process which, through ceaseless struggles and confrontations, transforms, strengthens, or reverses them; as the support which these force relations find in one another,

thus forming a chain or a system, or, on the contrary, the disjunctions and contradictions which isolate them from one another; and lastly, as the strategies in which they take effect, whose general design and institutional crystallization is embodied in the state apparatus, in the formulation of law, and in the various social hegemonies." (92)

38. Pierre Bourdieu, "Social Space and Symbolic Power," *Sociological Theory* 7/1, 17.
39. Elizabeth W. Fernea and Basima Q. Bezirgan, eds., *Middle Eastern Women Speak* (Austin: University of Texas Press, 1977).
40. Fernea and Bezirgan, *Middle Eastern Women Speak*, xx.
41. Elizabeth W. Fernea ed., *Women and Family in the Middle East: New Voices of Change* (Austin: University of Texas Press, 1985).
42. Fernea, *Women and Family in the Middle East*, 3.
43. Lois Beck and Nikki Keddie, eds., *Women in the Muslim World*, (Cambridge: Harvard University Press).
44. Beck and Keddie, *Women in the Muslim World*, 1.
45. Margot Badran and Miriam Cooke, eds., *Opening the Gates: A Century of Arab Feminist Writings*, (Bloomington: Indiana University Press, 1990).
46. Badran and Cooke, *Opening the Gates*, ix.
47. Sattareh Farman-Farmian, *Daughter of Persia: A Woman's Journey from her Father's Harem Through the Islamic Revolution* (New York: Crown Books, 1992), xiii.
48. M. Ettehadiyeh and C. Sa'dvaniyan, eds., *Khatirat-i Taj os-Saltanah* (Tehran: Nashr-i Tarikh-i Iran, 1982).
49. *Andarun* refers to the private quarters of a home.
50. As quoted in A. Najmabadi, "A Different Voice: Taj os-Saltaneh," in A. Najabadi, ed. *Women's Autobiographies in Contemporary Iran*, (Cambridge: Harvard University Press, 1990): 22.
51. Huda Shaarawi, *Harem Years: The Memoirs of an Egyptian Feminist*, trans. by Margot Badran (New York: The Feminist Press of the City University of New York: 1986).
52. Other autobiographies of Middle Eastern women include Fadhma Amrouche, *My Life Story*, trans. by Dorothy Blair (London: The Women's Press, 1988); Jehan Sadat, *A Woman of Egypt* (New York: Simon and Schuster, 1987); and Raymonda Tawil, *My Home, My Prison* (New York: Holt, Reinhart, and Winston, 1980).
53. Simin Daneshvar, *Savushun*, trans. by M. Ghanoonparvar (Washington, D.C: Mage, 1990).
54. Farzaneh Milani, "Veiled Voices: Women's Autobiographies in Iran," in A. Najambad, ed., *Women's Autobiographies in Contemporary Iran* (Cambridge: Harvard University Press, 1990), 6–7.
55. Ava Molnar Heinrichsdorff and Abu Bakr Bagader, eds., *Assassination of Light: Modern Saudi Short Stories*, (Washington, D. C.: Three Continents Press, 1990).

56. Alifaa Rifaat, *Distant View of a Minaret,* trans. Denis Johnson-Davies (London: Quartet Books, 1983).
57. For example, see Farzaneh Milani, "Forugh Farrokhzad: A Feminist Perspective" (Ph.D. Diss., University of California, Los Angeles, 1979), and Michael C. Hillman, *A Lonely Woman: Forugh Farrokhẓad and Her Poetry* (Washington, D.C.: Three Continents Press/Mage Publishers, 1987).
58. Nahid Rachlin's novels include *Foreigner,* (New York: Norton, 1978) and *Married to a Stranger,* (San Francisco: City Lights, 1983). Shusha Guppy has written *The Blindfold Horse: Memories of a Persian Childhood,* (London: Heinemann, 1988). Ehsan Yarshater has written an excellent review of Guppy's work, which appears in *Iranshinasi* (Spring 1992), 23–24.
59. See Etel Adnan, *The Arab Apocalypse* (Sausalito, CA: Post-Apollo Press, 1989); Miriam Cooke, *War's Other Voices: Women Writers on the Lebanese Civil War* (Cambridge: Cambridge University Press, 1987); Miriam Cooke, *Gendering War Talk* (Princeton: Princeton University Press, 1993); Evelyne Accad, *Sexuality and War: Literary Masks of the Middle East* (New York: New York University Press, 1990).
60. Abraham Marcus, *The Middle East on the Eve of Modernity: Aleppo in the Eighteenth Century* (New York: Columbia University Press, 1989).
61. Leila Ahmed, *Women and Gender in Islam* (New Haven: Yale University Press, 1992); Fedwa Malti-Douglas, *Women's Body, Women's Word: Gender and Discourse in Arabo-Islamic Writing* (Princeton: Princeton University Press, 1991).
62. Deniz Kandiyoti, ed., *Women, Islam, and the State,* (Philadelphia: Temple University Press, 1991); Kumari Jayawardena, *Feminism and Nationalism in the Third World* (London: Zed Books, 1986).
63. Billie Melman, *Women's Orients: English Women and the Middle East, 1718–1918* (Ann Arbor: University of Michigan Press, 1992), 8.
64. Lila Abu-Lughod, "Fieldwork of a Dutiful Daughter," in Soraya Altorki and Camillia Fawzi El-Solh, eds., *Arab Women in the Field: Studying Our Own Society,* (Syracuse: Syracuse University Press, 1988), 158.
65. Erika Friedl, *Women of Deh Koh, Lives in an Iranian Village* (Washington: Smithsonian Inst. Press, 1989), 5.

PART ONE

The Reconstruction of Tradition

CHAPTER ONE

Gender, Tradition, and History

Juan R. I. Cole

When we say that identity is constructed, we challenge commonsense views of nation, ethnicity, and gender. Many embrace the premise that ethnicity and nationality are "natural" and primordial: this view is exemplified by the French historian who describes Bonaparte as if he had been not a Corsican, but a Frenchman, and by the urbanite who expresses blind generalizations about the national character of immigrant groups. These ascribed national identities, along with sexual ones, are presumed to be givens, and are conceived as relatively undifferentiated. It is not very difficult to deconstruct this conception of a nation, whether Italy, Iran, or Israel: the supposedly uniform and static national identity combines a congeries of very different linguistic and ethnic groups assembled only at particular points in history. Furthermore, this union is the result of concerted, creative political and military action, rather than the natural culmination of inexorable ethnic affinity.[1] As Thomas Laquer has shown, ideas about sexual identity (which have varied greatly throughout history) can similarly be shown to possess constructed elements.[2]

In the Muslim Middle East, governments during the period 622–1750 were characterized by various forms of tribal feudalism, creating highly patriarchal societies. In the nineteenth century, the shift to peripheral agrarian capitalism disrupted many family and family-based institutions—without necessarily creating new forms of support for women. The rush to industrialize after about 1930 had, by the early 1990s, produced a number of Middle Eastern countries that are fifty percent urban, and fifty percent literate. These countries have substantial proletariats, but suffer from relatively low economic growth rates because of inefficient industries and bloated bureaucracies. This new social formation has created a variety of polities, from Turkey's tenuous parliamentary democracy to the authoritarian populist regimes of Iran and Iraq.

The increasingly industrialized countries of the Middle East have adopted a number of conflicting policies toward women; these policies are grounded in political philosophies that range from the neopatriarchy of Iran to the Kemalist liberalism of Turkey. As these societies become fully industrialized and largely urban, we may expect further transformations in identity, including gender identity, although these changes may not mirror the directions taken by the societies of the North Atlantic. Several Middle Eastern countries, Turkey in particular, have begun to undergo a demographic transition to low population growth. Other countries are growing very rapidly, and are subject to all the strains such growth places on societies with limited resources; much of the burden falls on women. These societies have only begun to experience the impact of the information and computer revolutions, which may be expected to introduce even greater changes in self-conception.

The vast changes in women's roles and status through Islamic history have been only lightly documented, but the extant research is highly instructive. Judith Tucker showed the immense impact on the family economy and the position of women of the bureaucratic and military reforms in nineteenth-century Egypt, as well as of the incorporation of Egypt into the world economy as a producer, primarily, of cotton.[3] The work of Tucker and a host of other historians of Middle Eastern women has safely buried the idea that there were any enduring set of circumstances that typified "traditional" society.[4] Veiling, itself a potent symbol of Islamic tradition in Western writing, was in premodern times a highly classed institution, practiced only by the elite. Veiling appears to have greatly increased as a practice during the colonial period (roughly 1830–1956). In an Orientalist corollary to Heisenberg's uncertainty principle, the intrusive presence of Westerners appears to have helped produce the phenomenon (widespread veiling) that they observed.[5] In short, the notion of tradition as a stable foil for the dynamism of modernity has been demolished, as the diversity and volatility of premodern extra-European societies has come to be better appreciated.

We say, then, that identity is constructed. Employing the passive mood, we conveniently manage to avoid ascribing agency. Who fashions our identities? The three essays that follow, on the reconstruction of tradition and of gender in the modern Middle East, offer some insights into this question. Zehra F. Arat looks at the Turkish Republic and the issue of women. For Western feminists, Turkey, Tunisia and Iraq stand out among Middle Eastern countries in having enacted legal reforms that made women more equal to men than they had been under the Ottoman Empire. Arat asks two probing questions in this regard. What was the original intent of the legislators who adapted the Swiss legal code to modern Turkey? And, under these laws, are women equal to men? Although a vigorous women's movement existed in republican Turkey, it was small and comprised of literate upper-class women. They were not in a position to enact legislative reform on their own.

Rather, the chief impetus for the alteration in the status of women came from the circle surrounding Mustafa Kemal Atatürk, the nationalist hero and subsequently President for Life. While the changes Atatürk and his legislature initiated no doubt offered women advantages over the Ottoman codes (based for the most part on a nineteenth-century rationalization of medieval Muslim jurisprudence), these changes were dictated to women in the same way as other modernist projects were imposed on the general population. The motive behind them appears to have been, in part, a desire to emulate Western Europe and to win the praise of Western officials and observers. The welfare of local women was only one impetus for the new laws, and perhaps a less important motive than winning the accolades of Western men. Another motivation was the promotion of a successful Turkish capitalism, for which the human resources of the entire nation (and not only the male half of it) were felt necessary.

Atatürk's Turkey, Arat argues, raises the question of whether feminists are well advised to see an authoritarian, paternalistic dictate as "state feminism." How feminist these decrees were can be deduced from the region's realist fiction of the time, which reports veiled elderly women scurrying through back alleys, avoiding the public eye lest the police espy their veils and rip them from their faces. The paternalism of Atatürk's own role is symbolized by his practice, as president, of "adopting" a series of girls and young women, some of whom became his surrogate wives.[6] There is little doubt that new roles and ideals for women were constructed in the 1920s and 1930s. It seems equally clear that the predominant agent was the male-dominated state (in so saying I do not wish to minimize the importance of the Turkish women's movement of that time; I simply wish to see it in perspective). Arat's second main point is that the Swiss civil code of the 1920s hardly created a feminist paradise, and that its implementation in Turkey left large spaces wherein women's subordination continued unabated, to the extent that spousal abuse is still not actionable under Turkish law.

Milani and Hessini examine particular women's self-constructions in post-revolutionary Iran and contemporary Morocco, neither of which most observers would categorize as feminist. Milani discusses gender categories in the poetry of Simin Behbahani, focusing upon the image of the gypsy in her *Ghazals*. The gypsy woman is a figure well known in classical Persian poetry, yet in her gender indeterminacy, her boldness, mobility, and unconventionality, the gypsy appears to suggest new possibilities to Behbahani for the behavior of Iranian women generally. "O gypsy with the yearning for liberty, stamp your feet," she soliloquizes.[7] Utilizing figures from Iranian folk culture, Milani argues, allows Behbahani to express a woman's yearning for more freedom without appearing to become a cultural traitor by emulating or exalting Western women as models. Here another player is instanced in the shaping of our gender identities, the Other, the foreigner (also described by Arat). Behbehani's poetry represents a woman's voice that also seeks to eschew a Western model, and her vision of the gypsy slaying feminine silence by her song appears to have provoked less controversy than has others' forthright advocacy of Western-style feminism.

As noted earlier, veiling is not a monochrome, universal, "traditional" practice in the Middle East. It has a history, like any fashion, which interacts with rising and falling subcultures. It was practiced by some Assyrians, but not by the Babylonians. Upper-class Byzantine (European Christian) women veiled, as did upper-class Sasanian (Iranian Zoroastrian) women. The Qur'an does not actually mandate veiling, though it urges women to cover their "adornments" and says the wives of the Prophet should speak from behind a veil. The latter appears to have been a special honor rather than a generalizable practice. Because pre-Islamic Arabia had a torrid climate, and because pagan women went about quite freely in public, even appearing on battlefields to cheer on their men, one suspects that the "adornments" the Qur'an wished covered were situated below the neck. Certainly, no verse actually mentions covering the hair or head or face. Mention of veiling occurs in the sayings attributed to the Prophet, which most Muslims believe to have the force of law. From a contemporary academic point of view, however, these sayings are extremely problematic, having been collected from oral sources two centuries after the Prophet's death, and they probably reflect folk practices of the Abbasid empire. It should be emphasized however, that the majority of Muslims believe that their voluminous collections of the Prophet's sayings constitute sound bases for religious law.

The resurgence of veiling, often across social classes, in the postcolo-

nial period is a complex and multivalent phenomenon, as Hessini demonstrates. It has been argued that lower-middle class women often employ
veiling as a statement of upward mobility. Hessini emphasizes that
veiling can also be seen as a way of creating a status group among
women that cuts across social classes. She focuses on the reasons that
some literate, urban, middle class women have begun to veil. She finds
that these women emphasize the modernity of their veiling, insofar as it
reflects a conscious choice and expresses their individualism. She finds
that Moroccans hold an ideal of social and public space as gender-
differentiated and as offering a sense of personal privacy. In postcolonial,
capitalist societies, this ideal is increasingly difficult to implement in
practice. Women of the professional class go to coeducational colleges,
and work in mixed-gender offices. Veiling is one way for women to
redifferentiate social space, even in the new, mixed-gender environment,
a way of recovering their privacy even in public and of refusing to
become a spectacle. From the point of view of these Moroccan conservatives, veiling helps protect women from sexual harassment and strengthens the public moral code. Hessini stresses, as have many others, that the
veil can also be a statement on the recovery of cultural authenticity for
postcolonial women oppressed for decades by foreign, imperial rule.
Veiling, as practiced by the city-dwelling, educated women who talked
to Hessini, is therefore the farthest thing from "traditional." It is a new
response, made by educated young women, to contemporary problems
in a postcolonial setting.

Gender identities in the modern Middle East have been shaped by
many forces. Middle Eastern women themselves have constructed a
diverse set of identities. But they have hardly done so in a vacuum, nor
do they agree upon the values that should shape those identities. They
disagree across social classes (as in Algeria or Afghanistan, where many
upper-middle class women marched against the prospect of a Muslim
fundamentalist state while large numbers of poor and lower-middle class
women supported the Muslim right). Many educated women throughout
the region fear the consequences of the repeal during the 1980s in Iran
and Egypt, under the influence of an organized Muslim Right, of what
these women saw as profeminist laws that had been enacted in the 1970s.
But their disagreements cut across class as well, with some educated,
middle-class women declaring themselves in support of the fundamental-
ists.

The modern state, with its rationalized bureaucracy, has been a
primary force for change, as in Kemalist Turkey.[8] The psychological

dynamics of the attitudes of indigenous state actors toward the capitalist core areas also has been crucial for the shaping of indigenous culture. Whereas Turkish women's fates were powerfully influenced by Atatürk's desire to emulate his Western brothers (and overthrow his Islamic father, the sultan-caliph, with all his laws), Iranian women's destinies have been molded by Khomeini's desire to avoid emulating the Western father-figures of imperialism (and to establish a fraternity of Muslim brothers within). Although not directly discussed by Arat, Milani, or Hessini, capitalism has remade the class structures and infrastructures of modern Middle Eastern societies, and these changes have had vast implications for women. Colonialism assaulted the Middle Eastern sense of autonomy and cultural identity. In Algeria, the French devalued Arabic, derided Islam, and attempted to create a class of gallicized compradors who would help them rule, even as they usurped the country's best land for *colons* and their lucrative vineyards. In such circumstances, Muslim women became, for the lower-middle classes, potent symbols of national authenticity; such conditions led to an increase in such practices as veiling. Moreover, the European impact did not end with the decline of colonialism. Contemporary American and French gender norms have a transnational influence, both through immigration and return migration, and through magazines, television, and films. Gender identities and roles, especially as they are inscribed in the discourses of law and institutions, are arenas of continual contention, which are negotiated and renegotiated between women and men, and among women of different classes and generations. Contrary to the assumptions of modernization theory, social change is not unidirectional. The contingent and negotiated character of gender identity and roles ensures that they remain in flux.

REFERENCES

1. Benedict Anderson, *Imagined Communities: Reflections on the Origin and Spread of Nationalism*, rev. ed. (London: Verso, 1991).
2. Thomas Laquer, *Making Sex: Body and Gender from the Greeks to Freud* (Cambridge: Harvard University Press, 1990).
3. Judith Tucker, *Women in Nineteenth-Century Egypt* (Cambridge: Cambridge University Press, 1985).
4. Beth Baron and Nikki R. Keddie, eds., *Women in Middle Eastern History: Shifting Boundaries in Sex and Gender* (New Haven: Yale University Press, 1991); Lois Beck and Nikki R. Keddie, *Women in the Muslim World* (Cam-

bridge: Harvard University Press, 1976); Nahid Yeganeh and Nikki R. Keddie, "Sexuality and Shi'i Social Protest." In Juan R. I. Cole and Nikki R. Keddie, eds., *Shi'ism and Social Protest* (New Haven: Yale University Press, 1986).

5. Juan R. I. Cole, "Feminism, Class, and Islam in Turn-of-the-Century Egypt." *International Journal of Middle East Studies* 13(1981):387–487; Nada Tomiche, "The Situation of Egyptian Women in the First Half of the Nineteenth Century." In W. Polk and R. Chambers, eds., *Beginnings of Modernization in the Middle East* (Chicago: University of Chicago Press, 1968) 171–184.

6. Vamık D. Volkan and Norman Itzkowitz, *The Immortal Atatürk: A Psychobiography* (Chicago: University of Chicago Press, 1984).

7. Simin Behbahani, *Dasht-e Arjan* [Arjan Plain] (Tehran: Zavar, 1983), 43.

8. Deniz Kandiyoti. "Women, Islam, and the State: A Comparative Approach." In Juan R. I. Cole, ed., *Comparing Muslim Societies* (Ann Arbor: University of Michigan Press, 1992).

CHAPTER TWO

Neotraditionalism in the Poetry of Simin Behbahani[1]

Farzaneh Milani

Most contemporary Iranian writers belong to one of two antagonistic camps. Many assume, too often and too unambiguously, that modernity in Iran is a by-product of Western influence. For them, "modern" is synonymous with "Western" and all things indigenous are labelled as regressive and retrograde; Iran's native literary tradition is considered dead, or else urgently awaiting renewal. A second group argues, with equal conviction, that Western encroachment has caused Iranian society to degenerate. Both camps remain locked in endless, baroque polemics with the West. The relentless emphasis on "heritage" is, in fact, a perverse way of paying homage to the West, homage paid in the form of what seems to be its opposite—the obsessive insistence on a separate, self-sufficient "Iranian" tradition that is "great," "authentic," and "old."

There are, however, a few contemporary Iranian writers such as Daneshvar, Golshiri, Behbahani, and Parsipur whose works revolve around the themes of continuity and change. Their writings gracefully blend the old and the new, and are free from the unanalytical rejection of anything "Western" or "Iranian." These writers neither affirm nor negate Iranian or Western literary traditions. Instead, they prove the instability upon which the dialectic between the two traditions is played. In these writers' work, the discourses of "modernity" and "tradition" no longer compete: they complement each other. In the hands of these authors, the discourses transform, restructure, and reconstruct each other. Their work contains various manifestations of modernity, a modernity that does not have the West as its reference point, and is not necessarily opposed to or in conflict with Iranian, Islamic, or Western traditions.

I do not mean to imply that modernity, as a concept or a vision, is resolved in this body of writing. Modernity has been, and continues to be a central epistemological, aesthetic, and ethical problematic of contemporary Iranian literature (and history). What I see as refreshingly liberating in this new literary movement, however, is the fact that it neither advocates a return to "pure" ethnic origins and values nor accepts the exclusiveness of Western models of individualism, democracy, objectivity, women's rights, gender relations, and so forth.

Freed from obsessive preoccupations with "authenticity," these writers find tradition and modernity neither opposed nor in conflict. They promote individual rights *and* offer access to an inspirational Iranian tradition. This domestication of modernity decentralizes the Western cultural and literary discourse. It challenges, even rejects, its hegemony. By refusing to perpetuate or rigidify the Iranian/Western dichotomy and polemic, it establishes, even promotes, the possibility of cross-cultural dialogue.

The poetry of Simin Behbahani may provide the best refutation of the conceptual and taxonomic divisions between "traditional-therefore-Iranian" and "modern-thus Western." She integrates an exclusively classical tradition with a distinctively modern vision. Her mastery of a classical ode is remarkably unconventional. Her mastery is unconventional because of its content, the way it overturns the paradigm of man-as-gazer, woman-as-gazed, and also because it revives a popular genre considered "dead" by many contemporary poets such as Ahmad Shamlu and Forugh Farrokhzad.

Simin Behbahani was born in Tehran in 1927. She grew up there and was married before finishing high school. The marriage ended after sixteen years and three children. Years later, Behbahani married Manuchehr Kushiar. In a productive career spanning four decades, Behbahani produced seven poetry collections and an autobiography titled *That Man, My Companion of the Road.* Her first book, *Broken Setar,* was published in 1951. Between 1956 and 1983, six other books of poems were published. This is a prodigious output, considering that Behbahani was a full-time high school teacher for twenty-nine years, a housewife, and a mother of three children.

Unlike Forugh Farrokhzad, another contemporary woman poet, Behbahani has been virtually neglected by the literary establishment. While her work has attracted the attention and admiration of an ever-growing number of readers, few scholars have written about it. Not a single book has been devoted to the study of Behbahani's life or poetry. For several decades, she has been neglected by literary critics and excluded from anthologies. Until now, none of her poems have been translated into English. Only recently has Behbahani been given some overdue recognition. Against difficult odds of neglect, slight, economic hardship, and divided loyalties, Behbahani has earned her prominence by the strength of her personality, her talent, and her perseverance.

As one reads through Behbahani's collected verse, one sees a wide variety of experiments with forms. Ultimately, she transforms a conventional and mainly masculine poetic form. Her strongest work is found in her creative use of *Ghazal*, a lyric ode that consists of seven to twelve monorhyming couplets. In an age characterized by violent breaks with the past, Behbahani has consistently challenged reactionary views of tradition. Working with inherited verse forms, she has become an innovative technical master, and has found a complex and distinctive voice. Her neotraditionalism stands out against the dominant spirit of her time, the desperate search by self-consciously modernist poets for new forms that would enable them to break with "tradition."

Etymologically, a *Ghazal* is a short lyrical poem a man writes about a woman. *Ghazil*, the writer of a Ghazal, has come to mean "a man who makes love to women." In other words, men traditionally wrote Ghazals, women listened to them. They rarely wrote Ghazals or rather they rarely published them. Simin Behbahani changed the old order. In her love poems, man becomes the object of love. Rarely a spectator of his own desirability in Ghazals, he is finally desired in a female-authored Ghazal. For centuries it was the prerogative of the man-*Ghazil* to choose his partner and to display his desire. He was neither chosen nor could he expect a woman to display sexual attraction: women "knew" that it was improper to show public interest in a man. For centuries, *Ma'shuq* [the beloved], which is a word not linguistically gender-marked, has meant "woman" or "effeminate man." In Behbahani's Ghazals, the traditional scheme is overturned: beloved becomes the lover, the observer becomes the observed, the spectacle turns into the spectator. She blocks the masculine gaze, subverts man's role as the surveyor, and removes woman from the category of object-to-be-seen. She becomes the seer, the surveyor, and gains power, agency, and control.

> The stars have closed their eyes, come.
> The wine of light flows through the veins of the night, come.
>
> In the night's lap I've poured so many tears
> That twilight has blossomed and the dawn has blossomed, come.

In my mind's sky your memory etches lines of gold
Like a shooting star, come.

I've sat so long with the night telling my tale of woe
That night and I have turned pale with sorrow, come.

If you'll see me again when I die,
Know that the time has come, come.

When I hear anyone's footsteps I imagine them to be yours,
My heart beating so hard has burst out of my breast, come.

You didn't come when the sky was full of star like grapes,
Now that the dawn has picked them one by one, come.

You're the hope in the heart of Simin-the-broken-hearted,
Don't make me feel any more hopeless, come.[2]

Behbahani gives man new life in the Ghazal by giving him clearer focus. After centuries of posing as the "poet" or the "lover," man becomes the "muse" or the "beloved." Many poems epitomize such a reversal of gender-bound representation, violation of mores, and the subversion of power, propriety, and tradition. The poems violate the very definition of Ghazal. By demanding a new literary space for women, they represent a self-assertiveness quite different from the passivity of the "typical" ideal Iranian woman. This new assertiveness can even express lack of desire—here is an elegy to the death of love:

O, lost from my heart,
lost from my side,
lost from my mind,
don't look,
I can't bear your eyes,
don't look:
your black eyes evoke
only bitterness and sorrow.

O, lost from my heart,
tell me the truth,
why have you come back tonight
with the memories?
If you've come back for the one
who stole your heart,
I'm not she: She's dead,
I am her shadow.

I'm not she:
my heart is dark
my heart is cold,
her heart knew lust
and love's wildness.
Passion for you
possessed her, loving idol,
no matter where she was,
when, or with who.

I'm not she:
My eyes are mute
my eyes are silent, in her eyes hid
so many conversations,
and the melancholic love
of the night-hued narcissus
held more mysteries
than the blackness of night.

I am not she:
yes, it's been a long time
since a smile blossomed
on my pale lips from your love,
but on her lips laid always
a smile that gave life
like moonlight
on flowers covered with dew.

Don't look at me:
I can't bear your eyes.
The one you want from me,
I swear is dead.
She was in my body,
and I don't know the moment
when I ceased to know
what she saw,
what she did
where she went,
and why she died,

I am her tomb,
her tomb,
rubbing camphor's cold sorrow
on her warm flesh.

She is dead
and in my breast
this loveless heart
is a stone
I've placed at the tomb's head.[3]

Behbahani's neotraditionalism extends beyond her work with verse forms. Her Ghazals explore feelings that are at once personal and social, at once individual and political.

You said—it's grapes.
I said—I don't see any.
You said—believe me,
I'll pick you a bunch.
This is the garden of history
and these the vines that bear fruit
in such abundance and types.
You made the motions with your hands
as if you were picking grapes.
In my beliefs—I said,
there is no room for such jest.
You said—just close your eyes
and open your mouth,
and I'll let you have a taste
of these sweet firm grapes.
I did as you told me.
Oh, how salty it is!—I said.
It tasted like blood.
I felt nauseous, I felt sick
I spat it out, to find out
the eyeball that was in my mouth.
It seemed the roof with all its weight
collapsed on my head
and the world began to whirl like a windmill
and blood rained from the moon and the constellations.
It's grapes—you said.
I screamed, eyeball![4]

For her themes, too, Behbahani dives deep into her culture and finds familiar motifs to revitalize and be revitalized in her poetry. In the tradition of Scheherazade, the ultimate storyteller, she tells stories to entertain, instruct, and incite. She questions the existing order of things. She challenges the status quo. She demands change. Often, she relies on familiar tales to make radical statements.

> "I'm scared of snakes," I used to tell you,
> "really scared," and in jest
> you would make a snake from a piece of rope.
> "This scares me," I would tell you in despair.
> And when you tied two false snakes on your shoulders
> I cried, "brother, I'm scared!"
> And when you declared "I am Zahak!"[5]
> In pain, I screamed, "cruel, heartless,
> murderer, cannibal—I'm scared."
> You laughed and said, "It's just a game."
> And I said, "I'm scared of games that end in massacres."
>
> The snakes became alive, your laughter changed to horror.
> You came to me, begging, "Stop it, I'm scared!"
> I shook my head in anguish, "now there's only fear."
> How many brains have you wrenched from their skulls
> since then for your own protection.
> Today snakes don't frighten me
> as much as loved ones.[6]

The series of sixteen poems dedicated to *Kowlis* are a fascinating reappropriation and reappraisal of a familiar figure. The Persian word *Kowli,* translated roughly as "gypsy," is dazzlingly rich in connotations in Iranian popular belief. Behbahani's poetry fully exploits that wealth. A Gypsy—always a woman in her poetry—is a mutant. Ambiguous and unclassifiable, she has an amorphous social status. She has no home of her own, and is constantly wandering. She is socially and culturally marginal, but refuses to be domesticated. Not recognized in her capacities as wife, mother, daughter, she has no family-bound existence. She has a reputation for aggressive nonconformity. Presented as "victim"— homeless, exiled—she is also endowed with magical powers. She can turn bodies into texts; she can read palms; she tells fortunes; she intuits the past and divines the future. She is resilient, she is a survivor.

A Kowli is mobile and her mobility affords her visibility. Unmindful of rules of modesty, she has a public presence. To appreciate the significance of her freedom to roam at will, one should recall the normative immobility of women in Middle Eastern societies. Neither segregated nor immobilized, a Kowli is unburdened by many of the restrictions imposed on women.

Another powerful challenge presented by the Kowli is her public voice. Her name is, in fact (somewhat negatively) associated with voiced existence. In a preface to a collection of her poems, Behbahani reminisces about a childhood ear infection: "The doctor interpreted my infantile screaming as *Kowligari* [gypsy-like] and told my mother, 'this girl will avenge you.' "[7] Behbahani's identification with the Kowli is thought-provoking, and this short sentence shows in a nutshell a Kowli's ambivalent position. Although condemned, she is also admired; although abased, she is also exalted. If she is, as so many legends about her suggest, unruly and loud, she can also demand her rights and defend those of others. Behbahani's fascination with this familiar social outcast, her portrayal of the Kowli as liberated and liberator, is a radical way of questioning society's conventional mores about femininity.

As a social type, a Kowli transgresses properties and boundaries. As the image of the sovereign individual in a culture that does not highly value autonomous individuality—especially in a woman—she can continually recreate her self and her myth. Her repeated journeys–whether literal (from one village, city, even country, to another) or figurative (from one universe of definitions and meanings of femininity to another)–defy laws of seclusion and segregation. The figure of the Kowli unavoidably challenges the narrow definitions of womanhood in Iran.

Behbahani recognizes subversive potentials of this figure of the Kowli. Rather than importing a Western model or inventing a new heroine, she appropriates what is already there. The reliance on the culturally familiar has proved to be a fruitful strategy. In the last few decades, any defiance of conventions, flaunting of family authority, and challenge to patriarchal authority have been automatically interpreted as a desire to "Westernize." Feminism, a word for which there still is no Persian equivalent, has been readily labelled and dismissed as "Western," an imitation of Western ways, a surrender to foreign powers.

During the mid-nineteenth and early twentieth centuries, Babism [a religious faith proclaimed in Iran] was used by anti-feminists to justify their condemnation of those who fought for women's rights. Later, the target of anger switched to the West. Over time, women's emancipation became a major grievance of nationalistic reactionaries.

Any secular Iranian feminist confronts formidable problems. On one hand, she needs to challenge historically ingrained forms of gender domination. On the other hand, she has to disentangle herself from the conveniently labeled "Western imperialism,"–betraying indigenous culture to alien infiltration and domination. This struggle is sometimes internalized and doubly hard to confront. In fact, the domination exercised by Western powers extends from political and economic control to outright assertions of cultural superiority. The Iranian feminist has been blamed, time and again, for not representing Iranian women or having their best interest at heart. In the face of enormous class differences, ethnic variables, and educational gaps, I don't know how anyone can claim to represent all Iranian women. Still, Iranian feminists have been criticized for their focus on bourgeois issues affecting only bourgeois women. Their alleged failure to address the needs and aspirations of tribal, rural, and lower class women has been a major grievance and a ready platform to undervalue and even negate their efforts.

The poetry of Simin Behbahani, despite the radical connotations of her neotraditionalism, has been spared such damaging categorization. Although it is impossible to account for this in terms of any simple or obvious "causes," and although Behbahani has never been the center of hot literary debates, it remains significant that her relentless advocacy of an autonomous, unconventional female identity has never been condemned. Perhaps Behbahani's use of familiar idioms has been the saving grace. In the figure of the Kowli, Behbahani casts a familiar figure in a new, heroic mold. She questions received interpretations of the Kowli's life, and uses the reinterpretations to promote radical change. She revives and subverts mythologies that govern patriarchal thinking. By reinterpreting the figure of the Kowli, she asserts her power rather than her victimhood. She turns the figure into a triumphant image of female autonomy.

The following poem, "Kowli Poem Number 13" advocates and celebrates the transcendence of three central cultural fears: women's visibility, women's mobility, and women's voice:

> Sing, O, Gypsy, in homage to being, sing
> To register your presence in people's ears, sing.
> Eyes and throats burn from the smoke that trails monsters
> Scream if you can, of the terror of this night. Sing.
> The secret of the monster's life hides in the stomach of a fish
> that swims in waters to which you can't reach.
> Every maiden holds the head of a monster on her lap
> like a lump of coal in silver wrapped.

The rapacious monsters have plundered from the pretty maidens
The silk of their cheeks, the agate of their lips.
O, Gypsy, with the yearning for liberty, stamp your feet,
To receive an answer, send a message wit their beat.
There is a purpose to your existence in the scheme of things
Draw a spark, make a fire, stamp your feet.
Ages dark have crushed your body, warping it inwards,
To remain not a mere trace on a rock, rise up, break out.
O Gypsy, to stay alive you must slay silence!
I mean, to pay homage to being, you must sing.[8]

REFERENCES

1. This is a revised version of a chapter that appears in *Veils and Words: The Emerging Voices of Iranian Women Writers* (New York: Syracuse University Press, 1992).
2. Simin Behbahani, *Gozine-ye Ash'ar* [Selected Poems] (Chicago: Midland Printing, 1990), 106. All English translations are by Kaveh Safa and Farzaneh Milani.
3. Behbahani, *Gozine-ye Ash'ar*, 73.
4. Behbahani, *Gozine-ye Ash'ar*, 221.
5. Zahak is the monstrous king who has two snakes growing out of his shoulders after being kissed there by the Devil. To stop the snakes from torturing him, he had to feed them every day with the fresh brains of two youths.
6. Simin Behbahani, *Dasht-e Arjan* [Arjan Plain] (Tehran: Zavar, 1983), 129.
7. Behbahani, *Gozine-ye Ash'ar*, 13.
8. Behbahani, *Dasht-e Arjan*, 43.

CHAPTER THREE

Wearing the Hijab in Contemporary Morocco: Choice and Identity

Leila Hessini

They tell you fairy tales, too, you women of the West, fairy tales, which like ours, have all the appearance of truth.

Zeynab Hanoun, *Women in Islam*

When I applied for a Fulbright Research Grant in 1988 to North Africa, I proposed to probe the legal and social status of women in the contemporary Muslim context of Morocco. As an Arab-American of Maghrebian[1] origin, I was particularly interested in issues related to the status of women in North Africa and Maghrebian concepts of women's empowerment and liberation. Once in Morocco, in the Fall of 1989, I began auditing classes at the Université Muhammed V. Courses in Islamic law and the Moroccan Personal Status Code provided me with indispensable insights into the legal aspects that underlie and control Moroccan Muslim family structure.

Through daily encounters with students and observation of the interactions between men and women, I soon learned that dress was not only socially conditioned but also a way to assert one's identity. Several of the women in my courses wore the hijab and djellaba;[2] they were often the most outspoken and articulate in the class. They projected identities of veiled women that contradicted the widespread Western belief that equates the veil with female subservience. It is rarely considered that assertive Muslim women may deliberately choose to wear the veil.

I therefore chose to investigate why increasing numbers of educated and professional women in Morocco are wearing the hijab and what that choice represents for them. There are three reasons the study focuses on educated urban women. First, being educated, and having access to written documents, these women presumably had a fairly solid background in the tenets of Islam. Second, these women were likely to have made a deliberate decision to wear the hijab. Third, their choice was likely to be a personal one,[3] and not the result of the cycle of poverty, unemployment, and ignorance, commonly held responsible by Westerners for the growth of fundamentalist Islamic movements.

The research for this study was performed in Morocco, in conjunction with my Fulbright Research Grant, between October 1989 and May 1991. Interviews for the research were held in Rabat and Casablanca, and were conducted in Arabic and French. The interviews took place in a variety of contexts: some in my home, others in the interviewee's home or the home of mutual friends, and still others in empty university classrooms. The interviewees decided on the locale and usually chose a context where we were alone, with no other observer present. Thirty formal focus-groups and individual interviews took place; in addition, I had numerous informal discussions with men and women about the relationship between wearing the hijab and the search for a sense of Muslim identity. The women ranged in age from twenty to forty. The majority of them were university students, but several were professionals. While my sample was small,[4] it could nonetheless be seen as representative of educated Moroccan women who made a deliberate personal choice about their religion and its outward expression.

Why would women deliberately choose the veil? Why would they confine themselves to what many in the West consider an oppressive system dominated by men? While various research has been done in recent years on veiling movements,[5] this study examines how Moroccan women are actively redefining tradition and modernity in an ever-changing world.

The term veil needs clarification. It is often used to cover a broad range of garments, from the traditional Moroccan veil that covers most of the face, to the contemporary Muslim hijab which leaves the face uncovered. Some consider the traditional veil to be provocative, because it underscores a woman's eyes, and may attract men. Also in the past, the wearing of the veil was often associated with social class and geographic origin. In cities, upper class women would tend to wear the veil in public, while rural women, not usually veiled in their own villages, would wear the veil while traveling.

The hijab differs from the traditional veil because it is not necessarily a symbol of class distinction; on the contrary, it is often used as a unifying symbol shared by Muslim women. The adoption of the veil is part of a widespread movement toward Islamic authenticity. For many Muslims this means searching for an identity in tune with their heritage and devoid of Western values. They are insisting on a revised, more genuine practice of Islam, one based on indigenous cultural norms as well as on the values inherent in traditional Islam.[6]

The wearing of the hijab[7] is redefined for these women in a new, contemporary context. The hijab differs from the traditional veil, not only as a garment, but also in the wearer's mind. According to the women interviewed in this study, the hijab differs from the veil because the wearer is convinced of having made a deliberate, personal choice. One interviewee, Sou'al,[8] explained that "my mother has always worn the veil, but she knew nothing about Islam. She wore the veil out of tradition, whereas I wear it out of conviction." Another woman, Wafa, suggested that women who wear the hijab are "true believers," whereas women who wear another type of veil may be doing so because of habit. Other women maintained that the hijab is a modern version of the veil that Muslim women wore during the Prophet's time.

My essay is divided into three parts. The first section contextualizes the phenomenon of the "reveiling" movement. The second section focuses on the reconstruction of a gender identity within the previously-defined context. Section three investigates the reinterpretation of Islamic women's identity in this contemporary context.

Hijab: Spatial Map of a New Identity

Are men and women equal? I don't understand your question.

Aicha, psychology student, twenty years old.

Aicha's conception of the equality of men and women also surfaced in other interviews. Although gender equality has always been at the center of the struggle for women's rights in the West, it seemed foreign and irrelevant to the Moroccan women I interviewed. For them, societal equilibrium was based not on equality between the sexes but on the division of gender roles, which found its most overt expression in the division of physical space.

Moroccan society divides space according to male and female roles. In the West houses are divided into spaces with specific purposes (bedroom, living room, dining room); in Morocco the space inside homes is more flexible. The division is made not primarily by function but in terms of private and public space. Private space is reserved for the family and is considered a "female" space; public space is designated as a "male" area. The division of space parallels the division of gender roles: women fulfill their roles inside female space, the interior of the home, while men fulfill their roles in public space, that is, almost anywhere outside the family dwelling.

This division of roles is based on the notion that the sexes are innately complementary rather than equal. Men and women have specific duties in separate domains. The notion of equality implies that men and women have the same dispositions, capabilities, and objectives. As such, they can fulfill the same functions. In Western societies, these identical societal functions lead to the notion of competition between the sexes. The Moroccan women I interviewed strongly criticized Westerners' substitution of competition for complementarity. They saw competition as destabilizing and dehumanizing. For these women, the reconstruction of an authentic Muslim identity takes into consideration familial and societal needs that supersede individual aspirations.

Map of Private Space

Several researchers have investigated the dichotomy between what constitutes acceptable behavior in public and private space.[9] Foucault focused on the ownership of power, how it is institutionalized and who decides what is acceptable in public and private space. Keddie and Baron (1991), while acknowledging the dichotomy between public and private behavior, have underscored the fluidity of these socially constructed boundaries. As noted later in this essay, the women I interviewed do not necessarily subscribe to a static portrayal of public and private space, or its relationship to societal order. While they tend to believe in an ideal structure, they also acquiesce to the realistic demands of contemporary Morocco. As such, they acknowledge that they have new roles to fulfill, without disrupting societal cohesion and the stability of the family.

The existing social order revolves around codified roles within the family. Each member has a function to fulfill in order to assure the maintenance of societal cohesion. The designated leader is the father; the mother plays the role of educator. The father works outside the home and supports his family, while the mother maintains the household, educates the children, and trains them in religious and cultural traditions. These roles are believed to be divinely ordained such, they are beyond question.

This social map is reflected in the Mudwanna, the Moroccan Personal Status Code.[10] Enacted in 1957, the code is inspired by the Shari'a, the Islamic law based on Maliki Rites[11] that governed the Maghreb, and specifies women's and men's duties and prerogatives. Article 36 of the Mudwanna identifies the wife's duties to her husband as:

1. fidelity;
2. obedience according to accepted social proprieties;
3. if possible, breast-feeding the children;
4. management and organization of the household;
5. deference towards the husband's father, mother, and close relatives.

In other words, the wife's duties center essentially around functions inside the house and focus on sexual morality, submission,[12] and family responsibilities.

Division of space also plays a deciding role in the interactions among family members. The mother is responsible for the children's education and for the transfer of religious and cultural traditions. By conveying tradition and cultural loyalty, one of the female's primary tasks becomes the maintenance of family stability. While the definitions of the house's public and private spaces are quite flexible, men seldom dare to venture into the kitchen. Because women spend a great deal of time there, their idea of space is formed by the kitchen's architecture, a small room secluded from other parts of the house. Women are thus conditioned to confine themselves to "their" space: a tiny area exclusively designated for them.

Map of Public Space

The idea of public space emphasizes the boundaries of male domination. The Mudwanna defines public space by citing the duties of the husband. According to article 35, he is responsible for

1. financial support (i.e., food, clothing, medical care, and housing);
2. equal treatment with other spouses (in case of polygamy);
3. authorization for his wife to visit and host her parents, within the limits of socially accepted norms;

4. protecting the wife's total freedom to administer her possessions independent of the husband's control (the husband has no power over his
wife's possessions).

Thus the husband's duties are essentially financial in nature while the
wife's are predominantly moral. Parallel with these duties lies the notion
of space; the husband's financial obligations are achieved in the outside,
public space. The most important duty seems to be the nafaqa, financial
support as stated by law, including providing food, clothing, medical
care, and housing. This obligation is clarified in article 115: "Every
person is required to provide for his needs with his resources, except the
wife whose upkeep is the responsibility of her husband."

A multitude of problems are created by the legal requirement that the
husband support his wife and family. In contemporary Moroccan society,
many women work, are heads of households,[13] and are often required to
contribute to the family income. However, Moroccan legislation has not
been modified to accommodate this reality. As a result, the gap between
what the Mudwanna specifies and what people actually do grows larger
every day.

The identification of public space with the male is an unmistakable
reality in Morocco. When walking along Rabat's Avenue Muhammad V,
one cannot avoid noticing that the coffee shops and movie theaters are
frequented exclusively by men. Women dare venture only into select tea
salons. Furthermore, men are free to sit in public places or just hang out.
Women are not welcome in these spaces. Consequently, in the streets,
they are almost always in motion.

Hijab: Reconstruction of Gender Identity

What occurs in a society in which the clearly structured division of space
is no longer possible? How is space divided once women possess duties
outside their "assigned" private realm? How do these women, who
are professionals or students, feel about women and work, women in
"masculine" space, and how should women reconcile the work outside
the home with the work inside?

The majority of the women I interviewed said that it is often difficult
for a family to manage with only one salary, and that women should
therefore work outside the home, provided their professions don't interfere with their primary duty: the care of the family. The belief that
"women should work outside the home" contradicts the Moroccan Per-

sonal Status Code's injunction to men to bear sole financial responsibility for their families. How then do these women justify this discrepancy? Some stated that women have a role to play in the development of the country, and should work outside the home. However, they also said that in an ideal Islamic society, women should stay indoors. As Aicha explained: "If she can stay home, it's better because it avoids problems; problems inside the small family as well as inside the big family." Others, such as Fatima, placed the blame of current unemployment on women: "Women have invaded all the positions of work, and this has created a problem for men who no longer have jobs."

To support their conviction of men's prerogatives over women and men's responsibility for women, the interviewees often quoted the following surah:

> Men are in charge of women, because Allah hath made one of you to excel over the other, and because they spend their property (for the support of women).[14]

Some Muslims have interpreted this surah to mean that Allah preferred men over women. For others, however, this is an inaccurate understanding. This sentence needs clarification. The word excel is translated from the Arabic word qawamoon, which means "to take care of, to assume the burdens of, or to defray the costs of."[15] When considering this surah, one must take into consideration the context in which the Qur'an was revealed. The interviewees claimed that Allah had chosen men over women solely when it came to financial matters. This view is consistent with conditions in seventh-century Arabia, where societal structure required men to assume economic responsibility. This duty has remained constant over fourteen centuries and is of utmost importance in relation to male/female dynamics in twentieth-century Morocco. The women interviewed generally agreed that the husband's duties are much greater than the wife's. Almost all concurred with Layla who said, "a man has many more duties than a woman! It's up to him to take care of her financially. Even if she has money, she isn't required to spend it on the family. She can keep it all to herself!"

No interviewee ever mentioned the idea that a woman could work for her own personal or professional fulfillment. When asked about that possibility Souraya answered: "she has enough work to do in the home!" Houria responded differently:

It is important that women who wear the hijab pursue advanced studies and obtain high positions [as doctors, lawyers, etc.]. If we do so, we will project a good image and set a good example for others. We will show others how to practice the real Islam. I would like to influence others into wearing the hijab.

The great majority of women interviewed agreed that in today's society, women can enter into traditionally masculine space. They also stated that in order to avoid disrupting societal equilibrium, the division of space and the distinction between the private and public worlds cannot be overturned. Men and women must be separated; therefore women wear hijabs, which are defined as "any partitions that separate two things."[16] Women can enter men's public space only by remaining shielded in their private space. Nadia clarified this point: "Wearing the hijab shows that women have a role in the society. Of course I am for women who work outside the home. If not I wouldn't be for the hijab, because inside their households, women don't wear the hijab!"

The veil therefore is a symbol of interiority. Because a woman's space is interior, she is permitted to move through the exterior only if she remains separated from it. Without the veil, societal equilibrium is threatened, if not disrupted.

The veil's reassuring effect is evident in Fatima's words:

I remember going to the city with my veil. Everything was so different from the village life. People, gestures, and actions seemed so hostile and brutish. I was afraid, I didn't belong. I clung tightly to my djellaba because it protected me. I hid inside the layers, as if they were my mother's womb.

Sou'al reaffirmed this need for security: "One day I had these strange dreams in which I would forget my veil, and I felt completely naked. Now I can never go out without my hijab."

Interiority Versus Exteriority

The concepts of interiority and exteriority are fundamental to the structure of North African societies.[17] One wonders if the rigidity of the division of space will lessen when women have worked in the masculine sphere for a longer period. Will men move into the feminine sphere? The interviewees gave a variety of responses when asked whether a man should help in the household: "Yes, he should help, as the Prophet did"; "No, but he should hire someone to help his wife;" and "She can do it on her own, it isn't difficult work!"

While the responses vary somewhat, the general consensus is that even if women work outside the home, a woman's domestic status is not changed. Hadija explained: "A woman can be a doctor, a lawyer, or whatever she wants, but she always has the same position inside the home which is to be responsible for the upkeep."

Therefore if women who have jobs outside the home still have the same function inside the home, can one speak of a woman's sense of liberation in the public sphere? How does a woman reconcile the dichotomy of having a certain status and relative freedom in masculine space, while remaining subjected to a subservient, traditional role in *her* space?

Religion Versus Social Reality

Nowhere in the Qur'an are women specifically enjoined to be veiled. Proponents of the veil most often cite the following passage:

> And tell the believing women to lower their gaze and be modest, and to display of their adornment only that which is apparent, and to draw their veils over their bosoms.[18]

Despite this surah's focus on modesty rather than on garb, all the interviewees insisted that it meant that Muslim women are required to wear the hijab. When asked about the historical context of the revelations of the Qur'an, the usual response was: "what was written then is applicable now" or "Islam is adaptable to all countries and to all centuries." Souraya explained:

> the evolution that has taken place over the years (fourteen centuries) is actually on a very superficial level. Humans have basically stayed the same, with their same needs and anxieties. Humans remain human. They still have the need for stability and security. Even with all the evolution that has taken place on other levels, this will never change. Humans remain human.

This idea, that "humans remain human" while society evolves, implies a sense of antagonism between the two. In this view, humans are born with a set of static characteristics, immune to the evolution of society. A person's gender carries a specific group of characteristics that determine one's destiny. The interviewees emphasized the immutable aspect of women, analogous to the French "éternel féminin." According to them, woman was created from the "not straight" rib of man. Woman was created weak, emotional, and capricious. Her destiny is programmed from birth: she is doomed to the role of a secondary citizen. She is incapable of change; as from the beginning "humans remain human," and "woman remains woman." Man was created strong, level-headed, and firm. His destiny is also determined from birth: he is to occupy positions of power and control. These characteristics cannot be challenged, because they are considered truths that exist beyond time and evolution. However, evolution has taken place, and the roles of men and women have altered. Societal evolution cannot be negated. How then do these seemingly opposing notions coexist?

It must be noted that when considering the interviewees' religious opinions and influences, they all stated that they had grown up not understanding Islam and that their parents had failed to show them the correct path. The notion that Islam, as religion, had been something foreign to them in their upbringing came through again and again, as Wafa explained: "You must understand that our parents did not know much about Islam. We were not raised correctly, they didn't teach us to follow the correct path." Malika developed the same idea: "I began praying when I was seven years old, but it was out of the need to imitate my parents. My mother, though illiterate, says her prayers, but she just repeats the same verse that someone in her family taught her."

These women believe that they were raised with no understanding of Islam and that their parents practiced it incorrectly. They also believe in an idealized, remote religious past, during the time of the Prophet, when true Islam was said to have been practiced. Agreeing that only Islam can create a functional society, they asserted repeatedly that capitalism leads to chaos, communism is passé, and that secularism, as practiced in Tunisia, is against divine will. These women felt deceived not only by their families, but also by society. Both failed to provide the "truth." Consequently, to what or to whom could they turn?

Ideal Versus Real Practice

The "ideal, genuine" Islam yearned for by the interviewees is the one practiced during the Prophet's time, and as stated by Jamila, "practicing the true Islam is the only thing that can save us." The women gain hope from that ideal; their desire is not simply to re-create that past but to re-create the ideal of that past. The hiatus between Islam as ideal and Islam in reality manifests itself in the wish to reconstruct this utopian past. Linked to this ideal is the belief that an authentic Islamic society is an egalitarian society. Sou'al elaborated:

> If we applied the Shari'a [Islamic law], the inequalities today would no longer exist. There would be the Zakah (the giving of alms, one of the pillars of Islam), there would be no poor because the rich would be required to give to the poor. There would be no adultery because women would be dressed in hijabs and ample clothing. Women would only work if necessary, therefore there would be more job opportunities open to men.

The idea that the practice of the "real Islam" would alleviate most social problems shows that the interviewees' believe many Moroccans today are practicing a faith that somehow deviates from the "straight path."

When asked if a "real Islamic society" exists today or if one existed in the past, the majority replied that the ideal was practiced only during the Prophet's lifetime. How do these women practice their faith in a corrupt society? The following quotes demonstrate the conflict. Malika said:

> I worked [as a physician] for five years but had to stop working two years ago because I couldn't work and apply my Islamic ideals. To work in such a society, one must have secular ideas. Islam is a way of life which I can't apply in such a system where it's only money that is important.

Fatima stressed the belief that "even if we are convinced of our faith, we can't practice it. I have friends who would like to wear the hijab, but if they did they would lose their jobs!" Another woman, Hadija, told me that "the hijab is a way for me to retreat from a world that has disappointed me. It's my own little sanctuary."

The hijab is used as a shelter, a way in which to withdraw from a society that has disappointed women, a society in which they are "treated as sex objects" and that uses "money as a trap." Wearing the hijab (and djellaba) gives a certain sense of anonymity. Being able to remain incognito diminishes the differences between social classes and is perceived as a step toward a more egalitarian society. Furthermore, the veiled women are no longer judged by their physical appearance, dress, or jewelry; they are instead considered for "their personality, and their minds." Competition is reduced, leading to a more egalitarian world. Nadia said: "My religion saved me. In a world where there is no justice, I now believe in something that is just. I now have something I can count on."

The need to practice the "real Islam" is related to the widespread influence of unorthodox religious practices such as the marabouts and fortune-tellers. Wafa said: "My parents thought they were believers but they would go to the marabout, which [is a practice] I now know is against Islam." However, many Moroccans do not find any contradiction in practicing what some would consider as being two different religions; for them, they are tenets of the same Islam. For the interviewees, however, any person who thinks that "he or she can predict or alter the future is... direct[ly]... violat[ing]... the [teachings of the] Sacred Books." The question, which Islam are we talking about? arises. What is the "real Islam" and, more important, who is its interpreter?

Hijab: Religious Significance Reinterpreted in Contemporary Context

Why do some women feel secure in public only when wearing the hijab? What is the basis for this sense of being uncovered? Morocco is a rapidly changing society influenced by contrasting value systems, one anchored in Muslim tradition and the other inspired by Western norms. The women interviewed feel that they have no control over the systems that are shaping their lives and that the influence of Western values is pernicious. Because they feel powerless, their identities are continually being redefined and questioned. How do women confront a multifaceted perception of the self? Aicha explained: "I feel more like a woman when I wear the hijab and not like the type of woman you see on billboards." These women feel the need to wear clothes that project a Muslim identity and refute an imitation of the West. To them, Muslim women should dress neither like men, nor like nonorthodox Muslims. When a woman wears the hijab, she has made a deliberate choice that shows she belongs to a group that overtly professes ethical standards in tune with Muslim values.

While allowing a Moroccan woman honorable access to men's public space, the hijab identifies the role she has assumed. Likewise, when a Moroccan woman chooses not to wear the hijab, she allows society to draw potentially contrary conclusions about her. In that context, how is identity defined, formed, and reconstructed?

Veiled Protection Versus Nakedness

I wear the hijab because I don't want to go out naked.

Djamila

If one believes that all women who are not dressed in hijab are "naked," where exactly does nudity begin? In the West, to be naked means to be unclothed. For the Moroccan women interviewed, the concept of nudity is different. A woman is naked if she dares show the shapeliness or outline of her body in public. Doing so means that she wishes to provoke and attract males, which in public is considered taboo. As Sou'al observed: "Look how women dress today. They wear such tight-fitting clothing, it's like they were naked. It's as if you showed a candy to a child and said 'look, look. . . but you can't have it.' " Souraya added: "Look at women today who wear short skirts, and lots of makeup to go to work. Do they really go to work, or are they thinking of other things? "

Thus, wearing jeans, skirts, blouses, or any clothing that outlines the body provokes men and can only lead to adultery. If adultery occurs, women are held more responsible that men.[19] Moreover, Moroccan law gives a woman the right to divorce only in specific circumstances;[20] catching her husband engaging in an adulterous act is not listed as one of the reasons, yet a woman's adulterous behavior is anathema. Why are there such different consequences for the same offense? This is based on the deep-rooted belief that by nature women excite and provoke men. As a consequence, women are presumed guilty for anything illicit that may happen to them. When they wear the hijab, however, they are protected from men, and possibly from harm. By protecting women, the hijab maintains and protects societal order. Being unveiled signifies being unprotected. It follows that if women in jeans venture into public space, they are, in essence, nude and without defense. At the same time, they can potentially disrupt the stability of society. Women in the hijab, on the other hand, are "clothed" and therefore protected. As long as women remain covered, i.e., separated from men, the mixing of the sexes does not occur. As a result, family honor, the basis for social equilibrium, is assured.

Veiled Protection Versus Impurity

When asked how wearing the hijab had changed their relationships with others, most women concurred with Jamila: the women "gained more respect from men and women and had more respect for themselves." Habiba commented: "Since I began wearing the hijab, men no longer bother me in the streets." The idea that women must be covered in order to merit respect is rooted in the division of space and in assumptions about fundamental differences between men and women. Although most of the interviewees stated that men must also follow a dress code (they must be covered from navel to knees), they stressed the belief that men and women are different and should not be compared. Aicha explains: "Look in the streets, it's the men that try to pick up women and not the other way around!"

Since any attempt to display one's beauty is a direct attempt to disrupt society, women who wear the hijab do not wear make-up or jewelry in public. A woman is permitted and encouraged, however, to "make herself beautiful" for her husband at home. Sou'al reasoned: "I have some friends, a woman and her husband, and when she is at home she doesn't care what she wears, and she puts on a type of scarf like maids wear. But when they go out, she spends an hour in front of the mirror to make herself beautiful and who does she do this for? For the men outside?"

To summarize, in Morocco, a woman may obtain a sense of dignity by staying in her private space or by wearing the veil, which keeps her in a private space in public. Venturing uncovered into public space upsets the social order. Because a woman's honor is the basis of family integrity, the loss of her honor only leads to chaos. How do women deal with the fact that their entire family's reputation depends on the sexual morality of its female members?

The hijab becomes the means by which females assert the sexual ethics required of their gender in the Muslim order. Wearing a veil represents purity of intention and behavior. It is a symbol affirming that "I'm clean" and "I'm not available." As a consequence, women wearing veils affirm the expectations of the society. By not questioning these expectations, they attain a certain degree of respect. The acquisition of honor, in such a morality-conscious society, leads to power, even if it is only symbolic.

Veiled Protection Versus Isolation

Wearing the veil also increases a woman's mobility. As Latifa explained, "When I wear the hijab I can do anything—go to the university, go shopping, and be with my classmates." Women who wear the hijab are liberated from parental apprehension and free to enter areas they might avoid if unprotected (i.e., unveiled). Layla said, "Now that I wear the hijab, my father no longer worries when I go out."

The hijab vitiates potential jealousy. If the wife goes out covered, her husband no longer feels threatened by other males. She is free from the harassment of men in the street. At the same time, she feels more respected by the population at large and gains more respect for herself. The veil becomes a way to acquire spiritual and ethical liberation while increasing mobility.

From a Western standpoint, the hijab may seem confining and re-stricting. For most of the women I interviewed, however, it provides physical and emotional security as well as a sense of group identity and self-worth. In a society still plagued by the vestiges of colonialism and subjected to tremendous cultural pressures, the hijab becomes a symbol of stability that stems the unsettling tide of uncontrollable change in an unknown future. Women in hijab are looking for an Islamic identity in tune with their heritage and devoid of Western materialism and values. In essence, they are requesting a revised, more genuine practice of Islam, one based on indigenous cultural norms, as well as on the values inherent in Islam.

Unfortunately, the country's drastic technological transformation as-sociated with modernity, has not been accompanied by parallel cultural changes, throwing Moroccan society into an abyss between two con-trasting sets of values. On the one hand, Moroccans can choose the values of traditional Sunni Islam; on the other, they can adopt a nonin-digenous version of Western secular materialism.

When women wear the hijab, they obtain respect and freedom. In this sense, the hijab, which is often perceived by Westerners as a tool of male domination, may ultimately be a liberating force for some Moroc-can women. However, this choice is made within a patriarchal frame-work. It is a conditioned reaction and can exist only within prescribed norms established by men for women.

The wearing of the hijab, while providing some level of self-respect and dignity, nevertheless also perpetuates the old dual vision of women as both temptresses and blameless pillars of sustenance for men. That mystique negates the evolution of female roles. The hijab serves a paradoxical purpose: it simultaneously challenges and underscores the notion of the unchanging, eternal female and her associated traditional roles. In essence, then, in Moroccan society, females who wear the hijab represent a major element of real and imagined permanency and societal cohesion in a male-dominated world subject to drastic change.

REFERENCES

1. *Maghreb* refers to Western North Africa, including the countries of Morocco, Algeria, and Tunisia.

2. The *hijab* is a large scarf that covers the back of a woman's head. It is folded around the chin, covers neck and shoulders, and leaves only the face visible. The *djellaba* is a long, loose-fitting, opaque gown; its design is to avoid suggesting any body shape or implying any sexual provocation. The hijab and the djellaba thus cover the entire female body, except for face and hands.

3. The term *personal* is used in the context of Morocco, a theocracy. Unless born into a Jewish or Christian family, all Moroccans are born and die Muslim. Saying, therefore, that one is Muslim doesn't necessarily mean that there has been an individual choice. Women who have made the decision themselves to wear the Islamic attire have most likely made a "personal decision" regarding their religious conviction.

4. It is important to remember I conducted my research in the fall of 1989. I started interviewing veiled women after two Moroccan girls were forbidden to wear the hijab in a public high school in a Paris suburb. According to French education officials, the dress code was enforced because of the veil's religious symbolism, which was considered unacceptable in a secular setting. Around that time, two French journalists interviewed King Hassan of Morocco; he announced on Moroccan and French television that Muslim women were not required to wear the veil. Because King Hassan carries the title of Commander of the Faithful, his assertion bears the seal of religious authority. However, many women who wear the hijab felt betrayed by the king and were reluctant to openly discuss their decision to veil.

5. See, for example, Arlene MacLeod, *Accommodating Protest: Working Women, the New Veiling, and Change in Cairo* (New York: Columbia University Press, 1990); Carla Makhlouf, *Changing Veils: Women and Modernization in North Yemen* (Austin: University of Texas Press, 1979); and Sherifa Zuhur, *Revealing and Reveiling* (Albany: State University of New York Press, 1992).

6. It should be noted that the belief that Islam invented the veil is erroneous. While some Muslims interpret various surahs as instituting the veil, the notion

of a veil in the Prophet Muhammad's time was nothing new. See Maxime Rodinson, *Europe and the Mystique of Islam* (Seattle: University of Washington, Press, 1987).

7. Throughout this paper I will use the word "veil" and "hijab" interchangeably to refer to the contemporary Islamic veil advocated by the fundamentalist Islamic movements for Muslim females.

8. Sou'al is a fictitious name, as is the case for all the interviewees' names quoted in this study.

9. This research includes Michel Foucault *Archaeology of Knowledge*, second ed. (New York: Routledge, 1990); Nikki Keddie and Beth Baron, eds., *Women in Middle Eastern History: Shifting Boundaries in Sex and Gender* (New Haven: Yale University Press, 1991); and Leila Ahmed, *Women and Gender in Islam: Historical Roots of A Modern Debate*, (New Haven: Yale University Press, 1992).

10. Government of Morocco, *Mudwanna: Le Code du Statut Personnel* (Maroc: Association pour la Promotion de la Recherche des Etudes Juridiques, 1983).

11. Since the Prophet's death, many schools of law and interpretation have been formed. In the Sunni tradition, there exist four primary schools: the Hanafi, Shafi'i, Maliki, and Hanabali. The Maliki school is dominant across North Africa.

12. For many Muslims, the word *submission* does not carry the negative connotations that it may for Westerners. Instead, it suggests devotion, respect of others, and harmony with a divinely ordained status.

13. See the study, *Les Femmes et Le Travail*, La Direction de La Statistique, (Rabat: Centre de Documentation, 1988).

14. *The Glorious Qur'an*, Mohammad M. Pickthall, trans. (Albany: State University of New York Press, 1987), surah Women, v. 34.

15. Unless otherwise indicated all Arabic/English translations are taken from J.M. Cowan, ed., *The Hans Wehr Dictionary of Modern Written Arabic* (Ithaca: Spoken Language Services, 1976).

16. This definition can be found in Cyril Glassé, *The Concise Encyclopedia of Islam* (San Francisico: Harper, 1989).

17. Margot Badran amd Miriam Cooke, eds., *Opening the Gates: A Century of Arab Feminist Writing*, (Bloomington: Indiana University Press, 1990).

18. *The Glorious Qur'an*, surah The Light v. 31.

19. The Moroccan Penal Code states in article 418: "Murder, wounds, and blows are excusable if they are committed by the husband against his wife and her accomplice at the moment when he catches them red-handed committing adultery." Therefore, the husband not only has the exclusive right to take the law in his hands, but he may furthermore be excused if he harms or kills his wife.

20. A woman can ask for a divorce for the following reasons: divorce due to lack of maintenance (article 53); divorce due to a damning vice (article 54); divorce due to ill treatment (article 55); divorce due to a husband's absence (article 56).

CHAPTER FOUR

Turkish Women and the Republican Reconstruction of Tradition

Zehra F. Arat

Compared with their counterparts in other developing countries, especially those in the Muslim world, Turkish women enjoy considerable civil and political rights and are more visible in the public domain. As early as the 1920s, they gained legal rights, including the right to choose their own spouse, initiate divorce, and demand child custody. In 1923, free elementary education was made mandatory for both sexes. Women were granted the right to vote and run in municipal elections in 1930, and in national elections in 1934. Consequently, although these rights were not equally enjoyed by the entire female population, many Turkish women gained access to education, public office, and employment opportunities—they had acquired rights comparable to those of women in industrialized countries. In fact, the statistical indicators of female representation among professionals in Turkey has been more impressive than those in many Western countries; figures from the 1970s indicate that one in every five lawyers and one in every six doctors in Turkey was a woman;[1] and Turkey ranked third among all nations, following the United States and Canada, in recruiting women into academia.[2]

What do these indicators signify? Some take them as evidence of the emancipation of Turkish women and attribute it to the efforts of Mustafa Kemal Atatürk, and the "Kemalist reforms"of the 1920s and 1930s.[3] Others point to the uneven utilization of these rights and point to the gap between urban upper- and middle-class women and rural lower-class women. Some of these analysts—without questioning the founder's

This article is reprinted from a slightly longer and different version published in *Women and Politics* 14:4 (1994).

sincerity in seeking the emancipation of women—argue that the impact of Kemalist reforms has been limited because of the power of conservative groups and Islamic tradition, especially in rural areas. It is true that the representatives of traditional ideology were quite vocal in the Grand National Assembly, the legislative body established in 1920. They questioned cabinet ministers who initiated progressive programs and, at times, forced them to resign.[4] Mustafa Kemal Atatürk, however, did not interfere in these parliamentary debates. His supporters today explain his silence not in terms of indifference or concurrence, but as a calculating strategy stemming from his cautious character. According to this line of argument, he presented ideas but did not defend them in the parliament when they faced resistance. Instead, he preferred to repeat them in public speeches, so he could gain support among the public, who in return would put pressure on the representatives.[5]

Another explanation for the limited impact of the reforms emphasizes the socioeconomic context and holds that impact of the reforms have been limited because the reforms preceded economic development. Turkey, a largely agrarian society, lacked both a sizable bourgeoisie and an industrial working class—therefore, women's rights could not be absorbed by its small, apolitical female labor force. The "state feminism" of Kemalism, therefore, fell short of having a national impact, and of bringing about full liberation.[6]

This paper dwells on the last argument, and illustrates that the stimulation of Western-style economic development and modernization led Kemalist reformers to grant some rights and create some opportunities for Turkish women. Development and modernization in Turkey meant Westernization, and the Kemalist reforms attempted to reorganize life by the replacement of the Islamic patriarchy with that of a secular Western one. Kemalism sought to improve women's lives only to the level prevailing in the West, where the female was still perceived as the "second sex."

Kemalist reforms were *not* aimed at liberating women or at promoting the development of female consciousness and feminine identity. Instead, they strove to equip Turkish women with the education and skills that would improve their contributions to the republican patriarchy by making them better wives and mothers.[7] With a goal of socioeconomic development, these reforms are hardly feminist, and their perception of the role of women and definition of womanhood would not qualify them to be taken as "state-sponsored feminism," as done by some analysts.[8] Kemalism ignored the notion of gender domination in the same way it denied class conflicts. The only legitimate struggle in this one-party state was the struggle against the military and economic threats by the foreign powers that had occupied the country after the First World War. Its corporatist nationalism recognized no special interests or any conflicts of interest. The population had to be united around the "national goal," and should be ready to sacrifice all other demands for the "nation" and "country." Thus, the education and participation of women were seen as tools for national development rather than as means that would enable them to create an individual consciousness to exist "for themselves" or develop a collective consciousness to form a gender class. The following pages analyze the patriarchal structure of the Kemalist regime[9] at three levels, in the context of its rhetorical, legal, and administrative policy frameworks. Within these frameworks one can observe that words and deeds were not contradictory; rather, they were consistent in the reconstruction of traditional society within a new, nationalist context.

Rhetorical Framework

Speeches by Mustafa Kemal Atatürk, the founder of the Republic and state ideology, provide the grounds for analyzing the rhetorical framework of Kemalist reforms. His speeches demonstrate that Atatürk held women in high regard as productive and reproductive forces. Nowhere in these texts, however, does he acknowledge women's rights or present the proposed changes as opportunities that women can use, or should use, to fulfill individual needs or potentials.

Atatürk perceived women as a social force with both positive and negative impact. In 1923, although he starts a speech arguing that "we should believe that everything on earth is the product of women," he quickly adds that their contribution has not been always positive. He holds them responsible for the male lethargy during the Ottoman era: "we used to have some false notions about the Sultans. They were consequences of our mothers' futile suggestions."[10] The acknowledgment of women's social contribution, nevertheless leads him to recognize their potential use for social change. He continues:

> If it is found to be sufficient to have only one of the two sexes that compose a society equipped with the contemporary needs, more than half of that society would remain weak.... Therefore, if knowledge and technology are necessary for our society, both our men and women have to acquire them equally.[11]

Following these egalitarian statements, however, Atatürk highlights motherhood as the most important function and virtue of women. He then defends the education of women, not as their right—as an end in itself—or as a means to liberate women, but as means of improving the quality of parental care so that the next generation of men will be reared better. In his words:

> The most important duty of woman is motherhood. The importance of this duty is better understood, if one considers that the earliest education takes place on one's mother's lap. Our nation had decided to be a strong nation. Circumstances today require the advancement of our women in all respects. Therefore, our women, too, will be enlightened and learned and, like men, will go through all educational stages. Then, women and men, walking side by side, will be each other's help and support in social life.[12]

"Walking side by side" implies cooperation, but it does not necessarily mean that men and women would have the *same* responsibilities. A division of labor between the sexes is treated as inevitable, if not essential, and the primary function of women is mothering. "Learned women" are expected to put their knowledge into practice first at home. After all, as he states in another speech, "it is the woman who gives a man the earliest words of advice and education, and who exercises on him the initial influence of motherhood."[13] Thus, Atatürk attributes men central importance and assigns women a peripheral role, as indirect facilitator of the modernization process. In the modern society that he envisions, however, mothering requires additional and more advanced qualifications for women. He argues:

> The education that mothers have to provide to their children today is not simple, as it had been in the past. Today's mothers have to attain several high qualities in order to bring up children with the necessary qualities and develop them into active members for life today. Therefore, our women are obliged to be more enlightened, more prosperous, and more knowledgeable than our men. If they really want to be the *mothers of this nation*, this is the way.[14]

Atatürk, like many other nationalist leaders, stresses education because of its transformative capacity; he designates education as the most effective way of changing the traditional mentality into a modern, secular mind.

In addition to emphasizing education, his approach to modernization also stresses the importance of dressing more like Westerners. He provides a strict dress code for men and offers suggestions for changes in outfits and appearance for women. His discontent with the prevailing clothing style and its symbolism is apparent in a speech that he delivered in Kastomonu, on August 30, 1925:

> In some places I see women who hide their faces and eyes by throwing a piece of fabric, a scarf, or something like that over their heads, and when a man passes by, they turn their backs to him or close up by sitting on the ground. What is the meaning and explanation of this behavior? Gentlemen, would the mothers and daughters of a civilized nation assume such an absurd and vulgar pose? This is a situation that ridicules our nation. It has to be corrected immediately.[15]

Here again, the goal is not to free women from social control, but to transform Turkey into a "civilized nation" acceptable to the West. Although Atatürk himself saw the linkage between look and outlook as more than spurious, in several other speeches he reflects his concern about Westerners equating Turkish women's excessive covering with a state of ignorance. For example, his address to the residents of Izmir, on January 31, 1923, deals with this issue:

> In our towns and cities foreigners' attention focuses on the way our women cover themselves. Such observations lead them to assume that our women don't see anything. However, covering, that is required by the religion, to be stated briefly, should be in a simple form which would not be a burden for women and disturb decency. Covering should not be in a form that would isolate woman from her life and existence.[16]

Atatürk's sensitivity toward Europeans' perception of Turkish women is most evident in his speech to the Women's Branch of the Red Crescent, delivered on March 21, 1923:

> Despite all the sacrifices and services by our women, and all their competence that are no less than those of men, our enemies and the shallow observations that are ignorant of the soul of Turkish women make some attributions to our women. There are some who state that our women live an idle life, have no contact with science and knowledge, are not involved in the civilized life and public life, our women are denied of everything, and they are kept away, by Turkish men, from life, world, humanity, and business gains. . . .

. . . . Honorable ladies, this image that misleads our enemies originates especially from our women's appearance, their way of clothing themselves and concealing their faces.[17]

Although a change in women's appearance and a moderation in veiling was suggested, women were not allowed to act or dress freely. On March 21, 1923 when he addressed women in Izmir he criticized some women for "mimicking the European conduct and behavior" and carrying their clothing style to the extreme by wearing "insufficient clothing that cannot be presented as an outfit even at the most liberal ball rooms of Europe."[18] The new modern woman was also warned that in her reformed appearance, she was not supposed to overdo and imitate the promiscuity of the western women, but maintain her modesty. In order for women to join men in public life, he urged Turkish women to wear "attire that is recommended by the law of God and commanded by our religion" and to assume "a virtuous attitude."[19] This meant that the ideal Turkish woman had to be "asexual," as she had been the "comrade-women" during the national struggle against the European occupation, and she was now expected to be "sexually neutral" in the work life to preserve her honor and chastity.[20]

Despite these criticisms of women's appearance, especially that of excessive concealment, no policies were adopted to alter the situation. The Dress Codes of 1925 outlawed traditional outfits for men, but did not touch either the women's garments or the veil, an instrument of psychological and physical segregation of sexes. In 1935, a ban on veil was proposed at the national congress of the Republican People's Party, but no legal action was taken by the state, and such a ban was carried out only in a few municipalities.[21]

Legal Policy Framework

During the early years of the Republic, the Grand National Assembly, as the representative organ of sovereign people, had been busy writing laws that reorganized practically every aspect of life. The laws dealt directly or indirectly with gender relations, and some of them made specific references to the role of women in the society and distinguished it from that of men.[22]

In 1926, the Grand National Assembly adopted the Swiss civil code as the basis of its civil law, which included family law. Civil law abolished polygamy, prevented child marriages by imposing minimum ages for marriage[23], and recognized women as legal equals of men in certain areas (e.g., as witnesses in courts; in inheriting and maintaining property). It also granted women the right to choose their spouses, initiate divorce, and maintain their maternal rights, even after divorce. All of these had been limited or unrecognized in the Islamic law, which had served as the principal source for the Ottoman legal code. However, the civil law failed to establish full legal equality between the sexes and contained several clauses that placed men first among equals. This is not surprising, because gender inequality also pervaded all Western legal and social systems. It should be noted, however, that the Swiss model did not conflict with the values of Switzerland's conservative Catholics, and it was not the most progressive model that could have been adopted.

The major accomplishment of civil law was the establishment of state control over the institution of family. Before the adoption of civil law, marriage and family were arranged according to the Islamic tradition, which treated marriage as a binding private agreement performed before two witnesses. Although an imam usually blessed the union, no legal respresentative was required to oversee the marriage contract. Similarly, the marriage could be ended by verbal repudiation. The civil law, on the other hand, introduced a set of detailed statutes that organized not only marriage, but also engagement and divorce.

The law banned polygamy and recognized the nuclear family as an institution to be organized and protected by law. Although the law's general principles and articles treated the husband and wife as legal equals, the division of labor in the family and the rights and responsibilities of each spouse, explicitly stated in the law, presented a highly inegalitarian picture.[24] The articles of the law that established male dominance in marriage can be summarized as follows:[25]

> Man is the head of the union of marriage (Article 152/I).
>
> The right and responsibility of deciding the place of residence belongs to the husband (Article 152/II).[26]
>
> It is the husband's responsibility to provide for his wife and children (Article 152/II).
>
> Although the father and mother share guardianship responsibilities, if there is a disagreement, the guardianship right is given to the father (Article 263).
>
> As their guardian, the father (not mother) has the right to benefit from the income of his children and keep the extra income (after the needs of the children are met) for himself (Articles 280 and 281).

The union of marriage is represented by the husband (Article 154).
Although the wife has some representative rights, they are limited to legal representation in matters that deal with providing "the continuous needs of the house" (Article 155).
The wife can take a job or engage in a craft only upon the "explicit or implicit permission" of the husband (Article 159/I).[27] The husband, on the other hand, can require his wife to contribute to the family budget to "a reasonable extent" (Article 190).
Upon marriage, the wife must use the husband's family name (Article 153/I).
The wife is responsible for taking care of the house (Article 153/II). However, she is never given the premier role, and in fact, as pronounced in article 153/II, "to the extent that she can, the wife serves as the assistant and consultant of her husband to pursue the happiness of the family."

The legal framework preserved the sexual division of labor and institutionalized women's social and economic dependence on men. The society henceforth has not treated "work" as a right of women, or as a means for fulfilling her individual needs.[28]

Moreover, the impact of the civil code's more egalitarian articles was mitigated by those that favor men. For example, although the law grants the wife the right to initiate divorce, and the divorce suit must be filed with the court in the plaintiff's residential district (Article 136), because the law also requires the wife to take husband's residence as her legal residence—even if they are separated—the authorized court is *de facto* always in the husband's venue.

For remarriage, the law imposes a restriction only on women. According to Article 95, "the woman who becomes a widow due to the husband's death or divorce, or nullity of her marriage, cannot marry again unless 300 days passed after the death, divorce or verdict of nullity." No such waiting period is required for men.

Virginity of the woman has been emphasized, and the discovery of its absence has been included among the conditions that would result in the annulment of marriage. Even contemporary legal authorities argue that "according to the moral and social rules of our country, the late discovery that the wife who was assumed to be virgin was not a virgin constitutes a 'substantial error in quality,' by man, both subjectively and objectively."[29] Similarly, the judicial interpretation of the tasks and responsibilities assigned to the women by the civil law reinforced the inequalities, and divorce requests of husbands have been granted on some grounds—if the wife was raped,[30] or she failed to perform the skills of cleaning and cooking[31]—because they would cause severe quarrels and disharmony in the marriage.

Although the unequal treatment of sexes by the civil law is often justified on the grounds that it protects women, it should be noted that no statutory arrangements have been made to protect the wife or children against an abusive husband or father. The continuous physical and psychological abuse of a wife can be used by the woman as a ground for divorce, but she cannot raise criminal charges against him, because no such crime has been recognized or defined by the law. On the issue of abuse, the relationship between the husband and wife is treated as a private affair and the state does not assume a protective role.[32]

In addition to the statutes in the civil code, unequal treatment of sexes can be found in the criminal and labor laws. The gender biases and restrictions imposed on women by the criminal law—legislated also in 1926—are particularly explicit over adultery and abortion. Adultery, which establishes a ground for divorce according to the family law, is also considered as a threat to public morality and pronounced a criminal act (Articles 440–444). The unequal treatment of the husband and wife lies in the separate definitions of adultery for each sex and the penalties assigned for each. While one incident of sexual intercourse is enough for a married woman to be charged for adultery (Article 440), a man can only be prosecuted for having a continuous relationship with another woman that resembles the relationship of a husband and wife (Article 441). Moreover, the husband only can be charged with the crime of adultery by his wife if the accomplice is an unmarried woman. If the accomplice is a married woman, however, the wife's complaint is not adequate to bring up the charge; the adulterous wife's husband is required to file the complaint.

The criminal law also denied the reproductive rights of women. Articles 468 and 469 banned abortion and sought the prosecution of anyone who had (or assisted in) an abortion.[33] The statutes that organized work life were not free from gender bias either. Labor law contains legal restrictions upon women's participation in the work force and public life. Article 68, for example, prevents women of any ages from working underground or underwater. It further restricts employment for women by banning them from jobs that involve physically demanding, dangerous and poisonous activities, on the grounds that these would threaten the reproductive function of women. Consequently, women have not been able to seek employment in relatively high paying jobs such as in mining, construction, or the heavy metal and manufacturing industries.[34]

Public administration comprised another area of employment denied for women. Based on the principle of unitary government, the Turkish national government is highly centralized; the law enforcement and policy implementation at the province and town levels are administered by governors who are appointed by the cabinet. These gubernatorial posts, the office of *Vali* in provinces and of *Kaymakam* in towns, were kept closed to women.[35] Although the law has no explicit gender restrictions for such appointments, by excluding women from the post-bachelor training programs required for these posts, governments denied women's right to hold such offices.

There is an obvious contradiction between the exclusion of women from public administration and the establishment of women's electoral rights (they were allowed to run for municipal governments in 1930, and for parliament in 1934). The contradiction deepens if one accepts the commonly stated argument that Turkish women were enfranchised at a time when they did not show a viable political presence. Some recent studies reveal that there *were* active women's organizations and movements. In the early 1920s, some women, organized as the Turkish Women's Federation, raised political demands. However, they were manipulated into sacrificing their interests for the sake of national unity. Atatürk himself talked them out of their attempt to establish a political party in 1923.[36] Later, he discouraged the Federation's attempt to nominate its own parliamentary candidates for the 1927 elections.[37] Similarly, women's demands for membership to the political party were denied in the 1930s.[38] If women's demands were successfully suppressed, why was not their demand for suffrage also ignored? The explanation lies in Atatürk's sensitivity to Western perceptions of the new Turkish regime. Tekeli argues that Atatürk was concerned about Western impressions of his regime as a dictatorship. His defensive attitude led him to encourage "democratization" in the 1930s. Thus, women's suffrage was a symbolic move, a part of democratic image-building that would distinguish the Turkish one-party rule from the other monolithic systems of the time, especially from Hitler's rule in Germany.[39] The manipulation of women continued after their inclusion in the electoral process, however, and suffrage did not result in further politization or independent political acts by women. Although women candidates acquired 4.5 percent of the parliamentary seats in the 1935 national elections, all 17 women were hand-picked by Atatürk. They all were characterized as "docile" women who "did not cause any problems at the parliament, [who] quietly performed duties that were assigned to them, did not speak or question much, were completely dedicated to "Atatürk's principles," and enthusiastically assumed the duty of being the symbol of those principles." [40]

Administrative Policy Framework

The effect of administrative policies on women can be best illustrated in the area of education. Education is not only a significant institution for development, but also a major agent of political socialization. Also, as demonstrated in the excerpts from Kemal Atatürk's speeches, the Kemalist regime assigned considerable value to the education of women. Despite the rhetoric, however, education policy appeared to be less than egalitarian; in fact, it reinforced traditional gender roles. The patriarchal indoctrination that took place in the earlier years of the Republic can be seen in three interrelated topics: the segregation of the school system, the segregation within coeducational schools, and the overt sanctioning of the sexuality of female students.

Although there were some advocates of coeducation, during the first years of the Republic, coeducation was established only at the primary education and university levels; middle schools and high-schools remained segregated. Although equal education for both groups was highly valued, and the number of schools for females continued to increase— sometimes even at the expense of schools for males—the number of schools for females remained at a fraction of those for males. While there were 72 middle schools for males and none for females during the 1923–24 academic year, for the next academic year the number of schools for males were reduced to 56, and 8 middle schools were opened for female students. In the 1925–26 academic year, these numbers changed to 54 and 15, respectively. [41]

Coeducation in the middle schools was initiated during 1927–28 academic year. [42] However, it took almost a decade, until the 1934–35 academic year, for high schools to start becoming coeducational—even then, it was allowed only in those cities where there was only one high school. [43]

However, while the middle and high schools with academic emphasis were gradually being integrated, segregated educational system was kept at teachers' schools, vocational and technical schools, and in adult education. It should be noted that vocational and technical schools were highly preferred by the public for their daughters' education. During the 1942–43 academic year, only 26 percent of the total female enrollments in secondary schools was in academic middle schools and high schools, while the vocational and technical schools absorbed the other 74 percent.[44]

The curricula of the vocational schools demonstrate striking gender–based differences. Some schools were geared toward training skilled industrial laborers or technicians, but those designed as girls' schools, especially the Girls' Institutes, emphasized home economics, child care, cooking, and sewing. According to official statements, the curriculum of these girls' schools aimed at "providing girls with theoretical and practical education that would train them in managing hygienic, orderly, economical, and tasteful homes, allowing them to establish cheerful and happy marriages, and therefore, making them contributors to the social development of the country."[45]

Table 1 reports the earliest available enrollment data that would allow comparative analyses. It shows that Girls' Institutes, along with the health care schools that specialized in nursing, child care, and midwifery—all reinforcing traditional female roles in the society—enrolled *only females*. Furthermore, even among these female-oriented schools, those that offered professional training that could lead to employment constituted a small portion of the total female enrollment. Females were not represented in eleven vocational schools which provided industrial training that would lead to employment. On the other hand, nearly half of the all female students were educated in the Girls' Institutes.[46]

The vocational schools that specialized in teaching "feminine work" that did not cultivate intellectual development, creativity, or independence, hardly prepared their students for employment. Moreover, the limited number of career-oriented schools that were open to female students led to mostly labor-intensive and low-wage jobs that did not allow women to participate in decision-making processes at work.[47] Consequently, the specialization and recruitment in vocational schools resulted in an educational system that perpetuated traditional gender roles. The differential treatment of sexes also was evident in the curricula of other secondary schools.

The 1924 law of Unification of Instruction (No. 430) sought secularization, centralization, and standardization of the curricula for the schools that provided same level of education and issued the same type of diplomas. Although the law eliminated regional or inter-institutional

TABLE 1
FEMALE ENROLLMENTS IN VOCATIONAL SCHOOLS, 1942–43

School type	Total Number of Females	Females as a Percentage of Total Enrollment	Percentage of Total Female Enrollments
TEACHERS' SCHOOLS			
Elementary ed.			
6 year schools	837	8.65	11.55
3 year schools	1576	60.47	21.75
Vocational ed.	236	55.92	3.26
BOYS' ARTS & CRAFTS INSTITUTES	—	—	—
Girls'	3471	100.00	47.90
Boys'	—	—	—
Construction	—	—	—
TECHNICAL SCHOOLS	—	—	—
TITLE/LAND REGISTRY	9	11.54	.12
RAILROAD	—	—	—
FINANCE	4	2.62	.06
COMMERCE			
Middle School	254	17.20	3.51
High School	167	14.87	2.30
CONSERVATORIES	200	54.49	2.76
FINE ARTS	78	28.06	1.08
TAILORING	56	60.21	.77
POLICE	—	—	—
HEALTH CARE			
Physician's aide	—	—	—
Nurse-Lab aide	148	100.00	2.04
Child Care	31	100.00	.43
Midwifery	127	100.00	1.75
AGRICULTURAL			
Regional farming	—	—	—
Animal health	—	—	—
Forestry	—	—	—
Mechanic	—	—	—
DISABLED (DEAF–MUTE–BLIND)	52	38.52	.72

SOURCE: Mine Tan, *Kadın: Ekonomik Yaşamı ve Eğitimi*. Türkiye İş Bankası Kültür Yayınları. (Ankara: TISA Matbaası, 1979), 206–207.

differences, it fell short of fulfilling the "separate but equal" principle for male and female students enrolled in regular middle or high schools.

Some subjects taught at schools were identified as feminine or masculine and were introduced only to the "relevant" group. When physical education and military instruction were first incorporated into the curricula of middle schools and high schools, they were taught only to boys. Girls were taught sewing, embroidery, home economics, and child care instead. Later on, these two courses were added to the curricula for girls, but classes were segregated, even at integrated schools. Moreover, the nature of the instruction and activities were different. For example, approximately twice as much time was allotted for military instruction for boys, and their classes involved military training instead of just civil defense. At various points in their education, male students were assigned extra time in science laboratories or were sent on field trips that would complement their history and geography classes. At the same time, girls were instructed in modern techniques of housekeeping.[48]

The 1924 curricula for the Teachers' Schools for Elementary School Education were also segregated. While schools for males and females were identical in the distribution of academic and professional classes, the differential treatment was clear in applied courses. Agriculture was offered only at Teachers' Schools for males, and male students spent twice as much on creative subjects such as painting, hand crafts, and calligraphy. At female schools, those hours were spared for courses of sewing, home economics (laundry, ironing, and cleaning), embroidery, and child care.[49]

While schools were being integrated, the curricula also underwent change. By the late 1930s, some uniformity had been established in the academic curriculum; male and female students studied mainly the same material, and they were taught in the same classrooms for most subjects. However, some separation in the schedules prevailed. Boys and girls attended different sections of physical education, on the rationale of biological differences; arts and crafts classes divided the students on the basis of traditional gender roles.[50] Once a week, boys attended arts and crafts classes that were usually called El İşi (handiwork). During the same time periods, girls attended Ev İşi (housework). While boys were instructed in crafts such as bookbinding, woodworking, and paper marbling, girls were trained in cooking, pickling, baking, sewing, and child care.

These courses had been included in the curriculum to develop students' constructive and creative skills, self-esteem, and independence, as well as to uncover their aptitudes and talents. In practice, however, they were more likely to suppress these traits. Instead, they tended to encourage conformity to gender-based identity formation and behavior. This kind of segregation and specialization, occurring during adolescence (when children are highly conscious of their sexual identity and of the definition of sex roles) must have been a conscious effort at indoctrination.

In middle and high school classes where girls and boys were taught in the same classroom, they were usually seated separately. Girls were often clustered together at one side of the classroom or in the front seats. Similarly, to the extent it was allowed by the architectural design of the school, boys and girls were directed to use different gates and doors to enter or exit buildings. This segregation of social space within the school building was geared to control the sexuality of both males and females (although especially the latter, who have been subject to further humiliating suppression).[51]

Female students were subject to tremendous scrutiny by their teachers.[52] Any reflection of femininity was closely sanctioned, and school personnel often responded to unauthorized behavior by scolding, insult, or punishment. Not allowed to wear makeup, girls had to follow strict codes that applied to their hair and dress. The students' hair was required to be short, or pulled back in braids or pony-tails. Any headware or accessories—except for bobby-pins and plain straps used to secure the hair—were forbidden. Similarly, uniforms were designed to be simple, with long hem lines and included thick and dark colored stockings (usually brown or black). All of these practices point to a consistent effort to mold young women into "asexual" female citizens and workers. Increasing women's access to education, when combined with unequal treatment and tight social control, did not inhibit patriarchal biases, but resulted in their reproduction in all domains—both old and new.

Conclusion

With the secularization of marriage, education of women, and the inclusion of women into the electoral process, the Republican regime distanced itself from the Islamic heritage of the Ottoman Empire and reinforced the development of a secular ideology that would legitimize the new state.[53]

In spite of these reforms, the Kemalist state continued to employ a traditional definition of female roles and emphasized reproduction and child care as the primary functions of women. Treating women as symbols and as tools of modernization and Westernization, rather than as the equal and full partners of men, the Kemalist reforms *intended* to achieve little in changing women's lot. The principles laid out in Atatürk's speeches were enacted through policies implemented under his leadership, as well as in those formulated by the subsequent governments. Female education, for example, was promoted mainly with a concern about women's influence over their male offspring, because they were the children's first instructors. Hence, a "feminized" curriculum was developed to transform "backward females" into competent mothers and practical wives.[54] By reforming some instutions that already included women (e.g., family) and expanding women's roles in others (e.g., schools), the Kemalist regime was able to reconstruct and legitimize patriarchal structures.

The restrictive effects of the Kemalist reforms and mentality continue to the present. To this day, both education and employment of women have remained limited; they have been mostly accessible to upper class urban women, but have failed to liberate even that segment of the population. Research indicates that the education of women in Turkey continues to lag much below the education of men, and even among educated women, participation in the labor force remains small.[55] Scholars agree that education in Turkey has not helped change gender roles or stimulate female participation in economy and public life; rather it has served as a process of reproducing the patriarchal ideology,[56] or as a means of obtaining social prestige.[57] Those women who work outside the home do so to meet the economic needs of the family; they do not enjoy "financial independence."[58]

Nevertheless, there is always the possibility that women, like all oppressed groups, will realize their construction and demand change. The feminist movement(s) that has gained spread and viability since the 1980s can be taken as an evidence of this awareness.[59]

Thus, as one of those women, I have attempted to explicate the historical roots of this construction; only by scrutinizing the limitations and intentions of the Kemalist reforms can we comprehend the structures that regulate women's actions in contemporary Turkey. Only then can we remove the facade of social equality and move towards a society of justice and symmetry.

REFERENCES

1. Ayşe Öncü, "Uzman Mesleklerde Türk Kadını," (Turkish Women in Professional Occupations), in Nermin Abadan-Unat, ed., *Türk Toplumunda Kadın* (Women in Turkish Society), Sosyal Bilimler Araştırmaları Dizisi 1., 2nd. ed. (İstanbul: Araştırma, Eğitim, Ekin Yayınları, and Türk Sosyal Bilimler Derneği, 1982), 253–267; 253.

2. "Eastern Bloc" nations are not included in ranking. Fatma Mansur Coşar, "Women in Turkish Society," in Lois Beck and Nikki Keddie, eds., *Women in the Moslem World* (Cambridge: Harvard University Press, 1978), 124–140; 136.

3. A. Afetinan, *Tarih Boyunca Türk Kadınının Hak ve Görevleri* (Turkish Women's Rights and Duties throughout History). Atatürk Kitapları Dizisi: 3 (İstanbul: Milli Eğitim Basımevi, 1982); Emel Doğramacı, *Status of Women in Turkey*, 3rd ed., (Ankara: Meteksan Co., Inc., 1989); Tezel Taşkıran, *Cumhuriyetin 50. Yılında Türk Kadın Hakları* (Women's Rights at the Fiftieth Anniversary of the Republic), (Ankara: Başbakanlık Kültür Müsteşarlığı, Başbakanlık Basımevi, 1973).

4. Tunalı Hilmi Bey and Hamdullah Suphi Bey were criticized for their support of women's suffrage and coeducation, respectively.

5. Nermin Abadan-Unat, "Toplumbilim Açısından Atatürk'ün Kadın Devrimi Üzerine Düşünceleri" (A Sociological Approach to Atatürk's Thoughts on Women's Reforms), Proceedings of the International Conference on Atatürk, Paper No: 66, Vol. 3, Boğaziçi Üniversitesi, November 9–13, 1981 (Bebek, İstanbul: Boğaziçi Üniversitesi Matbaası, 1981), 9 ; Mine Tan, "Atatürk'çü Düşünüş ve Karma Eğitim" (Atatürkist Thinking and Co-education), Proceedings of the International Conference on Atatürk, Paper No: 61, Vol. 3, Boğaziçi Üniversitesi, November 9–13, 1981 (Bebek, İstanbul: Boğaziçi Üniversitesi Matbaası, 1981), 12.

6. Deniz Kandiyoti, "Emancipated but Unliberated? Reflections on the Turkish Case" *Feminist Studies* 13:2 (Summer 1987), 317–338; Şirin Tekeli ed., *Kadınlar ve Siyasal Toplumsal Hayat* (Women and Political and Social Life) (Ankara: Bitikim Yayınları, 1982), 208.

7. Subordination of women's rights and interests to "national interest," is not unique to Turkey, but is a common practice in developing countries. For further discussions and examples see Nilüfer Çağatay and Yasemin Nuhoğlu Soysal, "Uluslaşma Süreci ve Feminizm Üzerine Karşılaştırmalı Düşünceler" (Comparative Reflections on the Process of Nation-Formation and Feminism), in Şirin Tekeli, ed., *Kadın Bakış Açısından 1980'ler Türkiye'sinde Kadın* (Women in the Turkey of the 1980s from a Women's Perspective) (İstanbul: İletişim Yayınları, 1990), 301–311; K. Jayawardena, *Feminism and Nationalism in the Third World* (London: Zed Press, 1988); Nadia H. Youssef, "Women in the Moslem World," in B. Iglitzin and R. Ross, eds., *Women in the World* (Oxford: Clio Books, 1976).

8. Deniz Kandiyoti, "Ataerkil Örüntüler: Türk Toplumunda Erkek Egemenliği-

nin Çözülmesine Yönelik Notlar," (Patriarchal Weaves: Notes on Dismantling the Patriarchal Hegemony in Turkish Society) in Tekeli, *Kadın Bakış Açısından*. 1990, 341–356; 351; Deniz Kandiyoti, "End of Empire: Islam, Nationalism and Women in Turkey," in Deniz Kandiyoti, ed., *Women, Islam, and the State* (Philadelphia: Temple University Press, 1991), 22–47; 42; Şirin Tekeli, *Kadınlar İçin* (For Women) (İstanbul: Alay Yayıncılık, 1988), 315. Although I mostly agree with the analyses of these scholars, I find their choice of term "state feminism" in defining the Kemalist reforms unfortunate. In order to call any movement or action feminist it should recognize gender inequalities and male domination, and by treating this as a political issue, it should take conscious measures to eliminate domination. On the other hand, both scholars agree that Kemalist reforms did not show such efforts or intentions. For a brief review and analysis of the discussions and reforms that addressed the "women issue" in Turkey, see Deniz Kandiyoti, "Women and the Turkish State: Political Actors or Symbolic Pawns?" in Nira Yuval-Davis and Floya Anthias, eds., *Woman–Nation–State* (New York: St. Martin's Press, 1989), 126–149.

I find the term "state feminism" as a more appropriate characterization of the so called "socialist regimes" which recognized the domination of women under capitalism and addressed it as a political issue, but fell short of identification of the roots of patriarchy, and thus failed to liberate women. For the feminism of socialist states, see Maxine Molyneux, "Women in Socialist Societies: Problems of Theory and Practice, in Kate Young, Carol Wolkoiwitz and Roslyn McCullagh, eds., *Of Marrige and the Market: Women's Subordination Internationally and Its Lessons* (London: Routledge, 1984), 55–90; and Lydia Sargent, ed. *Women and Revolution: A Discussion of the Unhappy Marriage of Marxism and Feminism* (Boston: South End Press, 1981).

9. The years that correspond to the Kemalist rule is a matter of dispute. The period that begins with the organization of the Grand National Assembly in 1920, or the establishment of the Turkish Republic in 1923, and end with the death of Atatürk in 1938 is commonly referred as the Kemalist rule or era. Given the fact that Kemalism—despite its originally vague definition and frequent redefinition—has been Turkey's "official ideology" (without any successful challenges at least till the mid-1960s), and its approach to women has not changed, I extend the chronological definition of the Kemalist era to include the 1960s.

10. *Atatürk'ün Söylev ve Demeçleri* (Atatürk's Speeches and Statements) 2 (1989): 89.

11. Atatürk, *Speeches*, 2:89.

12. Atatürk, *Speeches*, 2:89-90.

13. From Atatürk's hand written manuscripts of 1930 published by Afetinan and quoted in Emel Doğramacı, *Status of Women in Turkey*, 164.

14. Atatürk, *Speeches*, 2:156.

15. Atatürk, *Speeches*, 2:227.

16. Atatürk, *Speeches*, 2:91

17. Atatürk, *Speeches*, 2:152–153.
18. Atatürk, *Speeches*, 2:153.
19. Atatürk, *Speeches*, 2:154.
20. Deniz Kandiyoti, "Emancipated but Unliberated? Reflections on the Turkish Case," *Feminist Studies* 13:2 (Summer 1987), 317–338; 328.
21. Bernard Lewis, *The Emergence of Modern Turkey* 2nd ed., (Oxford: Oxford University Press, 1968), 271.
22. It should be noted that although later legislation introduced considerable changes, the laws that were related to women have been largely maintained until the 1980s when, as a response to the pressure from the accelerated women's movement (See Yeşim Arat's article in this volume), some minor amendments were introduced.
23. Originally, the minimum age was set at 18 and 17 for men and women respectively. However, in June 16, 1938, with a new law (NO. 3453) it was reduced to 17 for men and 15 for women.
24. In her book, *The Patriarchal Paradox: Women and Politics in Turkey* (Rutherford: Fairleigh Dickinson University Press, 1989), Yeşim Arat treats the civil code as the legal framework of the "republican patriarchy." See 33–34.
25. The essence of the civil code has been maintained till the 1980s. In 1984 the Ministry of Justice prepared a draft law that was directed to redress some of these inequalities. See Feyzi Necmeddin Feyzioğlu, *Aile Hukuku* (Family Law), 3rd ed. (İstanbul: Filiz Kitabevi, 1986), 182–183.
26. In practice, this clause has been used to maintain a husband's control and independence. Many court decisions advocated that "even if the wife owned a house and living there without paying any rent serves to the material interest of the husband, this might put him in the position of a dependent. Thus, it is the natural right of the husband to prefer his freedom over his material interest and to seek peace." See Feyzioğlu, *Aile Hukuku*, 86.
27. However, in the event of the arbitrary use of this right by the husband, the wife could appeal to the court to obtain the permission. This article is among the ones that were amended in favor of women in the 1980s.
28. Survey research from the 1960s and 1970s indicates that the main reason for women to secure work has been the need to provide supplementary income. Almost the entire income of the woman is contributed to the family budget, and working women tend to hand their earnings to other family members, usually to the husband. See Tekeli, *Kadınlar ve Siyasal Toplumsal Hayat*, 225.
29. Feyzioğlu, *Aile Hukuku*, 123.
30. Although the women is victimized and she is innocent, because the situation dishonors the husband in the community, the subsequent disharmony in the family caused by the rape is considered to be an acceptable ground for the husband to divorce his wife. See Feyzioğlu, *Aile Hukuku*, 312–313.
31. Decions by higher courts, however, discarded this as a legitimate reason for divorce in early days of the marriage, since the wife could not be expected to be an "experienced wife" yet. See Feyzioğlu, *Aile Hukuku*, 315.
32. Research indicates, however, that the physical abuse of women, especially

wife-beating, is a common practice in Turkey, and its victims are left to their own means to cope with the situation, and most of them lack even family support. See Şahika Yüksel, "Eş Dayağı ve Dayağa Karşı Dayanışma Kampanyası" (Wife-Beating and the Campaign of Solidarity Against Domestic Violence), in Tekeli, *Kadın Bakış Açısından*, 315–324.

33. In 1965, the Law on Population Planning allowed abortion only if the mother's life was in danger. The new Law on Population Planning (NO. 2927), enacted in 1983, legalized abortion during the first 10 weeks of pregnancy, but sought the condition of a health threat afterward, and suggested the imprisonment of the woman and her accomplices from two to five years. Moreover, for legal abortion, the law required the permission of a guardian for minors and of the husband for a married woman.

34. Gülten Kazgan, "Türk Ekonomisinde Kadınların İşgücüne Katılması, Mesleki Dağılımı, Eğitim Düzeyi ve Sosyo-Ekonomik Statüsü," (Women's Participation in the Work Force, Occupational Distribution, Educational Level, and Socioeconomic Status in Turkish Economy) in Abadan-Unat, *Türk Toplumunda Kadın*, 137–170; 145.

35. This has been the case until the recent appointment of a woman as the *Vali* of the province of Muğla in July 1991.

36. Zafer Toprak, "Kadınlar Halk Fırkası," (People's Party of Women), *Tarih ve Toplum* 51 (March 1988), 30–31.

37. Nükhet Sirman, "Feminism in Turkey: A Short History," *New Perspectives in Turkey*, 3:1 (Fall, 1989): 1–34, 13.

38. Tekeli, *Kadınlar ve Siyasal Toplumsal Hayat*, 215.

39. Tekeli, *Kadınlar ve Siyasal Toplumsal Hayat*, 214–217; Tekeli, *Kadınlar İçin* (İstanbul: Alay Yayıncılık, 1988), 289–294.

40. Tekeli, *Kadınlar İçin*, 300.

41. Tan, "Atatürk'çü Düşünüş ve Karma Eğitim," 17.

42. Tan, "Atatürk'çü Düşünüş ve Karma Eğitim" 18.

43. Tan, "Atatürk'çü Düşünüş ve Karma Eğitim," 19.

44. Mine Tan, *Kadın: Ekonomik Yaşamı ve Eğitimi* (Woman: Her Economic Life and Education). Türkiye İş Bankası Kültür Yayınları (Ankara: TISA Matbaası, 1979), 206.

45. From the curriculum evaluations of the Ministry of Education, as quoted by Tan, *Kadın*, 210.

46. Even in later years when women's participation in the formal economy and productive labor force increased considerably, the State Planning Organization found that among those who graduated from these institutes between 1958–59 and 1963–64, only 24 percent continued in higher education, 30 percent employed in an area which has little or nothing to do with the subject that they studied at school, and 41 percent stayed at home. See Tan, *Kadın*, 1979, 211.

47. Fatma Gök, "Türkiye'de Eğitim ve Kadınlar," (Education and Women in Turkey), in Tekeli, *Kadın Bakış Açısından*, 165–182.

48. Hasan-Ali Yücel. *Türkiye'de Orta Öğretim* (The Secondary Education in Turkey), (İstanbul: Devlet Basımevi, 1938), 145-236, Tables of Curricula.
49. Yücel, *Secondary Education in Turkey*, 229–230.
50. Segregation in these areas continues to be practiced today.
51. The information on school regulations is largely based on personal stories told by my parents, relatives, and family friends. My own generation experienced some of these policies in the 1970s. Although there has been some relaxation during the last two decades, most of such practices prevail even today, especially in small towns.
52. These regulations applied not only to the co-educational schools, but were common at vocational schools as well.
53. Tekeli, *Kadınlar ve Siyasal Toplumsal Hayat*; Kandiyoti, "Ataerkil Örüntüler," 341–356.
54. In line with the other Middle Eastern reform movements observed by Kandiyoti, "women's illiteracy, seclusion and the practice of polygyny were not denounced merely because they so blatantly curtailed the individual human rights of one half of the population, but because they created ignorant mothers, shallow and scheming partners, unstable marital unions, and lazy and unproductive members of society." See "Introduction" in Deniz Kandiyoti, ed., *Women, Islam, and the State* (Philadelphia: Temple University Press, 1991), 1–21, 10.
55. Kazgan, "Türk Ekonomisinde Kadınların İşgücüne Katılması"; Ferhunde Özbay, "Türkiye'de Kırsal/Kentsel Kesimde Eğitimin Kadınlar Üzerine Etkisi," (The Impact of Education on Women in Rural and Urban Sectors in Turkey), in *Abadan-Unat*, 171–197; Gök, "Türkiye'de Eğitim ve Kadınlar," Table 1, 174. According to the 1989–1990 statistics reported by the United Nations, 75 percent of young females (ages 15–24) are literate, and only 42 percent of the secondary school age group are actually enrolled. The enrollment rate in higher education is much lower, at 10 percent. For every 100 males enrolled in secondary schools, there are only 64 females. The enrollments in higher education and the average years of schooling for females are both half of those for male. Women constitute 33 percent of the labor force and 3 percent of the administrative and managerial staff. See, *Human Development Report 1993*. United Nations (New York: Oxford University Press, 1993).
56. Gök, "Education and Women in Turkey," 169-171.
57. Özbay, "Türkiye'de Kırsal/Kentsel Kesimde Eğitimin Kadınlar Üzerine Etkisi," *Abadan Unat*, 195–196.
58. Tekeli observes the psychological as well as economic oppression of "working" women, especially those of the "dutiful" civil servants who have represented the "educated new women" of the regime: "In reality this woman, too, is oppressed. The families . . . can hardly make it with the civil service salaries. After the long work hours, housework, child care, patching and sawing lie on their shoulders. Her husband, . . . does not only fail to share the household responsibilities with her, but, as the head of the family, he expects exactly the

same "attention, care and obedience that he would have received if he were married to a housewife" . . . These women who cannot change the relations within the family, despite their role and status in the state, accept double work and subordination, and in order to justify their oppression for themselves and in the eyes of others, they transmit the same role to their daughters. The next generation of these women who had never been actually equal or free, who could not even decide for themselves what they wanted to be, who could not find their identity, work at banks and offices, in thousands, and whenever they are squeezed between work and home will say "if there were no economic necessities, I would like to stay home, and be the woman of my house." " *Kadınlar İçin*, 316–317.

59. See Nükhet Sirman, "Feminism in Turkey." In this study of different women's movements in Turkey, Sirman defines the events of the 1980s as the development of a movement largely as response to the limited nature of and the restrictions imposed by the "state feminism" of the Kemalist regime. Despite their association with different, opposing orthodox ideologies (including the religious conservatives), she treats the proliferated women movements of the last decade as "feminist" because they have placed women at the center of the political debate.

PART TWO

The Reconstruction of Identity

CHAPTER FIVE

Gender, Identity, and Anthropology

Ruth Behar

Academic feminism has reached an interesting crossroads. Ten years ago, the authors of this book would have been writing about "women" in the Middle East. Now "gender" is the burning issue. Have we lost the courage to speak of women, plain and simple? I hope not. I want to think that studying gender is part of the new feminist desire to understand how the construction of identity, for women *and* men, has crucial consequences. At last, we are realizing that we all are in this together. On the female side (and I think I don't just speak for myself) there is a lingering fear of betrayal. But gender embodies hope: the hope that opening up feminism to include men will not, once again, make women invisible.

Since the sixties and the development of the women's movement, the juncture of feminism and anthropology has been defined in three ways. The first, the anthropology of women, sought to describe the lives of women across cultures;[1] the second, feminist anthropology, grew out of a desire to arrive at a universal understanding of the position of women as the second sex;[2] the third, and most recent, feminist ethnography, is informed by the new consciousness of ethnography as a form of writing and by the critique of white middle-class feminism made by women of color and Third World women.[3] Many anthropologists now also write about gender, but, on the whole, only women anthropologists continue to write specifically about women. Ultimately, the awkwardness of the relationship between anthropology and feminism has not yet been fully resolved.[4] At the moment, these approaches, which developed in dialogue with one another over time, exist somewhat messily within anthropology.

A mixture of these different anthropological approaches can be found in the four essays in this section. Erika Friedl, in her account of the women of Deh Koh, combines the anthropology of women with a generously reflexive feminist ethnography. Yeşim Arat, in her account of the Turkish women's movement, pursues the tradition of feminist anthropology with a keen attention to women's writing. Rachel Persico, in her highly personal account about growing up female in Israel, joins a rich anthropology of her own womanhood with the tradition of seeking answers to the large questions of gender inequality which is the hallmark of feminist anthropology. Leila Hudson, in her account of the Palestinian Intifada, offers an innovative form of feminist ethnography that is attentive to language, symbolic action, and reflexive understanding.

These four essays' range of concerns and styles suggest that many feminisms exist within Middle Eastern studies. As anthropologists, Erika Friedl and Leila Hudson seek to co-produce knowledge about the meaning of gender through interactions with their subjects. Yeşim Arat, on the other hand, focuses on feminist literary production and its connections with legal reform. Rachel Persico focuses on the masculine character of nationalist myths and her own sense of disenchantment with these myths. Yet there are also common threads that tie these essays together. The essays combine analytical and personal commentary in original ways, and do justice to the feminist tradition of enlarging the realm of the political. Rachel Persico's essay is the most explicitly autobiographical (and curiously, at the same time, the most explicitly political), but the other essays also use a first-person speaking voice without forgetting the politics at stake.

Each essay is written by a cultural insider. Each is an insightful exploration of cultural identity as well as an intriguing revelation of the identity of its author. Even though Erika Friedl is not Iranian, she has a near-native status in the small village where she has done long term fieldwork and developed close relationships with her informants. She is able to reflect on how her subjects' views about gender have changed over time, just as her own understanding has changed in response to unfolding currents of feminist research.

Yeşim Arat and Rachel Persico, as "native ethnographers," are both engaged in deflating the liberal myths of their native countries, Turkey and Israel. Arat and Persico point to social pockets into which women could enter, attain status, and even accumulate some power. But they also offer sobering reflections on how patriarchy has been reinforced rather than undermined by ideologies that merely appear to favor gender equality.

Whether the nation is called the "fatherland" or the "mother country" depends on national imagery. It also depends on the author's own relationship to homes regretfully abandoned or bravely reclaimed. This dialectic emerges clearly in the essays of Persico and Hudson. Rachel Persico writes about growing up in Israel, but she now lives in exile in the United States. She has decided she wants no part of a nation that glorifies war and reserves its highest respect for male warriors. For Leila Hudson, working among her Palestinian relatives and friends, marks a bittersweet return home. Hudson came to realize that political resistance also happens in women's everyday lives. Hudson's fieldwork was a way to forge a connection to the home she lost. Her text marks her connection to the nation that is being forged through women's routines, the rock-throwing bravado of young men coming of age, and the songs of the poets held in the tender magnetic strips of contraband cassettes. I hope it will not be long before the warriors of Rachel Persico's text put down their arms, and listen. . . .

REFERENCES

1. Rayna Reiter, ed., *Toward an Anthropology of Women* (New York and London: Monthly Review Press, 1975).
2. Louise Lamphere, "Feminist Anthropology: The Legacy of Elsie Clews Parsons," *American Ethnologist* 16/3 (1989): 518–533; Henrietta Moore, *Feminism and Anthropology* (Minneapolis: University of Minnesota Press, 1988); Michelle Zimbalist Rosaldo and Louise Lamphere, eds., *Woman, Culture, and Society*. (Stanford: Stanford University Press, 1974).
3. Lila Abu-Lughod "Can There Be a Feminist Ethnography?" *Women and Performance* 5/1 (1988): 7–27; Lila Abu-Lughod "Writing Against Culture," in Richard G. Fox ed., *Recapturing Anthropology: Working in the Present* (Santa Fe: School of American Research Press, 1991); Lila Abu-Lughod, *Writing Women's Worlds: Bedouin Stories* (Berkeley: University of California Press, 1992); Ruth Behar *Translated Woman: Crossing the Border with Esperanza's Story* (Boston: Beacon Press, 1993); Deborah Gordon, "Writing Culture, Writing Feminism: The Poetics and Politics of Experimental Ethnography," *Inscriptions* 3/4(1988): 7–24; Faye V. Harrison, "Anthropology as an Agent of Transformation: Introductory Comments and Queries," in Faye V. Harrison, ed., *Decolonizing Anthropology: Moving Further Toward an Anthropology for Liberation* (Washington, D.C.: American Anthropological Association, 1991); Micaela di Leonardo, "Gender, Culture and Political Economy: Feminist Anthropology in Historical Perspective" in Micaela di Leonardo, ed., *Gender at the Crossroads of Knowledge: Feminist Anthropology in the Postmodern Era* (Berkeley: University of California

Press, 1991); Chandra Talpade Mohanty, "Under Western Eyes: Feminist Scholarship and Colonial Discourses," in Chandra Talpade Mohanty, Ann Russo, and Lourdes Torres, eds. *Third World Women and the Politics of Feminism* (Bloomington: Indiana University Press, 1991); Judith Stacey, "Can There Be a Feminist Ethnography?" *Women's Studies International Forum* 11/1 (1988): 21–27; Kamala Visweswaran, "Defining Feminist Ethnography," *Inscriptions* 3/4 (1988): 27–44.

4. Marilyn Strathern, "An Awkward Relationship: The Case of Feminism and Anthropology," *Signs* 12/2 (1987): 276–292.

CHAPTER SIX

Notes from the Village: On the Ethnographic Construction of Women in Iran

Erika Friedl

Social science research on women in Iran and other Middle Eastern countries has provided contradictory reports on gender relations, women's identity, and women's life circumstances.[1] In a positivist frame, these differences reflect variations in the gender constructs that undergird the quantifiable aspects of society's laws, norms, and everyday practices. In matters of greater subtlety, such as gender identity, essentialist statements based on information from individuals beg the question of representation. Social scientists say they "collect information" in the field, as if information was lying around conveniently, waiting to be picked up, when, at least out of economic necessity, they have to choose some informants over others, and have to select from an overwhelming wealth of information. Published accounts of gender identities and gender relations invariably reflect the researcher's assumptions and theories that shape decisions about who will be heard, and who will be ignored.

The differences also reflect the influence that the observer's personality and conceptions exert on the observer's perception and analysis of gender issues: the identity of the observer/analyst and the identity of the women as perceived and described by the researcher are interlinked.

AUTHOR'S NOTE:
An earlier version of this paper was read at the 22nd Annual Meeting of the Middle East Studies Association, Los Angeles, 1988. The financial support for the research on which this paper is based, provided by the Social Science Research Council, the Wenner-Gren Foundation for Anthropological Research, the National Endowment for the Humanities, and Western Michigan University, is gratefully acknowledged.

Personality and methodology combine to screen the information chosen for the construction of gender identities.

Last, the differences may result from the very process of the creation of social knowledge, including gender identity, in the Middle East: ethnographic knowledge is largely a function of the dynamics of inter-personal relationships between observer and observed; because these interpersonal dynamics are variable, the conclusions drawn from them may differ.

The fragmentation of people's experiences is a problem encountered in all social science reporting. Analytic methodologies reduce informants' (i.e., real people's) experiences to static components in the formulation of generalizations, descriptions, or hypotheses. As a result of analysis, one loses sight of the real-life happenings that connect men and women and are the source and expression of shared meaning. Likewise, one loses contact with the interconnectedness people feel and express as members of families and communities. The concept of identity, thus, which is based on processes of individuation and a particular understand-ing of selfhood, easily turns into an ethnocentric concept when we try to define it for people who constitute themselves in ever-shifting relation-ships with others.

The following paper serves as a comment on these methodological problems, from the perspective of a village in Iran, which I call Deh Koh and where I have confronted these issues during some twenty-five years of longitudinal qualitative anthropological research.

My first point is a gripe about the question of representation.

Those of us studying gender issues in villages in Iran often are asked the following loaded question: "how representative are villagers of people in Iran ? "[2] "In matters of gender relations, is it permissible," the questioner asks, "to extrapolate even from one village to another, let alone to cities? " "Isn't the villager's sense of self bound to a small place and a small social circle with distinct customs and rules? Shouldn't one therefore look to the city to learn about Iranian culture, rather than to tradition-bound villages? " Such questions contain the unspoken, elitist assumption that a city is more typical for life in Iran and is therefore more representative of Iranian people than are rural communities. I hear these remarks whenever I say something that challenges stereotypical notions about women or gender in the Middle East. For example, when I talk about illiterate village women analyzing and critically appraising their situations, adherents to the conventional wisdom maintain that village women are tradition-bound, uneducated, and therefore accept their lot and the accompanying gender-myths without much reflection. "Surely," they argue, "there must be something especially progressive about Deh Koh if its women indeed can carry through critical analyses." Yet if I discuss androcentric or misogynist practices and beliefs, such as wife beating, the same colleagues advise me to confine my observations to Deh Koh, because one cannot draw general conclusions from this small, obviously backward village.

The majority of Iran's 64 million people live in rural areas—in some forty thousand villages.[3] Contrary to romantic and condescending stereotypes of isolated, forgotten, poverty-stricken, mud-walled obscurity, these villages are closely tied to towns and cities; their human surplus populated the cities in the past and is swelling them now, and city dwellers tend to keep their ties with relatives in the villages. Even in remote mountain hamlets, men and women consider themselves citizens of the state. They identify themselves as Iranians and Muslims, and increasingly are drawn into the state's affairs through schools, governmental agencies, radio, television, and state propaganda. Media attention, however, is focused on cities, as is social scientific inquiry. Village happenings pass unnoticed. Most writers and other traditional interpreters of village life belong to the urban middle class and bring their class-specific prejudices and romantic notions into the construction of villagers: the villagers become the "other" Iranians: inarticulate, downtrodden, and unimportant, except as metaphors for life's misery.[4]

Even if Iranian villages are not hotbeds of political and cultural innovations, they *do* furnish authentic, meaningful insights into women's affairs and gender relations. These insights complement, confirm, and contradict observations about urban areas. Frequently, Iranian middle class urbanites express surprise at the many similarities they see between their own experiences and those of the women in Deh Koh.[5]

Deh Koh, the focus of my fieldwork in Iran, is a relatively large village of some 4,000 people in a tribal region in the southwest of the country. The people are Luri-speaking Shi'ite Muslims, traditionally engaged in transhumant animal husbandry and farming. Since the mid-1960s, the area has become increasingly integrated into the wider socioeconomic structures of the state: administrative bureaucracies have replaced tribal power hierarchies; for some, formal education has opened a way into an urban-oriented middle class; roads established easy access to towns, where wage labor, trade, and crafts have created jobs that employ many from the ever-rising village population. As most everywhere in Iran, the population has outgrown the area's ecological and structural resources. In many respects, Deh Koh is a rather typical Iranian village.

Twenty-five years of involvement in one village forces one to face the challenge of change, even if the research is on other topics. The more often a particular topic like gender, for example, or women's identity, is explored, the more difficult it becomes to generalize and to make essentialist statements about it. Trained in the positivist, fact-chasing mode of the twentieth century university, I dutifully track facts and truth in the field, but meet only evolving personalities, evolving stories, evolving cultural patterns. Each time I visit one of my so-called informants, the situation has changed, however slightly; time makes it necessary for her to reinterpret the past, and to redefine herself and others, including me. If years lapse between encounters, the discrepancies often are so great that one is lured into heuristically sterile comparisons of conditions then and now that do little justice to the reality of change the people have passively experienced and actively shaped. If we indulge in this easy way out, we create ethnographic texts based on arbitrary, random pieces of information and insights that seem juxtaposed because the intermediary links in the process of their creation are denied. As ethnographers we are writing Culture *and* History. Yet one year, or ten, or even twenty-five years is not long enough to employ traditional historical methodologies: I am not dealing with documents but with the creation of documents; not with texts on paper but with people who change their minds and their behavior easily.

In everyday practice, gender attributes come in assemblages, in clusters, selected by each person from a variety of potential choices. Even small changes in a person's life circumstances, such as new neighbor, a move, or the availability of a new school, often dramatically effect changes in the choices, the assemblage of gender attributes, and thus in the person's gender philosophy and sense of self. For example, after the first woman teacher in Deh Koh, a young woman from a prominent local family, had started to teach successfully, a great many young women (and at least one each of these women's parents) accepted a career in teaching as fitting and desirable for women, while before, most had asserted that a woman's inherent weakness made higher education for women unhealthy and unadvisable, if not outrightly immoral. Twenty years later, these people again questioned if teaching was a realistic choice of work for women. This time, people looked at the gender attribute of women's alleged natural preference or duty to care for children and husband, which was said to be incompatible with teaching. At various points in this twenty-year continuum, such divergent gender attributes as women's weakness, women's intellectual talents, and women's duty (or preference) for home-making emerged as prominent factors in women's identities and choices for female activities. Not one of them, however, would have been the solid basis for an essentialist proclamation or even a generalization on gender it seemed to be at any given time: the other attributes also offered potential choices, contradictory as they might have been.

The chronological continuity of my research has proved to be important for a further, related problem: a quarter-century of observed and lived change very effectively destabilizes one's sense of memory, of recall, and one's confidence in the ability of people to record and store their own experiences. In other words, not only do people drastically change over such a long time, but past events, if remembered at all, begin to look different. With the different look, these events change their impact on the contemporary situation. After facts themselves have faded, pure cognition often motivates people to remember and to use memories to define themselves and to construct the reality of the day. For example, some fifteen years ago, a woman in Deh Koh told me that she wanted to renege on the promise of marriage of her daughter to a local young man of limited means when her daughter's high school diploma opened the prospect of gainful employment. After several months of complicated political maneuvering, the mother succeeded in extricating her daughter from the betrothal and in matching her with a more suitable fiancé. She was proud of her success and amused by her cleverness. When it turned out, however, that the jilted young man's family was offended, her satisfaction turned to concern, and the story changed: now she said that the young man himself had no longer wanted her daughter. An argument arose between the two families, and relationships were strained for a while. Fifteen years later, fences mended, the mother denies that there ever had been a broken engagement. According to her, the whole exciting affair never happened. This means that presently the story is of no consequence to anybody and is therefore best forgotten. Without knowing the twists and turns of the story over the course of fifteen years, however, the anthropologist at each stage in the development would have drawn widely different conclusions about gender relations and gender constructs, about women's identity and power—all of these conclusions would be true, but each would pertain to a different reality.

In another example, a young man in the village committed suicide about twenty years ago. At the time, men's suicides were unheard of, and the villagers were shocked accordingly. (Women's suicides were much more common.) Different explanations were offered, each one plausible, but the issue was not settled then. Fifteen years later, when I asked about it again, for some people the suicide had never happened. The man's mother said her son had died of a disease. Other people settled on "family quarrels" as a reason, thereby localizing the event where it did the least public harm: only the dead man's family carried blame. With these explanations, the suicide was particularized and the challenge to find a general explanation for suicides of men was avoided. Thus, gender notions regarding suicide and the "nature" of men and women remained intact. According to these ideas, men are rational and strong and thus resistant to the foolish loss of control that leads to suicide, while women are inherently weak intellectually and emotionally and thus are at great risk. Throughout the discussion, however, these gender attributes were not expressed. Later, during the Iran-Iraq war, a few young people who knew about the dead man labelled him *shahid*, a martyr, as if he had died on the battlefield. "Disease" refers to a natural cause of death; "quarrel" alludes to dishonor, and "martyr" to honor. None of these explanations seem to be situated in the local gender-discourse. Yet, this fact itself strongly suggests that some hidden gender construct is being defended, in this case by denying the challenging exception to the general assumption that only women are weak enough to commit suicide.

Over the years, I have tried four approaches to writing about change. The first attempt, at a time when I was unaware of the depth of the problem, was a "then versus now" inventory of the material culture in the village.[6] In it, women's objects emerge as different from men's, and as different from objects of earlier times, but there the description ends. What the gender-indexed objects signify or how they are used as markers of identity for men and women remained unexplored. The second attempt took the format of a Marxist historical analysis of women's input in the village economy.[7] The article was process-oriented, but on an abstract, generalizing level, where women and men were anonymous, mute actors in economic development. For the third attempt I used an evolutionistic approach to try to unravel different, seemingly contradictory, strands of women's behavior and the ideologies supporting the behaviors, and to link them to economic and political constellations at different times in the village's history.[8] Again I focused on the analysis of circumstances framing village women rather than on the women's understanding of themselves and on identity formation. The most ambitious attempt to deal with women and cultural change was a kind of narrative ethnography of women in Deh Koh.[9]

The decision to write *Women of Deh Koh* as a narrative grew out of a profound dissatisfaction with the fragmented insights into women's lives which most of the literature, including my own earlier writings, offers. Neither I, the observer, nor the people themselves feel that the traditional academic approach represents life on the ground. When people think and talk about themselves, about their lives, they do so in stories. Things and people and relationships are understood, structured, and remembered in narratives. The construction of gender and the revelation of identities happen in accounts of what people think and do, in the stories they tell about themselves and about each other. By adopting a narrative style to capture these stories I tried to recreate a level of reality in which women deal with quintessential challenges of life such as survival, meaning, inconstancy, both practically and philosophically. Although many scholars have taken existentialist approaches to ethnography, few have used it for social scientific writing about women in the Middle East.[10] We need more such experiments, because there is no "correct" way of dealing with change or fragmentation. Each experiment will contribute to balancing the inevitably reductionist and essentialist pictures of gender provided by established, traditional analyses.[11]

Research on gender inevitably reflects the researcher's own identity, questions, assumptions, and agenda that she or he explicitly or implicitly covertly brings into the field. My own case is a good example of the effects of shifts in awareness and orientation, as I took with me into Iran the mind-set, theories, and anthropological concerns of the day. When I started research in Deh Koh in 1965, I was a value-free, presumably non-gendered scientist optimistically prepared to cover all conventional ethnographic topics—all the "important" ones, at least. Male-female relationships (the term gender was not in use then) were not a very important theme; they emerged as a by-product of research on kinship (important) or family (important in a structural sense). Intricate matters, such as the dynamics of selfhood, or the philosophies of self and others, were submerged in the category "Islamic world view." This category was approached through the study of myth, religion, and ritual, i.e., areas where women were not highly visible, and preferably in formal analyses. Because I was fresh from a conservative university in Germany, with a traditional, i.e., unquestioned male-centered ethnographic point of view, I saw women mainly as informants on topics of their specialty:

child care, for example, or folk remedies—minor topics, to be sure. On major topics like history, politics, or religion, men were to be consulted—because men naturally were better informed and more involved in such public matters and they could speak about such issues with more authority than women could, "naturally."

The standing liberal-progressive gender assumptions for the Middle East at that time, of men and women being "separate but equal" was an effective heuristic blinder, blocking critical analysis and awareness of power relations. "Separate but equal" fit the local ideology, including Muslim theological proclamations on the subject, so it was even harder to recognize male-female differences as signs of a fundamentally gendered, unequal world. At the same time, I experienced much of what it meant to be a village woman, because I brought young children with me into the field. But personal experiences were not supposed to cloud the larger scientific vista, and so I ignored them. Sitting around with other women while mending clothes, cleaning rice, or watching children was time idled, misspent, as far as my professional conscience was concerned.

The expansion of feminist awareness and feminist literature in the early 1970s led me and others to pose explicit questions about women's issues. Women became topics of inquiry in their own right. The study of work, health, economic development, religion, now had two foci: men and women—separate, but no longer equal. Differences were expected and accepted as fitting into a hierarchical order, and the documentation of inequality between the sexes became a worthwhile undertaking. But this, too, was a path that led into a heuristic cul de sac: what do we actually know about men and women if we know that women are beaten by their husbands? That women lose economic niches in the course of national integration and economic development? That women have few legal rights? That they have little access to resources? And what is one to do about injustices? Do we embark on crusades to liberate subordinated Middle Eastern women? Are we to design new identities for them? To politicize them?

By dwelling on manifestations of dominance and subordination, I—and others—found soon that our insights were raising hostility and antipathy between Iranians and non-Iranians of both sexes. We were charged with employing a new, western-feminist ethnocentrism to supplant good, value-free science. Under the pressure of this criticism, we were forced to reexamine our vocabulary of feminine awareness and our evaluation of the feminine condition cross-culturally. What does "identity" mean in a society where individuation, in a Western sense is, at best, just beginning, or where it develops in directions different from ours, thus leading to a different understanding of women's liberation? Who is to be given the privilege to speak on behalf of Middle Eastern women? Are the opinions of educated Middle Eastern apologists any more authentic than the critical analyses of exiled Iranians or the assertions of women in the hezbollah? Women's identity, as soon as it is expressed, becomes a product of representation, and might reflect more easily the identity ideals of the spokesperson than the women's understanding of themselves. Speaking about women now necessitates the delineation of the frame in which one places them, if one wants to avoid being accused of hidden motives and tendentious reporting. It has become impossible to hide behind a claim of value-free scientific inquiry.

The critical evaluation of gender-identities and gender politics is a mine field. Having traversed it, I now find myself interested in questions that go beyond exposing inequalities, that have to do with learning more about the view from within, about evaluative views women have of their own existential situations as women, as mothers, as wives. This includes an interest in local evaluative concepts and processes, including critiques of any kind, but not in a relativist-functionalist mode, in which, for example, ideologies and practices women use to work the system are seen as supporting the system (they do, of course, and it needs to be said), but in the form of comments they actually make about their culture and about their situation within their society.

I will elaborate.

I see the construction of gender—in the village, of femininity and masculinity, of the roster of gender attributes, ideologies, and indices— as ongoing dialectic processes of challenge and defense, negation and affirmation, elaboration and destruction, all within the wider philosophy-supported frames of power in which gender is placed. In the case of Deh Koh, the frame is built of elements of Muslim theology, morality, and proscriptions of behavior, mixed with local notions about the workings of the universe, and so-called modern things and ideas, be they inspired by the Western or the revolutionary government.[12] Women do not have a fixed place in this frame; indeed, the frame is not even fixed. The frame is constantly shifting, as norms, cognitions, and relationships are negotiated and renegotiated. The fabric of reality that women weave is constantly unraveled and rewoven in critical appraisals of one's choices, assumptions, and logic. While we know and expect that particular matters can and are criticized everywhere, such as, for example, a breach of etiquette or an act of violence, we do not necessarily expect simple

Iranian village women to try to analyze critically, often with sophistica-
tion and clarity, the ideological underpinnings of everyday practices and
assumptions, even of the very foundations on which their lives are built.
Theology, philosophy, rituals of everyday life, and relationships with
things and people take on new meaning when seen through the critical
prisms of those who also create and use them. In the case of illiterate
and publicly subdued women in villages, these critical efforts go largely
unnoticed, unless they create practical problems for others, by resulting
in arguments or public fights.

Traditional ethnographies tend to present commonalities and
agreements ("norms") rather than diversities or dissent. Therefore, ethnographers tend to present their informants' critical interpretations of
conditions in their own culture as the exception or deviation that others
in the critic's culture judge them to be. For example, the ethnographer
easily may describe a protesting or argumentative woman as "sick" or
"bitchy" because the others see her that way, instead of inquiring into
the argumentative woman's view of herself as a woman in relationship
to the cause of her dissatisfaction. In the first case, the ethnographer,
although avoiding ethnocentrism, represents the point of view of those
who make her angry and misses an opportunity to find out how gender
is constituted in daily life. The ethnographer easily may ignore, as an
exception, a woman who comments sarcastically on the religious scrip-
tures' simultaneous claim of human equality and demand of wives'
obedience to their husbands—simply because such a woman is called an
ignorant and erring troublemaker by those defending religious authority.
In both cases, the ethnographer will be lured into examining the public
reactions to these women's behavior rather than into looking at the
background and logic of the women's discontent.

I suggest that we need to listen to women's dissent and criticism
carefully to establish the base from which women profile themselves. By
focusing on the critical components in women's utterances and actions,
we can learn how women construct themselves and others, how they
frame and place themselves in relation to others, in ways that avoid
ethnocentrism as well as tacit acceptance of the evaluative grid of those
who wield power over them. As I see it, women's criticism is not simply
an idiosyncratic negation or dismissal of that which is criticized, but an
attempt to construct and negotiate a different reality. We know very
little about Middle Eastern women's realities of life in this regard, and
equally little about how women think they fit into it.

While I have become increasingly aware of these problems over the last decade, my style of fieldwork has shifted from so-called participant observation in which the observer interprets cultural features with more or less confidence to one in which people are constantly encouraged to make critical and personal comments on their own culture. Put in postmodern language, culture no longer is an entity to be described, but a text that people create, read, and negotiate with the anthropologist. Gender "is" not, it emerges. Women's texts and performances are taken as interpretive and projective devices that metaphorically express the dynamics of constructing, questioning, defending, debunking, and modifying peoples' lives. For example, folk tales are read as storytellers' commentaries on gender roles, on power relationships, on conditions of life, on themselves; actions, and the supporting justifications are taken as expressions of opinions about choices the society offers; life histories or accounts of events are seen as emotional-rational-manipulative reactions to the ideas, expectations, and actions of others.

Such a style of fieldwork, with its emphasis on listening, prompting of associations, encouragement of opinions, on personal disclosure, affect, remembering, introspection, easily takes the form of what in a different setting would be called psychotherapy, and poses a serious ethical problem: how can an anthropologist justify getting women to reflect on themselves, on the limits of their own logic? On consequences of their beliefs? On results of attitudes? On child rearing, old age? Probing the glue that holds together the women's world may dissolve it; making women shake the kaleidoscope of their world will scramble and change their image of themselves and of others. If at least I knew that the women are better off emotionally or are better able to cope because of my probing interest and my sympathetic ear, I would not feel as uncomfortable as I indeed, feel.

The dilemma obviously is unsolvable. A different style of field research probably would make it less obvious, but there is no way to make it disappear.

This particular style of fieldwork developed out of the particular constellation of my own identity, my personality, the women's interests, and the questions that interest me and them. We know how ethnographic reality is created, and that the anthropologist's personality cannot be kept out of this creative process. We know this and do not lack attempts to live up to it in recent ethnographic writings, in order to sneak up on an ever-elusive ethnographic "truth," but I do not think we yet have found a satisfactory method. Inasmuch as I have kept myself out of the stories in the book on Deh Koh, the ethnography contained in them is very traditional: I pretend to be invisible, and everything in Deh Koh simply presents itself seemingly without my input.

Methodologically flawed as such an ethnography might be, the new ethnographies, in which the anthropologist offers self-disclosure, may be interesting to nosy readers like myself, but I for one don't find an ethnographer's childhood memories or favorite poems help create a better, i.e., contextualized, understanding of the ethnographic text. Bits and pieces of carefully selected ego-revelations in the text *do* provide, at best, a self-conscious identity collage of the writer, adding yet another layer of "truth" to the text. It is a constructed truth, and therefore as deconstructible as all others. It is far more helpful to be given information that lets the reader appreciate the style of fieldwork that produced the information and the text: the interactional patterns the author perfected; the kind of personalities that were congenial; the personae the author assumed; the stance assumed in the flow of the stories that were unfolding around—and with—the ethnographer. In fieldwork, personality traits are put to action in systematic ways, and actions are analytically better accessible than are character traits or filtered childhood memories.

Recently, a colleague and I were talking about our respective work in Iran; a problem arose that provides an example of the difficulties of trying to sort out the ethnographer's influence on the creation of an ethnographic text about women. Mary Hegland conducted ethnographic research on women in a village not very far from Deh Koh,[13] and at roughly the same time I was in Deh Koh. We wondered why neither of us had learned much about sexual matters from the women in our respective villages. Was this a reflection of our own reserve, which the local women discerned and employed in the construction of our identities, making them reluctant to talk about this topic? Or was it due to a hesitancy rooted in the personalities of the particular women we happened to associate with, women whose personalities were compatible with our own? Maybe other women would have been much less reluctant to talk about such matters, women who, however, probably found us less congenial than their reserved sisters did, and to whom we therefore had rather shallow ties. Was it a pattern of sensibility shared generally among women in our respective villages?

These questions are legitimate and normal for us, because we proceed on the assumption that facts are out there, if only we knew how to get them. However, we shall never know if we have encountered a fact. It is much more profitable and more honest to say that the particular way in which the women "read" us, the way we read them, and the way they perceived our reading of them (and vice versa), let us construct a reality, an interactional pattern, in which both anthropologist and "native" handled sexual topics with reserve. Dealing with sexual themes in this way lies within the cultural repertoire of the local women and the anthropologist. However, even if the cultural repertoire also allowed for other choices, it does not make our encounters and conclusions any less real or authentic.

The researcher's and the other women's identities exert mutual impact; by coming to terms with each other, anthropologist and the other women constitute each other. In order to sort out this interpersonal dynamic, most of us require more psychological insight, honesty, and time for introspection than we feel we can afford, especially so if the interaction is long and involved. The longer I stay in the village, the more I am shaped into an actor in the women's stories—I become a woman with different faces and different personae. I become more like all the other women, and affect each of them in different ways.

For example, the frequent visits I paid to a neighboring family in Deh Koh was turned by the youngest and most vulnerable woman in the house, a new daughter-in-law, into a tool of power: the esteemed foreign woman talked with *her*. For her, I became a source of self esteem at a time when few events around her could be used for this purpose. She constructed me into a VIP, whose high status rubbed off on her. For her mother-in-law, the matron of the house, my visits were catalogued as a small nuisance: the foreign woman, who obviously had nothing better to do than to visit other people, often came at a time when the matron would have liked to take a nap rather than be a gracious hostess. An older sister-in-law felt snubbed because the visits were not to her exclusively. For the young, unmarried woman high school student, who hoped against reason to become a teacher, my presence, and our conversations (resembling counseling sessions), triggered self-awareness and other subtle changes. They spilled over into her assessment of her goals and aspirations, and got knotted into a life story that was very different from those of the other women sitting around the same tea tray with the same foreigner at the same time.

The foreigner was the same, however, only to herself. In effect, I was appropriated by each of these four women and I was constructed into different personalities. The resulting interpersonal processes and relationships, all happening simultaneously, in turn shaped my understanding of these four women and, by extension, of women's identity and gender processes in the village.

How does one disentangle this web? The more familiar I become with the ways and means of women and men in the village the more I am being incorporated into their lives. As my involvement with the villagers intensifies over the years (or as I am opting out of village life at some points), the personae which my hosts and co-actors construct for me become part of myself and part of my ethnographic knowledge. Slowly, over the years, my own story gets lost somewhere in the other women's stories—and what kind of gender reality do I write about then?

REFERENCES

1. See, for example, Minou Reeves, *Female Warriors of Allah*, (New York: E. P. Dutton, 1989). In this book, Reeves deals with two such contradictory attributes of contemporary women in Iran.

2. Such sentiments are expressed mostly verbally in discussions following paper presentations, and thus are hard to document.

3. The National Census for 1986 gives a population figure of 49,851,384 (National Census of Population and Housing 1365 [1986], Teheran: Central Statistical Office, 1988). With an estimate growth rate of 3.2 percent, the population will have risen to over 64 million in 1994.

4. The Persian film *"The Cow,"* by D. Mehrjui, 1968, is a cinematic example of the negatively romanticized attitude towards villagers. Sattareh Farman Farmaian, in *Daughter of Persia* (New York: Crown Publishers, 1992), 267–9, describes the upper-class "use" of a village: for the city-wary, exhausted urbanite, her garden in the village provides the tonic of the simple life close to nature. The anonymous resident gardener is taken for granted.

5. This happens in discussions of my book *Women of Deh Koh: Lives in an Iranian Village* (New York: Viking Penguin, 1991), so frequently that even I am surprised by the extent of similarities in experiences expressed by women of all walks of life.

6. Reinhold Loeffler and Erika Friedl, "Eine Ethnographische Sammlung von den Boir Ahmad, Süd Iran" *Archiv für Völkerkunde* 21 (1967), 95–206. Reinhold Loeffler, Erika Friedl, and Alfred Janata, "Die Materielle Kultur von Boir Ahmad, Süd Iran" *Archiv für Völkerkunde* 28 (1974), 61–142.

7. Erika Friedl, "The Division of Labor in an Iranian Village," *Merip Reports*, 95 (1981), 12–18.

8. Erika Friedl, "The Dynamics of Women's Spheres of Action in Rural Iran," in Nikki Keddie and Beth Baron, eds., *Women in Middle Eastern History*, (New Haven and London: Yale University Press, 1991), 195–213.

9. Friedl, *Women of Deh Koh* (New York: Viking Penguin, 1991). The term "narrative ethnography" is also used in anthropology more narrowly for

writing in first person, a mixture of travelogue, diary, and reflective description.

10. The first book to pull together the range of scholarship on women in the Middle East was Nikki Keddie and Lois Beck, eds., *Women in the Muslim World* (Cambridge: Harvard University Press, 1978). The amount of writing on Iranian women has increased sharply since the revolution of 1978, but most academics continue to take descriptive approaches.

11. See for example, another, quite different approach for Arab women, in Lila Abu Lughod, *Veiled Sentiments* (Berkeley: University of California Press, 1986).

12. See Reinhold Loeffler, *Islam in Practice* (Albany, State University of New York Press, 1988).

13. Mary Hegland calls it Aliabad. See, for example, Mary Elaine Hegland, "Political Roles of Aliabad Women: The Public-Private Dichotomy Transcended," in Keddie and Baron, *Women in Middle Eastern History*, 1991.

CHAPTER SEVEN

Women's Movement of the 1980s in Turkey: Radical Outcome of Liberal Kemalism?[1]

Yeşim Arat

On February 4, 1983, Şule Torun addressed the Turkish readers of the weekly literary journal *Somut* with the following argument: The words "woman" and "man" do not reflect anatomical differences. Their meanings are socially constructed and embody differences far beyond the anatomical. Furthermore, these constructed differences create a hierarchy of gender. Consequently, men exploit and women are exploited. So-called feminists and feminist movements in the world protest this particular division. At the end of her short column, she concluded:

> Henceforth, in this corner, in this page, we shall analyze [the] history of feminism, this new radical viewpoint and the choices it offers in all aspects of life. Hello.[2]

This brief greeting in the 1980s introduced feminism in Turkey.

During the following years, small groups of educated, middle class women who called themselves feminists initiated a women's movement and collectively acted in protest of women's subjugation. Consciousness-raising groups, petition campaigns, protest walks, articles, journals, and institutions like the Women's Library defined the contours of the women's movement in Turkey. Ideological cleavages, a testimony to the movement's vigor, existed among the ranks of feminists. The main cleavage was between a younger generation, who called themselves feminists and began organizing in the early 1980s, and an older genera-

The author would like to thank the Middle East Research Competition of the Ford Foundation for providing her with the opportunity to work on this article.

tion, who preferred to call themselves Kemalist feminists (or egalitarian feminists) and became involved in the later 1980s.

In this paper, I shall focus on the younger generation of feminists who initiated the movement. My aim is to interpret the significance of the feminist movement against the background of the Kemalist tradition in Turkey. Kemalist reforms of the 1920s and 1930s had attempted to found a Westernized Turkey.[3] The monarchic Ottoman rule legitimized by Islam was to be replaced by a liberal, democratic, secular polity. While the Kemalists articulated the vision of a Westernized Turkey, their secularist politics were neither liberal nor democratic.[4] Ever since the foundation of the Republic in 1923, both state and society have waged war against Turkey's authoritarian and religious tendencies, in a continuing attempt to become liberal, democratic, and secular.

I shall argue that the women's movement was a conscious challenge to Kemalist reforms of women's status but that it unwillingly helped promote the Kemalist vision of a Westernized (namely, liberal, democratic, and secular) Turkey. I shall describe how the feminists grew out of and challenged the Kemalist reforms. Then, I shall trace how the feminist movement promoted liberalism, contributed to democracy, and upheld secularism in Turkey.

Kemalist Reforms and the Feminists of the 1980s: An Offshoot and a Challenge

Two Kemalist reforms were particularly repsonsible for dramatic improvements in women's lives—namely, the 1926 adoption of the Swiss civil code and the 1934 passage of universal suffrage. These two reforms also played significant roles in the Westernization process.[5] The civil code, which replaced the *Shariat*, was a secular blow to the Islamists; furthermore, it encouraged women's recognition as individuals within the polity. The 1934 Amendment to the Electoral Law, which granted suffrage to women, was a formal expansion of democratic rights; similar to the 1926 civil code, suffrage expanded individual liberties in a secular context. Meanwhile, women, especially those in urban areas, benefitted from these reforms, as they voted in elections or divorced their husbands or sought custody over their children.

Besides the reforms of 1926 and 1934, structural changes undertaken in the process of Westernization enhanced women's status. The reforms created an "opportunity space"[6] where men and women could improve their socioeconomic standing. Opportunity space allowed women, along with men, to be educated and work in the public realm. Consequently, a group of women, who could benefit from the new civil and social rights, emerged to educate themselves and work in public life.

Women who raised their voices in protest during the 1980s were able do so because, along with other factors, they had utilized the opportunity space created by Kemalist reforms. These women were educated, most were professionals, they had been abroad, or else were equipped to observe developments outside Turkey. Their mothers were the first generation to benefit from and revere these reforms. The younger generation could take these reforms for granted and evaluate them more critically. Consequently, the leading feminists challenged the adequacy of Kemalist reforms.[7] These reforms had brought women neither equality nor liberation. They invited women to the political and economic realms, but women still were not equal to men. In the private realm, women's subjugation to men continued, despite improvements in divorce, inheritance, and child custody laws. These women believed that the cause of women's exploitation was the patriarchal organization of society. They argued that the reforms had endorsed the patriarchy even when those reforms improved women's position in society. Feminists aimed for a more radical restructuring of society, where women were not merely "emancipated but also liberated"[8].

Accordingly, they were keen to differentiate themselves from an older generation of women who identified themselves as Kemalist feminists or egalitarian feminists.[9] Although the Kemalist feminists increasingly preempted the agenda of the younger, more radical feminists, the latter consistently remained anti-statist. The Kemalist feminists helped reform the state, at times collaborating with the Social Democrats through autonomous organization.

The radical feminists could pose a challenge to Kemalists, but they could not create the radical restructuring of society they desired. Instead, they helped redefine a more liberal, democratic, and secular polity in Turkey, for which the Kemalist reforms allegedly had been undertaken. I shall now sketch the prominent features of feminist activism in Turkey, and then relate how this activism could contribute to a Westernizing Turkey.

Feminist Movement of the 1980s

Şule Torun, whose greeting of feminism in 1983 was quoted at the beginning of this article, was a member of the group of professional women who regularly came together to prepare a feminist page for the weekly *Somut*.[10] This project, which lasted less than a year, helped sow the seeds of a feminist consciousness among the urban elite in Turkey. Those involved followed feminist activism abroad and developed feminist perspectives on Turkish issues. Later the same year, some of these women organized a publishing service and consultancy company called *Kadın Çevresi* (Woman's Circle). Located in İstanbul, Woman's Circle aimed to uphold women's labor within or outside the household. A book club was formed, which translated feminist classics and discussed feminist works. Meanwhile, women were organizing in Ankara as well.

In 1986, Ankara and Istanbul groups collaborated to launch a petition campaign to urge the government to implement the 1985 UN Convention on the Elimination of All Forms of Discrimination Against Women. The convention had been signed by Turkey in 1985 and ignored thereafter. With the petition campaign, the feminists initiated collective public activism for the first time. The women's movement prospered as the journal *feminist* emerged in March 8, 1987. Those who brought out the journal defined their goals as follows:

> We had been thinking on the nature of our exploitation for a while, but this journal gave us the courage to speak about that which is personal to us. As you know, we the feminists think the private is political.[11]

Even though the journal did not elaborate its theoretical stance in depth, there was a radical feminist inclination amongst its contributors, who criticized the patriarchal nature of women's subjugation. As Ayşe Düzkan, one of its prominent writers explained, "(the journal) brought a fresh breath to societal opposition . . . questioned hierarchy, even authority . . . (and) brought a frivolous, naive, cheerful definition to the word feminist that is customarily used as an obscene word." [12]

The same year, a campaign called Solidarity Against Battering was organized against domestic violence. The campaign began with a march in May and continued with a festival in October.

Meanwhile, the Association of Women Against Discrimination (Ayrımcılığa Karşı Kadın Derneği-AKKD) was founded. The association signaled a new stage in the development of the feminist movement, which heretofore had been against conventional institutionalization and hierarchic organization. In their program, the founders articulated the need they felt for the association:

We, a group of women who argue for the necessity of institutionalization in order to implement the UN Convention on the Elimination of All Forms of Discrimination Against Women and transform the patriarchal institutions, traditions, and values agreed upon institutionalization, bearing in mind the potential that surfaced in the petition campaign (for CEDAW) and founded our association on June 25, 1987. We invite all women who are against gender discrimination that is experienced in all avenues of life.[13]

Among women's groups, socialist feminists were most vocal and interested in charting their ideological distinctiveness. On May 1, 1988, the journal *Sosyalist Feminist Kaktüs* (Socialist Feminist Cactus) began publication. The women who brought out the journal had worked together in the Woman's Circle and the Solidarity Campaign Against Battering. In their own words, "they had lived through an important experience based on the common denominator of the women's struggle."[14] In this process, perception of different feminisms had become more stark. Socialist women had seen more clearly how they wanted to live according to feminist principles. They decided to bring out *Kaktüs* "to discuss and develop what kind of independent women's politics they aimed for."[15] The *Kaktüs* group argued that "ideology alone was not what generated male female inequality, rather the network of gender as well as production relations accounted for this inequality."[16]

In January 1989, Women's Solidarity Association was founded to promote the activities of feminists in Ankara.[17] Apart from the Woman's Solidarity Association, women who called themselves the "Thursday Group" were engaged in consciousness raising. Others who did not strictly belong to any of these groups and journals, but nevertheless played a prominent role in activating the women's movement, called themselves the dissident feminists.

In February 1989, the Feminist Weekend that took place in Ankara brought together feminists from Istanbul and Ankara. A campaign called "No to Sexual Harassment" began as a consequence of this meeting and in light of the resolutions made there. As part of this campaign, needles with purple ribbons were sold, so that women could protect themselves against assault. Feminist initiatives led Bakırköy and Şişli municipalities to open shelters for battered women. In the summer of 1990, feminists founded the Purple Roof Woman's Shelter Foundation.[18] Meanwhile, in the spring of 1989, the Women's Library and Information Center was founded by a group of feminists. The library helped further institutionalize the movement.

Beyond these activities that were initiated by feminists, the women's movement moved ahead protesting legal inequalities. In 1990, article 438 of Turkish criminal code was deleted. The article diminished the severity of sentencing in rape cases by two-thirds if the victim was a prostitute. Article 159 of the civil code, which made women gain their husbands' permission before they could work outside the home, also was abolished. Beyond its relevance for women, this feminist activism was significant in the wider context of Turkish political development.

Liberalism and the Women's Movement

Until recently, the Turkish polity lacked a strong civil society where groups or individuals could pursue their interests and raise their voices peacefully. The women's movement provided the opportunity for individuals and groups to stand up for women's interests. To the extent that liberalism is the ideology of individualism that respects the power individuals generate independent of the state, feminists promoted liberalism in Turkey. Despite the homage Kemalism paid to Western liberalism, a dominant state tradition shaped the Turkish polity. Feminists, in this milieu, aimed to win respectability for women as individuals. The feminists' diverse activities and colorful writings underlined how significant it was for women to claim their feelings and problems individually. The aim of feminist public activism was to create public awareness on this issue.

The journal *feminist* was particularly keen to encourage women to act personally. The journal addressed women as follows: "Dear women, write to us. Write to *feminist* in order to remember, to understand, to express and purge yourself, to build again, to save memories, and to exist."[19] Women wrote in response. Many did not use their last names, in order to distance themselves from their patriarchal heritage. Previously unvoiced questions came to the surface. Choosing not to have children, alternative living arrangements, abortion, and lesbianism encroached upon the political agenda. In *feminist*, İdil wrote,

> Just as politics is not merely the business of 'people who know better,' speaking and writing are also not merely the business of people 'who speak better' or 'who write better' ... Writing and speaking have traditionally been men's realms, therefore we are inexperienced and shy in these fields. On top of this, if we add on our lack of self-confidence, we remain unable to express ourselves. However, we should try to express

ourselves. If we want to speak our words ourselves, we should try to
write and speak. In our own style and manner.[20]

The journal encouraged women to have respect as individuals, and
claim their social rights and freedoms; *feminist*'s colorful pages (decorated with flowers and birds), staunchly defended individualism, which
was one of the most significant themes of the post-1980 women's movement.

Not all feminists were liberal individualists, however. The individualism was not a satisfactory goal for many feminists. In fact, many thought
it could impede restructuring of society. Restructuring involved equality,
individualism, and solidarity. It was impossible or unhealthy to mobilize
women before they could exist as individuals; however, an individualism
devoid of feminist consciousness would obstruct solidarity.

The 1980s women's movement could underline women's individualism as a feminist dictate and succeed in mobilizing women. Consequently, horizontal solidarity between women could generate power
from civil society. The feminists in Turkey did not found an institution
to increase women's representation in the parliament (similar to the
National Organization of Women in the United States). There were no
links with political parties and no concerted effort was made to send
women to the Grand National Assembly. However, for the first time
in Republican history, women could raise their voices without being
compromised by the State when they organized into protest groups and
established independent women's institutions.

The feminist women who initiated the movement and aimed to change
the patriarchal nature of society, precipitated an unexpected outcome.
While these women failed to transform society radically as they aspired
to, they contributed to the establishment of a liberal society where
groups could associate and raise power in civil society. Liberalism as an
ideology might have been premised on patriarchal assumptions that
betray liberal aspirations for equality or freedom.[21] However, to the
extent that a liberal civil society allows for the pursuit of feminist
aspirations, it is preferable to a muted, powerless society.

Redemocratization and the Women's Movement

In addition to acting as a liberalizing influence, feminist activism helped
democratize society. As mentioned before, the rights women were
granted during the 1930s served democratic functions. A polity where

women participated in political life met a formal requirement of a democratic society.

However, the women's movement shouldered a different democratic function in the 1980s. It did not increase women's numbers in political organs. Instead, a small group of women increased their participation in political life by speaking, writing, and engaging in protest and conscious-ness-raising. The activist groups which constituted the women's move-ment emphasized and attempted to practice internal democracy as they engaged in politics.

The women's movement was not democratic merely because a small group of women assumed an active democratic role in politics. Women's activism played its role in the transition from authoritarianism to democ-racy. O'Donnell and Schmitter, focusing on the disintegration of authori-tarian regimes, emphasize the importance of political actors and their political activism.[22] These exemplary individuals, along with groups possessing special privileges, frequently find themselves in unique posi-tions to precipitate the transition to democracy.

In the context of the military regime of the 1980s, feminist groups had special privileges. While other groups, including labor, students, civil servants, and political parties were supressed, women could engage in politics. Whether it was because women's groups and their activism were thought insignificant or because the vague concept of "women's rights" could root its legitimacy in Kemalist reforms, feminists could raise their voices in politics. During a period when political will was curtailed, these women were able to exercise their political will. By doing so, they underlined the significance of becoming politicized; as a consequence, they directly contributed to the process of redemocratization.

The women's movement also stood against the authoritarian state. Feminist women did not expect the state to liberate women. On the contrary, major activities were organized against state policies, laws, and the regime itself. Protesting the state which restricted civil rights and liberties (of women) was a significant contribution to the process of democratization. The campaign "Solidarity Against Beating" began in response to a judge's refusal to allow the divorce of a pregnant mother of three children who was regularly beaten by her husband. The judge claimed "you do not leave a woman's back without a stick, [nor] her belly without a kid." This statement infuriated the feminists and helped channel their anger into organized protest. Women also organized pro-tests when the Constitutional Court upheld criminal code article 438.

Women's writings and speeches were also part of the pressure exerted

on the government.[23] Daily pronouncements, laws, and bills were as-
sessed from a feminist perspective. Women criticized the civil code
reform bill, abortion law, censure and torture. They brought the torture
of women to public attention.

There were limits, however, to how much the feminists could contribute to redemocratization. Their demands and dissent were primarily
oriented to expand women's rights and liberties. Constitutional restrictions on civil liberties were not explicitly linked to women's issues.
Feminist protests against the state were based on the assumption that the
political system should be opened, but did not explicitly take a stance on
democratization.

Secularism and the Women's Movement

The most significant function of Kemalist reforms on women's status
may have been the strengthening of secularism. The equality envisioned
in the reforms of the 1920s and 1930s dealt a blow to the Shariat and
those who defended the Sharia, which was based on a hierarchic division
of labor between genders.

How did the new generation of feminists interpret the responsibility
of upholding secularism? In the 1980s, the state no longer sought to
supress Islamic groups; rather, it supported them. The socioeconomic
transformation that took place since the 1930s and the attempt of the
1980s regime to relocate political life beyond a right-left axis gave the
Islamist groups a new impetus and a new status.[24]

During an era when the Islamist groups were gaining strength rather
than being supressed, the feminists were a secular front. Secularism was
an indispensable prerequisite for the feminists. If one held that divine
will shaped social relations, it would be difficult to talk of male-female
equality and impossible to talk, in feminist terms, of women's liberation.
On the other hand, Islamic groups differed on women's place in Islam.
Some argued that the Qur'an proposed male-female equality.[25] A majority accepted that Islam proposed a hierarchic system built on a gender-
based division of labor. These groups maintained that this system was
based on divine justice, was righteous, and did not exploit women.[26] It
was difficult to reconcile Islamist groups with those who constituted the
women's movement whether they were mobilized to defend principles of
equality or women's liberation.[27] Under these conditions, the women's
movement was an important force in the secular wing.

For the liberal or Kemalist feminists within the women's movement, secularism was of primary importance. They neither believed that there could be egalitarian interpretations within the confines of Islam, nor that the hierarchic gender-based division of labor most Islamists upheld was just. Islam was the biggest threat to male-female equality. Islam was the basic problem of the women's movement. Some women even argued that before women's equality to men or liberation could be sought, a war had to be waged for secularism.

For the younger generation of feminists, women's liberation, rather than secularism, was the priority. They agreed that the hierarchic gender-based division of labor was unacceptable. Islam might or might not be open to egalitarian interpretation. In either case, the patriarchal context of Islam, which controlled every aspect of women's lives, could not be reconciled with feminism, which aimed to undermine patriarchal structures, reshape social relations and legitimize women's right to self-determination. Despite these fundamental divergences beyond the issue of male-female equality, the potential or actual threat of the Islamic groups was not considered to be more important than women's liberation.

Small groups within the women's movement even interacted with Islamist women. Ironically, these women, influenced by feminism, questioned gender-biased rhetoric in Islam at the same time they accused secular feminists of Jacobinism. As a result of these charges, feminists clarified their stances.[28]

The women's movement of the 1980s was a radical outcome of Kemalist Westernization. The 1930s Kemalist reforms and Turkey's subsequent socioeconomic development prepared the unique conditions where a women's movement influenced from the West could come into existence.

At the same time, the women's movement presented a radical critique of Kemalism. Feminists argued that it was not sufficient to approach the issue of women from the perspective of the egalitarian Kemalist reforms. Beyond egalitarian legal amendments that could be shaped by the state, feminists argued that patriarchal social relations in the private and public realm needed to be radically transformed. Private life, that the state neglected, had to be redefined and all forms of women's exploitation had to end.

Despite the controversy between Kemalist and feminist values, the women's movement helped promote the values of the Kemalists. Even though they had a marginal status in the polity, feminists helped spread liberalism, democracy, and secularism. By underlining respect for the individual and helping individuals generate power independent of the state, the women's movement played a role in establishing a liberal society. The Kemalist rhetoric of democracy was put into practice with feminist activism during the transition to democracy in the 1980s. The feminists were loyal to the secular ethic of the Kemalists, but at the same time, they worked to to reconcile secularism with democracy. Consequently, the women's movement used criticism and activism to help realize the Kemalist reforms.

Turkish feminists were less successful in creating radical change. Campaigns, festivals, demonstrations organized by women, journals, and magazine articles contributed less to the transformation of the patriarchal society than to the establishment of a liberal, democratic and secular polity. The women's movement reached its goals, to the extent that a liberal, democratic, and secular polity is a precondition for the transformation of a patriarchal polity. While a significant feminist consciousness emerged in urban circles, it helped strengthen a pluralist polity rather than animate a feminist one.

REFERENCES

1. This paper is a revised version of the article "1980'ler Türkiye'sinde Kadın Hareketi: Liberal Kemalizmin Radikal Uzantısı" which appeared in the quarterly journal *Toplum ve Bilim*, Spring 1991.

2. Şule Torun, " 'İnsanlar' ve 'Ötekiler' " *Somut*, February 4, 1983, 4.

3. Bernard Lewis, *The Emergence of Modern Turkey* (London: Oxford University Press, 1976).

4. Mete Tunçay, *Türkiye Cumhuriyeti'nde Tek Parti Yönetiminin Kurulması (1923–1931)* (Ankara: Yurt Yayınları, 1981).

5. For a critical evaluation of the Kemalist reforms on women, see Şirin Tekeli *Kadın Bakış Açısından 1980'ler Türkiye'sinde Kadınlar* (İstanbul: İletişim, 1990) 214–216; for an examination of their functional significance in the process of Westernization, see Yeşim Arat, *The Patriarchal Paradox: Women Politicians in Turkey* (N.J.: Associated University Presses, 1989) 23–33; for their role in nation-building, see Nilüfer Çağatay and Yasemin Nuhoğlu Soysal, "Uluslaşma Süreci ve Feminizm Üzerine Karşılaştırmalı Düşünceler." In Şirin Tekeli ed., *Kadın Bakış Açısından 1980'ler Türkiye'sinde Kadın* (İstanbul: İletişim Yayınları, 1990); for a feminist perspective on their limitations, see Zehra Arat, "Turkish Women and the Republican Reconstruction of Tradition." In Fatma Müge Göçek and Shiva Balaghi, eds., *Reconstructuring Gender in the Middle*

East: Power, Identity, and Tradition (New York: Columbia University Press, 1995).

6. "Opportunity space" is a concept Şerif Mardin uses to refer to the "totality of areas in society where new opportunities become available whether through the vacating of slots in the occupational pyramid, or the creation of new ones through social differentiation and mobility, or the decrease in population in relation to available slots in the manpower structure." [Şerif Mardin, "Turkey: The Transformation of an Economic Code." In Ergun Özbudun and Aydın Ulusan eds., *The Political Ecomony of Income Distribution in Turkey* (New York: Holmes and Meier, 1980), 28]. Reforms specifically designed to improve women's opportunity space were herculean tasks, especially in the Middle Eastern context. The modernizing leaders of Muslim countries such as Egypt and Iran that had most opened to the West were unsuccessful in improving women's predicament within the boundaries of the Shariat. See Nadia Hijab *Womanpower: The Arab Debate on Women at Work* (Cambridge: Cambridge University Press, 1988) 29–31; Eliz Sanasarian, *The Women's Rights Movement in Iran* (New York: Praeger Publishers, 1982) 79–105.

7. Levent Cinemre and Ruşen Çakır, eds., *Sol Kemalizme Bakıyor* (İstanbul: Metis Yayınları, 1991) 93–107.

8. *Birinci Feminist Haftasonu*, 11–12 Şubat, 1989, 84; Kandiyoti, 1987.

9. See Necla Arat, *Feminizmin ABC'si* (İstanbul: Simavi yayınları, 1991), for a definition of liberal feminism as one of its self-declared proponents defines it. Liberal feminists have been very active in post-1985 feminist politics. They founded University of İstanbul Women's Research and Education Center in 1990, which aimed to "defend and enlarge women's rights gained through Atatürk's Principles and Revolutions" (University of İstanbul Women's Research and Education Center, 1990 Objectives). They have been organizing widely-attended lecture series, turning them into well-publicized books, presenting their views on major political developments (including the raping of women in Bosnia-Herzegovina or the electoral success of the Islamists in local politics) through the media and collaborating with a well known professional public relations company to advance their cause.

10. Nükhet Sirman, "Feminism in Turkey: A Short History," *New Perspectives on Turkey* 3 (1989), 1; Şirin Tekeli, "Emergence of the New Feminist Movement in Turkey," in Drude Dahlerup, ed., *The New Women's Movement: Feminism and Political Power in the USA* (London: Sage, 1986), 179–199; Şirin Tekeli, "Women in the Changing Political Associations of the 1980s," in Andrew Finkel and Nükhet Sirman, eds., *Turkish State Turkish Society* (London: Routledge, 1990), 259–288; Şirin Tekeli "Europe, European Feminism, and Women in Turkey," *Women's Studies International Forum* 15, 1.

11. *feminist* 1 (1987), 34

12. *Birinci Feminist Haftasonu* (1989) 32.

13. "Ayrımcılığa Karşı Kadın Derneği Programı," Program of AKKD.

14. Sosyalist Feminist Kaktüs, "Neden Dergi Çıkarıyoruz," *Kaktüs* 1 (1988), 5.

15. "Neden Dergi Çıkarıyoruz," *Kaktüs* 1 (1988), 6.
16. "Neden Dergi Çıkarıyoruz," *Kaktüs* 1 (1988), 16.
17. *Birinci Feminist Haftasonu,* (1989), 20
18. *Cumhuriyet,* June 17, 1990.
19. *feminist* 1 (1987), 6.
20. İdil, "Bilim? Politika? Yazmak-Konuşmak?," *feminist* 3 (1987), 16.
21. Carol Pateman, *The Sexual Contract,* (Cambridge: Polity Press, 1988); Zillah Eisenstein, *The Radical Future of Liberal Feminism,* (New York: Longman, 1981).
22. Guilermo O'Donnell and Philippe C. Schmitter, *Transitions from Authoritarian Rule: Tentative Conclusions About Uncertain Democracies* (Baltimore: The Johns Hopkins University Press, 1986).
23. For an example of the assessment of sociopolitical developments from a feminist perspective, see Tekeli, 1988.
24. İlkay Sunar and Binnaz Toprak, "Islam in Politics: The Case of Turkey," *Government and Opposition* 18 (1983), 421–441; Nilüfer Göle, *Modern Mahrem* (İstanbul: Metis Yayınları, 1991); Richard Tapper and Nancy Tapper eds., *Islam in Modern Turkey,* (London: I.B. Tauris, 1991).
25. Hüseyin Hatemi, *Kadının Çıkış Yolu* (Ankara: Fecr Yayınevi, 1988).
26. Feride Acar, "Women in the Ideology of Islamic Revivalism in Turkey: Three Islamic Women's Journals." In Richard Tapper and Nancy Tapper eds., *Islam in Modern Turkey* (London: I.B. Tauris, 1991).
27. Yeşim Arat, "Feminizm ve Islam: *Kadın ve Aile* Dergisinin Düşündürdükleri." In Şirin Tekeli ed. *Kadın Bakış Açısından 1980'ler Türkiye'sinde Kadınlar.* (İstanbul: İletişim, 1990) 89–102.
28. For examples of the polemic that took place between Muslim women and socialist feminists, see Sedef Öztürk, "Kadın Sorunu Islamcıların Gündeminde Nereye Kadar? " *Kaktüs* 2 (1988) 38; Sedef Öztürk, "Eleştiriye Bir Yanıt," *Kaktüs* 4 (1988) 28–30; and Aysel Kurter et al., "Kadınlara Rağmen Kadınlar İçin" Tavrına Bir Eleştiri. *Kaktüs* 4 (1988) 25–27.

CHAPTER EIGHT

Growing up in Israel: A Personal Perspective

Rachel Persico

Contrary to the popular mythologies associated with Israel, the culture does not treat women as equals but is, rather, like the U.S. or Turkey, a Patriarchal Democracy. I will attempt to describe the specific ways in which Israeli culture relates to women and examine the impact it had on my own life, as a typical middle-class Israeli, Jewish woman.

I was born and raised on a kibbutz in what was purported to be a "New Society," to coin a phrase. The nation's founding fathers' and mothers' vision at the turn of the century, back in the diaspora, was to come here, we were told as children, and establish an agricultural community. In doing so, they would live close to the good earth, and share, among its members, absolutely equally all duties and privileges. Toiling the soil shoulder-to-shoulder, men and women would enjoy the fruits of that labor as equals. One of the central myths we were given as children was the story of how our particular kibbutz was instituted. It had to do with the Jews being oppressed back in Europe by the Goyim, the gentiles, from without, and by Ghetto mentality, being closely regulated by religion and tradition, from within. (If you've seen "Fiddler on the Roof," as I'm sure you all have, you'll know what I'm talking about.)

At any rate, it had to do with a whole generation of young idealists back in Europe who decided that it was time to stop sitting and waiting for the Messiah to come; it was time to take destiny into their own hands, to tear away the shackles of old and start anew in that empty land called Palestine. That empty land which, like the princess in the fairy tale, had been asleep for thousands of years, waiting for them to come and reawaken her with the kiss of their sweat and their tears.

When I grew up I was shocked to learn that the myth about the land

being empty was a lie, that in fact there was another people already on
that land, a local agricultural society numbering approximately seven
hundred thousand people. They were to become dispossessed by us, the
Jews, "returning" to Palestine. In fact, my own Kibbutz turned out to
have been built on the ruins of a Palestinian village. In his book *The
Birth of the Palestinian Refugee Problem*,[1] Benny Morris reports about
four hundred villages that were razed to the ground, their inhabitants
fleeing or being chased across the borders, to make room for the new
Israeli state. Growing up, the myth of "a land with no people to a people
with no land" was central to my education. It was therefore a shock to
discover that it was false.

The myth about absolute equality was shattered long before that. As
a girl child on the kibbutz, I noticed very early on that there were strict
roles for every individual to play. There were unwritten rules which, if
you did not follow, you risked being ostracized, being pushed out of the
group. Our class, my peer group, was equally balanced, 10 boys and 10
girls. When we first started working in fifth grade, doing two hours a
day of chores as a sign of our maturity, we were sent equally to all
branches of the Kibbutz economy. But as we grew up, the boys were
somehow directed more towards field work, where the big bonus was
that you learned how to drive a tractor, while the girls became assistant
care takers at the children's home, helping to take care of babies. The
same labour division was true for the grownups. The men did most of
the agricultural work and all the managerial work, while women were
occupied in caregiving, cooking, laundry, sewing, etc. At school, although most teachers were women, the headmaster was a man. The
secretary-general position of the kibbutz, the top position, was always
occupied by a man. Yet our childhood mythology included stories about
those wondrous women, the pioneers, who took part in the so called
"historical act of return," toiling the fields by day standing guard,
holding a gun by night.

As Debbi Bernstein points in her article about the subject in "Politikah" magazine:

> The myths about the role of women during the early settlement were
> created by men. Realistically while 43% of the men took part in the
> ground-laying work of building roads and working the land, only 5% of
> the women shared in that. . . while household chores were done by 27%
> of the women and only 2.4% of the men. These numbers are taken from
> a 1937 Census which also reveals a discrepancy in wage earned. While

36.8% of the men and only 5.3% of the women get the highest pay, 60% of the women and only 15% of the men are rated at the lowest wage.[2]

This matter of the wage, I suspect, is the reason why women were kept away from the most lucrative jobs. Sounds familiar? It is amazing how sometimes things seem to have been different and how much they actually stayed the same. In those days too, women were the ones who stopped working outside the home as soon as they had children and had to struggle with this issue. Here is a quote from a female member at the "Workers Convention" of 1926:

> At this time of work shortage, and while women are just starting to penetrate some fields, we must not ignore our biggest problem: the liberation of women. Should building a family really deprive us of our own identity? We must find a way for a woman union member who marries another comrade to remain a member of the union, on her own merit, not as a proxy to her husband. . . we must find a way to be liberated of household chores. . . .[3]

But women's needs were sacrificed for the so-called national good, and by the time I was born in 1953, all that was left was the myth, the essence of those words. Not their practice.

The inequality between men and women dominated every aspect of our life, though it was never acknowledged as such. For example, on the kibbutz, few pupils from every age group were encouraged to go on and pursue higher education. The numbers further indicated that most of these were boys, who as a rule, were directed towards "manly" professions like engineering and agricultural studies. When a women was sent out to school, it was presumed that she would become either a teacher or a nurse.

One of the most prominent aspects of kibbutz life had always been communal housing for the children. Originally this was established for ideological reasons, so that parents of both sexes were free to contribute equal working time for the sake of the commune. All children were brought up together in the children's home. Each peer group or class had its own teacher and set of two caregivers. As a child, you would spend most of your day at the children's home; you would go to see your parents around 4 p.m., spend the evening with them, and then you would be taken to the children's home for the night to be put down to sleep.

Most Kibbutzim in Israel have undergone a revolution of sorts, a revolution that was initiated by the women. Women who themselves were second or third generation Kibutzniks and had grown up in the system had learned through their own experience that communal sleeping quarters only ensured misery rather than provide equality of opportunity for both the parents and the child. Growing up almost exclusively with a peer group created children who were not very emotionally secure. The peer group could never replace parents in giving unconditional love. Instead, groups of children were known to be immensely cruel to the individual who may venture to be different. A child would have to bend and mold his or her behavior according to the strict rules of the group. As a result, psychological research suggested that kibbutz children tended to have a hard time attaching emotionally.

In recent years, women of the kibbutz started to demand that this system be changed. Those who objected, mostly men, pointed to the fact that children sleeping at home may hinder women's progress in the kibbutz. But the women insisted that this was a different issue and should be examined with equal seriousness but separately. The women won, today 99.9% Kibutzim have switched to sleeping arrangements that have the children sleeping at home. Paradoxical as it seems, getting the sleeping arrangements changed was the first victory of Kibbutz women in its long history, and what may initially appear to be a situation more restraining for women, has in fact, given them some power, the power that comes from success. These days, things are beginning to change, however slowly. Even though there is a theoretical consent to women's right for equality, in practice, women still do most of the caretaking jobs and it is the men who go out into the world and manage things. In recent years, many Kibbutzim have had a woman as general secretary, and more and more women have taken on managerial positions. Yet, at the highest echelons of Kibbutz politics, as well as in the Labor movement (which is now in control of the government), you would still find mostly men.

Although there has been some progress, women's powerlessness is pervasive throughout Israeli society where there is not one woman at the head of a large corporation or a financial institution. Israel is still a male dominated society where women are viewed as support systems, as mothers of the nation rather than as equals.

Personally, I was lucky. Since my parents were not members of the kibbutz but rather its employed Doctors, I was sent to a good high school in nearby Haifa and later persued higher education. Of my peer group, none of the women ever went to college. Even those who left the Kibbutz ended up doing "feminine" jobs like being a secretary, a kindergarten teacher, and a girls' Physical Education teacher.

Yes, they all served in the army. All Jews in Israel are compelled to serve. When I graduated from high-school, I was also drafted into the army. Another myth, the Israeli Army is reputed throughout the world to be not only invincible but also extremely sexy. All sorts of books and movies have drawn a picture of brave youth, fighting a relentless enemy, the women fighting shoulder to shoulder with the men, tearing pins off of hand grenades with their teeth, while their blond hair flows in the wind. . . Well, reality, as always, is much different. In the army, as in any other aspect of society, women are the auxiliary force. They do the clerical jobs and generally play a supporting role. Unlike the American military, you will never see a woman pilot of any kind in Israel Air Force, or as a commander of male soldiers. These days, some women are allowed to teach some training courses but that is as far as they go.

When I was in the army (1972-1974), in basic training you were told that your role was to be there to support "our boys." After basic training, when I was stationed in the divisional office, and expected to know how to type and file, and make coffee, as if that knowledge was, somehow, in my genes, I got into trouble. By the time I had been in the army for six months I was desperate at the thought that I would have to spend the next two years obeying orders concerned with typing and filing. When I was recruited to go to an officer's course I jumped at the chance. I knew that as an officer I would at least not be asked to type, I even imagined I may be able to actually do some good. When I graduated from officer's course I was stationed at a base in the Sinai where I became responsible for the welfare of some 70 girls. I was 19 at the time and thought I was oh so grown up. As it turned out I did not have much of an opportunity to examine my new found authority; after about a month, the 1973 October war began and all females were evacuated as soon as possible. That process took about a week, shipping the girls out on buses, in between air raids. I have to confess I was very glad I was not a man then; several of my male high school class mates who were also doing their army service at the time lost their lives in that war.

This brings me to a very important point, a possible hypothesis as to why women are not treated as equals in Israel. It appears to me that in a society like Israel's everything revolves around war: the possibility of it, getting ready for it, recovering from it. Serving in the army is not a matter of choice but is obligatory. Those who do the most dangerous job, or even appear to be doing it, will later have the most power in the societal structure. I suppose it is possible that women have made a subconscious choice, they prefer not to be called into the battlefield and in return have left all the power in the hands of men. It seems more likely, however, that men have prevented women from sharing in the battle so that they later will not have to share power with their sisters. It is as if, in the most basic terms, women have relinquished their power to their so called protectors. It is a tricky thing. I suspect many women would rather pay the price and have the power while many individual men would forego the privileges and choose not to serve in the army. As a society, it appears that Israel is locked into this position; women's secondary role in battle is reflected in all aspects of life.

The Arab citizens of Israel are totally denied, by the state, the opportunity to serve in the army. As a result, they are second class citizens, not privy to many of the financial privileges and educational and job opportunities of the Jews. In Israel, it is part of the convention that people in uniform are somehow better, they are revered, usually referred to as "our boys, our most prized possessions." And yet they are periodically, almost ritualistically, sacrificed to the gods of war.

This cycle of army service and privileges effects all other strata of the society; for example, in many work places, there is a separate rate of pay for male and female workers. Women as a rule make about 60% of men's wages, any profession that is dominated by women, like teachers or nurses is devalued and underpaid.

When I was in the army I was encouraged by my parents to go abroad to pursue an education. After completing my studies in communications and television production, I came back to Israel and applied for a job with the Israeli Broadcasting Authority, the only T.V. channel in Israel at the time. I wanted to work as a Camera Operator. This was extremely unusual. There were no women in that job at the time, and I did not think I had much of a chance of getting it. I suspect I was accepted not so much on my merits but rather because my new boss wanted to appear liberated and progressive. I was young and pleasant, and he thought it would be interesting to have a woman around, someone who would actually respect him as the boss. . . .

At that time, 1975, my presence behind the camera was so unusual that it was mentioned in several newspapers in the entertainment section. I was young enough then to think that I could overcome any prejudices and really show them what I could do. I lasted in that job for thirteen years. Initially I invested huge amounts of energy into proving that I could do the job just as well as any men. I carried heavy equipment, I was always available to rush to any assignment, and tried to do the best job I could. But after a few years it finally dawned on me that I would always be a kind of a curiosity, that I would never be judged on my merit but rather always as a woman, that I will never have a chance of proper advancement. I found that no matter how hard I worked, my paycheck was never as large as some of my colleagues'. Who, as my boss explained to me, were after all supporting a family. . .

When I worked at Israel T.V. (1975–1987) I was witness to other interesting phenomena. For example, there was only one woman technician in the whole building. There has never been a woman head of Television, and the only department head reserved for women is Children's Programing. Neither Television, Radio, or any newspaper's News Division in the country is run by a woman. On Israel Television, women reporters are not allowed to cover hard news, rather they cover entertainment and so called women's topics, and even that very rarely. Although there are two announcers in each evening broadcast, the woman is almost always only a reader of news, she never writes her own text. She hardly ever conducts interviews on the air, that privilege is reserved for the male counterpart who is usually the news editor and so is the center of the broadcast. Women who have political opinions, and express those freely, are usually frowned upon. Although ninety percent of the production staff are women, they remain behind the scene and the credit usually goes to the male star of the show. Women announcers are judged on appearance, and so, as they mature, they are routinely replaced by fresh blossoms, while males, as we all know, only gain dignity and authority with age. . .[4]

In Israel, most women work outside the home, it has always been that way. No household can survive on one salary, most find it difficult these days to survive on two. One of the greatest achievements of working women in Israel was the passage of law that ensures a paid maternity leave and protects pregnant women against being terminated from her job for as long as a year after she has given birth. Also, contrary to the situation in the States, there are affordable and satisfactory day care facilities for children from a very early age. Special provisions are made for single mothers in that they are allowed to work less and maintain the same pay and their medical expenses are paid for by the health insurance carrier which in many cases is the State in one form or another. Yet some people point to the fact that these kinds of provisions may cause employers to place women only in dispensable positions, so that when they go on maternity leave, they may be easily replaced. All of the above mentioned privileges only hold true if you are an employee. If you are a woman entrepreneur or a freelancer you basically have no rights, no big father to pay your health insurance, no special provisions for child care. You are, in fact, an entity not recognized by many institutions. I have a friend who is an author and a freelance journalist, she is prohibited by law from filing her own separate income tax return and can only exist on her husband's return. None of her professional expenses is deductible. For example if she were to hire a nanny or a cleaning person, she may not deduct this from her income tax. She only exists as an adjunct to her husband. One may deduce that independence for women is not a high priority with Israeli law makers.

In her book *Women in Politics*,[5] Dafnah Sharfman states that the legal situation in Israel puts women at an unequal position by law. Unique among Western democracies, Israel, just like Iran, gives the Clerics absolute power, by law, to be the final arbiters in matters of Marriage, Birth and Death. This means that judgment in these, the most personal of matters, is up to the religious courts and that in them, the laws of the Bible take precedence over the law of the land. This creates a situation where modern day disputes are decided according to ancient law, a law that still views the wife as the property of her husband, to be disposed of as he sees fit. The Hebrew word for husband, *ba'al*, literally means "owner." This creates a situation where, for example, a woman cannot actively divorce her husband. The divorce procedure is totally dependent upon his good will, and he has to agree to say the words and take part in the ancient ceremony before they may be divorced. Consequently there is a group of women in Israel, called *agunot*, whose husbands have refused to divorce them, sometimes for tens of years. These women can not remarry, as they are not divorced according to Jewish law, and they are helpless to do anything about it. They have to sit and wait for their husband to give them a divorce. If a wife, even a battered wife, leaves her home before she is divorced, the Clerical Courts can declare her a "mutinous woman" and can take her children and any rights to her own property, away. If a wife is alleged to have slept with one man while she was still married to another, by Jewish law she is forbidden to marry her lover even after her divorce *asurah le-be'alah ule-bo'alah*.[6] So if a husband knows that his wife is leaving him for someone else, he can go to court, get a judgment, and the new couple will be forbidden marriage, forever. There are plenty of other examples. I suppose, every institutionalized religion has its own rituals, and that is fine, if one freely chooses to participate. In Israel, however, there is no separation between state and church; there is no such thing as Civil Marriage. If you want to get married or be buried, you have to comply with Biblical law. And even then, a Jew may only marry a Jew, a non-Jew may not be buried in a Jewish cemetery etc. All of this of course contributes to the inequality of women.

And yet, Israel is often described as "the only democracy in the Middle East," and it is a democracy, of sorts, for its Jewish citizens. It is also the only western democracy that is forcibly occupying another people, and has an oppressive military rule over a population of about two million (2,000,000) Palestinians who have absolutely no rights. They spend much of their days under curfew confined to their homes. The Palestinians in the Occupied Territories can not vote or be elected to office, can not run their schools freely, can not travel freely or purchase land. Their property is robbed and so is their water supply. A Palestinian woman may be doubly oppressed. First by a culture-that views her subordinates to men and than by an occupying army that deprive her and her children basic freedoms.

Paradoxically, among Jewish Israelis, a group of women called the "Women in Black" are the bravest fighters against the injustices done to Palestinians. These women gather every Friday afternoon in central squares of some cities where they all wear black and carry protest signs that call for ending the occupation. Although these women have become a target for harassment by men who pass by in their cars, who spit at them, throw rotten fruits and eggs at them and shout obscenities, they have been relentless. A member of the group who conducted a survey of the most popular obscenities shouted at them illuminates the greatest fear of the Israeli male ego: "You sleep with Arafat. . . all of you sleep with Arafat. . . " they shout. Typical, universal, racist, male fear, all entangled with sex and ownership, their women will be taken out of their posses-sion and become the possession of the enemy.

To sum up, Israeli women, even though aware of the feminist revolu-tion, and even though at one point had one feminist member of parlia-ment, seem to have reverted in recent years to a less equal status. This, in my opinion, is related to the obsessive preoccupation with war, past, present and future, which has taken hold of Israeli society after the 67 war. The army has become the most revered institution, coupled with a simultaneous upsurge in religious and political fanaticism.

It appears to me that apart from the universal, traditional patrimony and dominance of men over women, which has to do with a struggle over power and resources, Israeli society may have been influenced by two powerful themes that have helped to shape it into the Patriarchal Democracy it is today.

The first one, I suggest is the centrality of the role of a powerful military establishment in this society. Every Jewish male is required to serve in the army, and unlike the women who share the same compulsory service, he alone is sent into the battle field and is asked to give his life for his country. This creates a culture in which soldiers are revered and given special privileges. This, in turn, constrains women, who serve in the army only as supporting, non combative operatives, into a secondary position, in which their rights are eroded. The large Israeli minority of Arab citizens, who are denied the opportunity to serve in the army, is in turn the least privileged and, in fact, becomes disenfranchised.

The other compelling theme is religion. Although the founding fathers and mothers of Israel purported to create a new, religion free society, the political Status Quo gives the religious minority enormous political power. In a country that defines itself as "The Jewish State" and in which there is no separation between state and church, in the personal realms, like marriage and divorce settlement, ancient biblical rules still dictate the court's ruling. These two particularly Israeli phenomena, the centrality of the military and of religion, fortify a rigid patriarchal society where the ultimate compliment to the only woman prime minister that country ever had, Golda Meir, was that she was "a real man."

REFERENCES

1. Benny Morris, *The Birth of the Palestinian Refugee Problem: 1947– 1949* (Cambridge: Cambridge University Press, 1987).
2. Debbi Bernstein, *Politikah Maga{ine* (Hebrew), 27:60 (July 1989).
3. Bernstein, *Politikah*, 61.
4. I left Israeli TV at the end of 1987. With the influx of cable, some superficial progress has has been made, but women are yet to gain power, as in editorial or managerial positions in the media.
5. Dafnah Sharfman, *Nashim u-Politikah* (Hebrew) (Haifa: Tamar Publishing House, 1988).
6. Literally translates "forbidden to her owner and to her lover."

CHAPTER NINE

Coming of Age in Occupied Palestine: Engendering the Intifada

Leila Hudson

The reinterpretation and adaptation of traditional gender roles to the exigencies of life under Israeli occupation is an important factor in the continuing durability of the Intifada.[1] While the historical context and local conditions that sparked the Intifada are well known,[2] questions about its structure and function are more difficult to answer. Why did a community that suffered under occupation for decades bond into a comparatively effective popular resistance? What keeps the Intifada going, in spite of its discouraging results? How did Palestinian society become more willing to endure both external and self-imposed economic hardship? How can the community rationalize allowing its youths and children to engage regularly in violent confrontations with heavily armed military force? In short, what are the social factors and dynamics that fuel the Intifada? Others have written about the local politics of the committees that coordinate the uprising.[3] I will focus on the culture which, it appears, was ripe for transformation in the late 1980s.

It has been noted by many observers that the Intifada coincides with the coming of age of a generation of Palestinians born into occupation in, around, and after 1967, when the West Bank and Gaza Strip were captured by Israel in the Six Day War. The Intifada's confrontational attitude[4] expresses the frustration of a population that becomes younger, larger, and more hopeless with each passing year. This gradual shift in the perspective of the population helps explain the change of mood in the occupied territories from one characterized by faith in extralocal processes to one characterized by active local resistance and confrontation. By the time of the Gulf War, however, the Intifada was losing steam. The Intifada proved costly for the Palestinians in economic and human terms. Israel's response to it was brutal.[5] While the focus of the Palestinian struggle shifted from the diaspora to the occupied territories, international sympathy for the Palestinian cause grew,[6] but many residents claim that life in the West Bank and Gaza was never more difficult and are pessimistic about their future. Why and how does the motivation for the Intifada persist?

It is appealing (and misleading) to believe that the Intifada's stamina is directly related to the turbulent adolescence of those born after 1967. It leads to the conclusion that the Intifada should have died after a short burst of tragic bravado. The institutionalisation, organization, and routinization of many types of social and economic resistance belie this interpretation. Although it provides a compelling metaphor, it is not the emotional response of a single generation that has energized the Intifada. The despair of the so-called Generation of 1967 or Children of the Stones did not simply arise from the ashes of their parents' hopes. How can the relationship between the generation raised under occupation and the Intifada be further specified?

A gendered approach to the study of the Intifada need not simply describe women's participation in the uprising.[7] This paper explores how people of both sexes anchor themselves in relation to traditional[8] discourses of gender while they experience and affect the transformation of their society. My attempt to view historical change through the lens of flexible paradigms of masculinity and feminity suggests that the traditional and the revolutionary are not necessarily contradictory; rather, they are overlapping and mutually reinforcing justifications for political action.

Interpreting and applying concepts of gender is a central leitmotiv of adolescence and young adulthood, and it is an aspect of culture in which a considerable amount of social energy is invested. Whether one accepts a set of gendered expectations from one's elders or redefines sex roles, nearly everyone must live up to or confront a cultural standard of gender. The Palestinians born in the occupied territories find themselves between a rock and a hard place. It is difficult for them to fulfill naturalized, "nonpolitical" ideals of masculinity and femininity that are tied to work, honor, independence, and family because legal restrictions and the limited economy do not provide opportunity for most of the population. At the same time they cannot abandon traditional values without risking the fragmentation of a largely patriarchal society whose only hope of preservation lies in solidarity.

The result is the widespread, implicit expression of gender categories *through* the explicitly political response of resistance. The trials and responsibilities that were always a part of becoming or being a man or a woman are now dedicated to the cause of resistance. People are ready to participate in the Intifada in spite of the intense pressures it exerts, because participation has become one of the few ways to mark the passage from childhood to adulthood. The processes of maturation and initiation to adult status and responsibility provide a model and a vehicle for the progressive and total political awakening that the Intifada strives to be. At the same time, the Intifada provides a new arena for constructing gender roles and assuming authority in a disenfranchised society.

Gender Imagery of the Intifada Songs

In this paper I use the word "traditional" advisedly. I use it to refer to conceptions of gender that are not informed by feminist views, are characterized as "natural" and socially necessary, and which carry expectations about kinship norms and honor obligations. In a traditional view, men's and women's roles are complementary and rarely overlap. Ideally, men's social life is active and public, while women's is private. Through their imagery, the songs of the Intifada[9] illustrate how the emergent norms of resistance draw strength from older, more securely entrenched discourses of men's and women's duties toward family and society. At the same time the poetic rhetoric articulates conceptions of masculinity and femininity that are unababashedly political and directed.

The poetry of the Intifada develops an organic vision, in which all parts of the community are bound together by descent from, and responsibility toward the land of Palestine itself. The songs' repeated depiction of the earth as a living relation and the reiteration of normative kinship values help to create a social atmosphere in which the risk-taking rebel is not alienated from his family and society but is fulfilling his duty toward them.

In many songs, the land figures prominently as an ancestress and victim, whose redemption is the duty of her human children. The song below addresses and anthropomorphizes (gynomorphizes?) the land and the Arab towns that are evidence of the Palestinians' connection to the land.[10] The land and the nation are exhorted to rise up in response to the male singer's lead.

I sing to you my land
Listen to me and rise up and repeat the tunes
I sing to every village and city
In whose streets we played.

In another song, the stones of Palestine are personfied, and the link
between the land and the inhabitants is reinforced. The young people of
Palestine express the anger of the land, and act to protect it.

The gun sang inside the refugee camp
And little children
Let the stone speak for itself
The generation of rebels is learning
For the sake of the land and its steadfast people.

Sometimes, kinship with the land is explicitly stated.

A voice was heard, boys, calling
[It was] the voice of my country and it said "my children
I am your mother, I am Palestine
And I've been calling to you for years."

Other parts of the song illustrate how kinship, honor, and the land
recur in the exhortative poetry of the Intifada. The mother Palestine
calls out to her sons, the *shabab* (young men). As long as they remain
insensible or immature, they are excused from her service. Once awak-
ened, however, they cannot rest until they have redeemed her honor.
The following verse portrays the earth as the beloved and the mother of
all.

To your land, the darling of the martyrs
Homeland of flowers, oh my dear mother
We offer the rebels.

In another song, the fighter and the land are linked in a cycle of
rebirth, causing a dead youth's mother to sing as in celebration of birth,
rather than wail in mourning.

The martyr gives us stones from his blood
From his blood the rose becomes red

> His mother trills for him in joy
> He has given his blood to the nation.

Finally, duty toward the land is linked to social relations within the community. A mother prepares herself for the sacrifices she will witness, by defiantly celebrating the uprising and offering herself and her family for the struggle. Notably the mother offers support, blood, and children, but not direct personal action:

> My mother trilled in joy
> She said "go arm yourself,
> For we do not shirk our duties.
> You want my children? help yourselves
> You want my blood? here's a portion."

The terminology of kinship refers both to immediate relatives and the community as a whole. In the next verse, a man tells his sister (*ukht*) and mother (*um*) to be strong and not interfere with the sacrifices he must endure. It should be noted that these terms are not used only to refer to blood relations: *ukht* can refer to any female contemporary; *um* can refer to any older woman.

> Oh sister and mother
> Do not worry
> If you see my blood
> Or if they break my arm
> Or my bones
> In the prison camp.

Here a young man alternates the words for "my mother" (*ummi*) and "community" (*umma*), playing on their similarity.

> My comrades returned without me
> Don't ever cry, my people
> Don't cry, don't cry, my mother
> My blood lives on as drops of oil
> That will light the dawn of freedom.

It should be stated that the singers and narrators of the all of the quoted songs are male, and that the act of performance is marked as a masculine act of self-assertion.[11] While women and girls may take part in performance, presentation, and confrontation, their participation is perceived as extraordinary.

The ambiguity of women's positions, the potential for both emancipation and suppression emerging in the social transformation of the Intifada is revealed in the next verse. It celebrates female participation in the male-dominated activity of stone-throwing, but takes care to reasert traditional feminine identity in the end. Note that the girl's speech is indirectly quoted, not directly assertive (as in the examples of mothers in the previous passages) Like her relationship to the listener, her relationship to her country, effected through participation in the violence of the uprising, is one of safely harnessed female sexuality.

> Cheers, cheers!
> What's this for?
> For the wounded
> And for the girl
> Who was not content with just shouting
> Who took up stones against the Zionists
> And threw them at them
> As in her loudest voice she cried
> "The land of my country is both my wedding and my veil! "

Much of poetry of the Intifada is suffused with appeals to honor and family.[12] These appeals help locate resistance in the organic solidarity of traditional culture. By doing so, the violence of the Intifada is made honorable, natural, and heroic.

Rituals of Confrontation and Manhood

Clashes with the Israeli army play an important part in the construction of young men's sense of gender roles. I will describe a typical incident.

One afternoon in the summer of 1989, Ahmad, a twenty-three year-old laborer, informed me that there would be a rock-throwing demonstration that afternoon. It was to take place in front of his house in Bethlehem; he invited me to come and watch.

His family lived in two rooms on the second storey of an Ottoman-era building in the heart of Bethlehem's old city. An eighteen year-old brother lay on a couch, his leg in a full cast. He had been shot a month earlier at a demonstration. His shin was broken in several places by an exploding bullet, which had left small metal particles scattered through his calf. He showed me his X-rays proudly. The seventeen year-old brother was currently imprisoned in Ansar III desert camp, serving time for throwing a Molotov cocktail at a police station. His portraits, adorned with ornate gold frames hammered from foil chocolate wrappers, hung on one wall. Ahmad's fifteen year-old brother was pulling on an old sweatshirt of his sister's over his own clothes and double knotting the laces of his sneakers. He grabbed several checkered headscarves to bring to his friends congregating in the narrow lane in front of the house. "God be with you," said his mother, looking up from her cooking as he ran from the house.

Ahmad, his sixteen year-old sister, and I watched from the window as the eight or ten shabab gathered in the five foot wide street spent about 15 minutes discussing tactics, adjusting their headscarves, shooing little children into their houses, collecting small piles of rocks to throw, and obstructing the lane with larger stones. A masked youth appeared, rolling a tire in front of him and someone produced a can of gasoline. After much coming and going, they realized they had no matches. "Kibrit, kibrit," they cried, slightly panicked. Several boxes of matches were tossed from windows overlooking the scene. In spite of the boys' exasperated attempts to clear the area of the ever-present three to eight year-olds, a group of excited little children had gathered in a doorway to watch and chant slogans before being yanked in to safety by anxious parents.

Within a few minutes the tire was burning nicely, and the shabab had found a discarded washing machine,which they added to their blockade. The tremendous clatter also was intended to attract the attention of the soldiers patrolling the market below. Once they had the soldiers' attention, they would run forward, crying "allahu akbar." When they got within range, they would launch fist-sized stones at the patrol and quickly retreat. While Ahmad kept up a running commentary on the action in the lane, his sister kept her eyes firmly fixed on the road winding into Bethlehem from the main highway, ready to alert the shabab of any danger approaching from the rear.

Within 15 minutes, the soldiers responded by firing plastic bullets and gradually ascending to the shabab's position. After each gunshot, the shabab scattered and took cover. The soldiers used the gap in stone-throwing to advance a few yards. Every now and then, a boy would spring out and hurl a stone, earning an immediate gunshot. By the time the soldiers were within twenty yards of the blockade, five or six shots had been fired. Most of the shabab had retreated behind the next bend in the lane and continued to hold off the soldiers with a hail of rocks. As we watched from the window, one boy fell. Before I had even understood what had happened, Ahmad was out the door and in the street. "Get out of here" he yelled to the boys, "I've got him." He dragged the wounded boy into a nearby lane. By the time the Israelis reached the washing machine, most of the boys had disappeared into side streets, and vaulted over retaining walls, tearing off their masks and overshirts and returning to normal life in some other neighborhood.

Ahmad's sister hurried me into the bedroom in preparation for a visit from the army. After a few minutes of frenzied activity, and the fabrication of alibis, it became apparent that the soldiers were not going to come. Just as abruptly as it had started, the event was over. Ahmad's father called for tea, and we speculated on the condition of the injured boy. Ahmad returned breathless and told us hat he had carried the wounded boy, a fourteen year-old, to a relative's house a few blocks away. The boy had been hit in the left thigh, but his wound was not considered serious enough to warrant the risk of going to the hospital. Ahmad's brother would stay with relatives in another part of town. The incident lasted about an hour and a half. Ahmad walked me home, and we picked up a few plastic bullets from the street.

Scenes like this take place every day throughout Gaza and the West Bank. Hundreds of boys and young men have been killed in these confrontations and thousands, including young children, women, and old people have been injured. There is a regularity and uniformity to the confrontations: the shabab have few other avenues of protest, and the the military's response is predictable. These incidents are not "riots" or "mob action," as many Israelis call them and as many outsiders perceive them. Massive actions involving large numbers of people of all ages and both sexes certainly occur after some Friday prayers, after funerals, or on national holidays, but the Intifada is embodied by local incidents initiated by the shabab.

This historical moment in the development of the Palestinian-Israeli conflict coincides with a historical moment in the lives of the Generation of 1967—the coming of maturity and the need to prove themselves worthy of social authority and responsibility. The ritual of demonstrating and stone-throwing seems to serve a fairly explicit role as a rite of passage in a society for which premarital sexual exploits within the community are taboo, and economic opportunities (and therefore the possibilities for marriage) are extremely limited. The gender, age, and sex of participants and the risky symbolic confrontation suggest a self-initiated test of manhood. As journalist Daoud Kuttab puts it, "To throw a stone is to be 'one of the guys'; to hit an Israeli car is to become a hero; to be arrested and not confess to having done anything is to be a man." [13]

The stone-throwings are characterized by a number of traits that distinguish them from arbitrary expressions of rage. Most importantly, the age range of participants is extremely limited. In the four demonstrations I observed, the main action was carried out by teen-agers ranging from approximately thirteen to eighteen. Younger children were always present beforehand, eager to serve in some secondary function—chanting, building blockades, fetching tires or gasoline—but they were an annoying distraction to the older boys when they tried to take on roles for which they were clearly too young. Based on interviews, Kuttab reports the shabab acknowledge the following formalized age-roles: seven to ten year-olds are often entrusted with finding and lighting tires, because this job is technically easy and not overly risky, occuring well before the arrival of the soldiers. Eleven to fourteen year-olds block the road with large stones. This age group also uses slingshots to hurl rocks, because they cannot throw as far as older boys. Fifteen to nineteen year olds, masked in scarves, Palestinian flags, or masks sewn for them by mothers or sisters, are the core of those who damage Israeli cars and taunt and occasionally wound Israeli soldiers and settlers. Participants older than nineteen direct the action from rooftops or windows, shouting instructions, warnings, giving information about the location of the soldiers, the type of weapons and ammunition used, and helping the wounded to safety. [14] This extreme specificity of roles was highlighted in an exchange between twenty-three-year-old Ahmad and his fifteen-year-old brother: "So," I jokingly accused my friend when he told me about the planned demonstration, "you really are one of the shabab." His little brother snorted with all the machismo a fifteen year-old can muster. "You think this old wreck is one of the shabab? You ain't seen nothing yet!" But the older brother's crucial role keeping watch, coordinating the action, and particularly in helping the injured boy was clear and appreciated.

The implicit function of confrontation as a rite of passage pins down the historical roots of the Intifada. The rite of passage, will be sustained as long as the oppressor allows no other way for boys to become men and as long as the culture of resistance legitimizes the sacrifices and violence. Children who chanted slogans two years ago are throwing stones now, and the shabab who threw stones can now sell their labor in the so-called "slave markets" of Tel Aviv, secure in the knowledge that they are men and that they have confronted the occupation, in spite of their apparent powerlessness.

The shabab and their families reinforce each other's participation in the uprising. No family has been untouched by the Intifada and the Israeli military's response to it. The woman whose son is in prison will boycott Israeli products with renewed defiance. The father will close his store every day. The boy whose entire family works for the Intifada will not fear alienating his family by involving himself in dangerous confrontations. As Ahmad told me:

> Before the Intifada my brothers were always a little rowdy, bullying kids in school, and stuff like that. My father was very tough with them. If they were caught throwing stones or getting into trouble he would get very angry with them. Since the Intifada started and he sees that everyone throws stones now, or does something at least, if he sees them lying around the house he says, "What's the matter with you? Get out there and throw some stones!"

Although boys have a well-defined road to adulthood, there is no corresponding rite of passage for girls. As in the time before the occupation, they take the long way.

Women and girls participate on the popular committees and take part in public demonstrations. Generally, however, they do not join the front line in potentially violent clashes. They march with the men and boys in larger demonstrations and funerals,and they also organize their own marches. They intercede with Israeli soldiers and attempt to prevent the arrest of men and boys. Many have been wounded, and some killed.

Women's active participation in the Intifada has certainly been acknowledged and encouraged, but their resistance takes forms that traditionalists would deem appropriate for women. For example, Abdul Jawwad reports about leaflet that appeared, on March 8, 1988, International Women's Day, in the name of the "Palestinian Women in the occupied territories." The pamphlet addressed "the large mass of heroic women, e.g. the mothers of martyrs and detainees and wounded, their wives, their sisters, their daughters, and all women of our people in all refugee camps, villages, and cities of Palestine who are united in confronting the policies of oppression and terror," and encouraged them to participate in popular committees, join labor unions, confront the Israeli policy of de-education, and develop their home economies. Furthermore, the pamphlet told women to prevent the arrest of young men by "considering any man arrested or injured as one of their sons and trying to rescue him."[15]

Most women are not a part of what Tamari calls "the revolt of the petite bourgeoisie"[16] or the labor movements, because they have been excluded from the mainstream commercial sector and labor market.

Assumptions about traditional "women's work" facilitate the conflation of noncommercial, marginal, domestic labor with women's labor. These assumptions allow the most vigorous sectors of the economy to slow down, without causing immediate social collapse and without debate about how increased costs will be shared. Because of their customary or presumed marginality in the mainstream economy, women's continuing or increased participation in productive activities outside the commercial zone is seen as natural and necessary. Strikes and boycotts, which are the most symbolically and materially hard-hitting aspects of the uprising, would not be possible if women could not absorb the jarring effects on community or household economies.[17] It remains to be seen, however, if women's increased political and economic activity will develop the possbilities for greater equality.

This essay has examined gender discourses in the Intifada culture— poetry and song, and ritualized confrontations with the Israeli army. In each of these forms, one finds people using traditional gender categories and conceptions to rationalize, generate, and motivate universal participation, symbolic action, and violence. The Intifada allows Palestinians to use these traditions to create a new culture, rather than to perpetuate the status quo.

Palestinian women are oriented by cultural images of femininity toward the emotional and economic support of men. Young men, on the other hand, tend to be unable to assume or maintain material responsibility for their families and yet feel the compulsions of traditional masculine pride and honor. The men express themselves through symbolic action, presenting an image of the Intifada to Israeland the world. Women's work consists of, among other things, maneuvering in the interstices of a faltering economy and making ends meet at home and in the community. Men's work consists of, among other things, representing the

Palestinian national struggle through confrontations with the Israeli occupation forces and the symbolic renunciation of participation in the Israeli economy. There has been an abrupt transition from the old attitudes to the culture of active resistance; this transition is anchored by inherited concepts of femininity and masculinity which naturalize a gendered division of political labor; without the division of labor, the Intifada might not have endured as long as it has.

REFERENCES

1. *Uprising* is the most common English translation of the word *Intifada*, which iterally means "a shuddering awakening from sleep, a return to consciousness, the shaking off of a burden." J.M. Cowan, ed., *The Hans Wehr Dictionary of Modern Written Arabic* (Ithaca: Spoken Language Services, 1976).

2. For general accounts of the Intifada, see Don Peretz, *Intifada: The Palestinian Uprising* (Boulder: Westview Press, 1990); Zachary Lockman and Joel Beinin (eds.), *Intifada: The Palestinian Uprising Against Israeli Occupation* (Boston: South End Press, 1989); Jamal Nassar and Roger Heacock (eds.), *Intifada: Palestine at the Crossroads* (New York: Praeger, 1990); and Michael Hudson (ed.), *The Palestinians: New Directions* (Washington, D.C., 1990). For accounts of women's participation in the Intifada and in the Palestinian resistance movement, see Philippa Strum, *The Women are Marching: The Second Sex and the Palestinian Revolution* (Chicago: Lawrence Hill Books, 1992) and Julie Peteet, *Gender in Crisis: Women and the Palestinian Resistance Movement* (New York: Columbia University Press, 1991). For accounts of human rights violations during the Intifada, see Al-Haq: Law in the Service of Man, *Punishing a Nation—Human Rights Violations During the Palestinian Uprising—December 1987–1988* (Ramallah, 1988).

3. For more information about the politics of the Intifada leadership and organization, see Ziad Abu Amr, "The Politics of the Intifada," and Islah Abdul-Jawwad, "The Evolution of the Political Role of the Palestinian Women's Movement," in Hudson, *The Palestinians*, 3–23 and 63–76. See also Lisa Taraki, "The Islamic Resistance Movement in the Palestinian Uprising," in Lockman and Beinin, *Intifada*, 171–182.

4. The Intifada manifests itself through commerical strikes, boycotts of Israeli products, civil disobedience, efforts to build economic and political infrastructures independent of Israel, demonstrations, and stone-throwing confrontations with Israeli soldiers and settlers who patrol the territories. Prominent West Bank personalities announced in January 1988 fourteen specific demands of the Intifada, including the end of Israeli "iron fist" rule, the release of political prisoners, the end to the policy of expulsion, a cessation of Israeli settlement

in the territories, minimal impingement by the authorities on Islamic and Christian holy places, the cancellation of all restrictions on political freedoms, and the termination of discriminatory policies against industrial and agricultural produce of the occupied territories. "The Fourteen Demands," *The Journal of Palestine Studies*67 (1988): 63–65. While the number of armed attacks on Israeli settlers, soldiers, and civilians increased in the 1990s, it still represents only a small precentage of the Intifada's confrontations. In this paper I deal only with the much more prevalent type of confrontation, in which unarmed Palestinians provoke well-armed and organized military and settler patrols.

5. See Al-Haq: Law in the Service of Man, *Punishing a Nation* and publications of the Database Project on Palestinian Human Rights in Chicago and Jerusalem for more recent accounts and statistics.

6. See Peretz, *Intifada*, 163–190, and Hudson, *The Palestinians*, 87–151.

7. For a discussion of women's history and gender history, see Joan Scott, "Gender: A Useful Category for Historical Analysis" in *Gender and the Politics of History* (New York: Columbia University Press, 1988), 28–53.

8. Realizing that the term "traditional" is highly problematic and all traditions historically constructed, I use the word for want of a better referent. In my usage here, traditional gender categories and norms are those that define gender terms of honor and kinship obligations.

9. The verses I use to illustrate my points come from songs on three of the most popular cassette tapes circulating around Bethlehem, Beit Jala, and Beit Sahour in the spring of 1989. The themes they illustrate seem more or less representative of other songs and poems with which I am familiar.

10. See Linda Layne, "The Dialogics of Tribal Self-Representation in Jordan," *American Ethnologist* 16 (1989): 24–39. Layne argues that the national identity of the young Jordanian monarchy as symbolized by the Bedouin tribalism of its pre-1948 population has been defined in contrast with the formation of a Palestinian identity based on its connection to the land and agricultural base.

11. These songs are easily placed in the context of masculine Arabic poetry in which the spoken word is a source of power and the skilled poet a hero. Palestinians are constantly reminded through these songs that the power to speak with authority and legitimacy and to be heard in the international arena is a vital weapon in their struggle for self-determination. At the same time, the lyrics reinforce an underlying consciousness that patience, endurance, and sacrifice are the necessary complements to the dramatic struggle for visibility and recognition carried out in the streets of the Occupied Territories. For background on self-assertion through speech, poetry and song, see Lila Abu-Lughod, *Veiled Sentiments* (Cairo: American University in Cairo Press, 1986), Michael Meeker, *Literature and Violence in North Arabia* (Cambridge: Cambridge University Press, 1977), and Steven Caton, *Peaks of Yemen I Summon* (Berkeley: University of California Press, 1990).

12. For example, this song is purely nationalistic and denies the importance of other social groupings such as religion or political party:

> Don't ask me which party I belong to
> Don't ask about my religion
> I am soil from this land
> My name is Arab of Palestine.
> —Mustapha al-Kurd, cassette, *Kinder der Intifada*, 1987.

13. Daoud Kuttab, "Profile of the Stonethrowers," in *The Journal of Palestine Studies* 67 (1988): 14–24.
14. Daoud Kuttab, "Profile of the Stonethrowers," 18.
15. Abdul Jawwad, in Hudson, *The Palestinians*, 70.
16. Salim Tamari, "Revolt of the Petite Bourgeoisie: Urban Merchants and the Palestinian Uprising," in Hudson, *The Palestinians*, 24–43.
17. Women employed outside the home tend to work in service occupations and light manufacturing or cooperative production. None of these activites are as directly or clearly linked to the Israeli economy as the production or trade of goods manufactured in Israel. In the summer of 1989, when I lived in a middle-class neighborhood in Beit Jala (a town on the West Bank, with a population of twenty-thousand), only one man had regular work, whereas all the women between the ages of 18 and 80 had jobs outside the home. All of the women continued to draw incomes or wages as teachers, nurses, cleaners, secretaries, babysitters, and co-op workers. At least two families were supported entirely by the wife's earnings. Older women and younger teen-age girls in the neighborhood were very active in the local women's co-op, which made pastries and embroidered handicrafts. By the summer of 1990, one woman was covertly running a small grocery store out of her living room and had used the profits to set up a makeshift felafel stand, which enabled her to support her unemployed husband and two sons.

PART THREE

The Reconstruction of Power

"Metaphors Can Kill": Gender, Power, and the Field of the Literary

Anne Herrmann

In the introduction to the current volume the editors insist on the dichotomy between experience and everyday practices as the subject of sociological inquiry, on the one hand, and identity formation as the result of textual analyses performed by poststructuralist critics, on the other. While the former seeks to uncover the *origins* of oppression, the latter is marked by its disconnection from material forms of social inequality. On the one hand, the real; on the other hand, representation.

At the same time, recognition is given to the fact that power refers not only to economic and political power, but also to "symbolic" power, power relations which inhere in the domains of "culture," such as language, education, religion, art, ideology, etc. While dispossessed of the former, women, as well as other oppressed groups, display higher levels of participation in the latter, thereby confirming what Peter Stally-brass and Allon White argue in *The Politics and Poetics of Transgression*, "that what is *socially* peripheral is so frequently *symbolically* central."[1] The prostitute offers a recurring example of such a figure.

What seems striking about the essays in this section is the way in which the "real" and forms of representation remain inextricably linked, that if gender relations and war are both about conflict, then one often functions as a metaphor for the other. On the one hand, language uses military metaphors to describe its own workings, as in "the battle of the books," a term which describes the ongoing controversy within literary studies over literary merit and social values. Toni Morrison opens her essay, "Unspeakable Things Unspoken: The Afro-American Presence in American Literature" (1989) with: "I planned to call this paper "Canon Fodder," because the terms put me in mind of a kind of trained muscular response that appears to be on display in some areas of the recent canon debates."[2] On the other hand, military conflicts are as much about struggles over linguistic territory as they are about geographical conquest. The anecdote taken from the press used by Anton Shammas which describes Arab women who "pass" as Jewish prostitutes dressed as female Israeli soldiers on the Gaza—so that local Gazans can "give it to the Israeli occupation"[3]—uses the figure of the prostitute as a metaphor of occupation—linguistic, geographical, and sexual. One discourse appropriates the language of militarized conflict, even as it debates the status of literary texts within an academic context; the other, in the form of a sensationalized news story, offers multiple layers of meaning based on relations between body and costume, land and language. At the same time, it genders these configurations in the relationship between pimp, prostitute and soldier by resisting military occupation through the sexual exploitation of women.

The figure of the prostitute as the site of occupation receives its complementary figure in the mother as agent of oppositionality. Miriam Cooke writes of "motherism"[4] as a form of resistance to military conflict when she argues that Mothers of the Intifada (like Argentinian Madres) resist the narrative of war that suggests that women weren't there when in fact they produce the "canon fodder" that turns bodies into corpses by repressing the role of reproduction. On the one hand, war polarizes the sexes by reducing gender differences to anatomical ones one possesses: either physical strength or the ability to engage in childbirth. On the other hand, cross-dressing (as participated in by women during the Algerian Revolution) augments the male army by temporarily refusing to recognize anatomical differences as meaningful. The opposition between cross-dressed female soldiers (who fight like men) and resisting mothers (who fight like women) recapitulates the difference of gender by privileging the feminine, what Cooke calls the "unarmed, disorganized, fragmented struggle"[5] of mothers. Instead one could argue that women who take on the roles of men make meaningless the very foundation of sexual difference, even if achieved only temporarily. Here, cross-dressing empowers women to participate in a conflict that has categorically excluded them (in spite of a long history of cross-dressed female soldiers) as opposed to literally (with their bodies) representing the conflict metaphorically (through their dress), as in the Shammas episode.

Conflicts in the Middle East, by blurring the boundaries between war and peace, blur the boundaries between men and women's rightful participation. Thus, women can no longer be expected not to write about war based on their lack of experience. At the same time the "authentic war text"[6] remains as much a matter of what constitutes a literary text as what constitutes the experience of war. The questions that Cooke raises are those that continue to be debated in the "canon wars": should it be written directly out of the war experience or after the war; can it hope to intervene in the war by negotiating violence or by constructing a counternarrative; is it art or is it propaganda? By suggesting that the conflicting discourses of wartime will serve to destabilize the illusory coherence of the "war myth," Cooke again privileges the feminine over the masculine, thereby reinscribing the gendered opposition, this time within discursive rather than military practices.

War as increasingly "technologized" foregrounds the role representation plays in its waging. On the one hand Cooke calls the Intifada a war "in the metaphoric sense."[7] On the other hand, in his discussion of the Arab-Palestinian male in Hebrew literature by contemporary male Israeli writers, Shammas speaks not of dead bodies (increasingly "unreal") but of dead texts. Modern Hebrew literature has turned "the dead language of the text into a normal, live language of con-text, territorially and otherwise normal." As a result of military occupation, a dead language has been revitalized in order to create, retroactively, "an imaginary Jewish state of the mind,"[8] a linguistic territory detached from social reality that relegates the Palestinian vernacular to a dialect. Military occupation results in linguistic occupation results in the occupation of the Arab/Palestinian male character within the contemporary Hebrew novel. Here literature does not attempt to represent experience but rather to substitute for it by turning a dead language into a living one in order to make a detour around the real dead, the bodies. War is about a territory we call language where we can ask of language itself whether it is dead or alive and what difference that makes. At what point does literature do no more than preserve an obsolete conflict in its metaphors?

Military conflicts are not the only conflicts women negotiate. Elizabeth Bergmann writes of conflicts not between nation states but between kinship roles as they are negotiated within the Arab Morrocan family. Proverbs become a means of "bargaining for reality,"[9] thereby once again resisting the opposition between reality and representation by offering a text that neither reflects nor distorts what lies outside of it. Instead, it encodes the negotiation of conflict as predicated on textual interpretation. While proverbs rely on limitless proliferation and self-contradictory meanings, interpretations are nevertheless limited by the power relation between husbands and wives: a wife depends on a husband and therefore can't bargain with him. At the same time, the most intense hostility occurs in the relationship between the wife and her husband's mother. The containment of power between husband and wife (men and women) involves the displacement of conflict onto the relationship between two women where the priority of birth (the son's mother) over marriage (the son's wife) in kinship networks remains eternally unstable and thus open to negotiation. What continues to remain nonnegotiable is the centrality of the son's position.

While the relationship between daughter and mother-in-law is predicated on hostility punctuated by the occasional "cease-fire," Diane Singerman examines the political component of informal networks where once again matters of power inhere in everyday activities rather than national politics. Marriage in the popular quarters of Cairo appears as financial transaction rather than psychological negotiation, but this time inflected by the war as continued military conflict effects migration opportunities and consequently requires the deferral of the marriage contract.

I would like to conclude by addressing briefly the anecdote involving Umm Tahir that Singerman inserts into a social scientific discourse produced through contact with 350 lower class women (and men). What is the effect of this novelistic scene, which involves naming one of the women and thus placing her within a plot? The scene ends with Umm Tahir saying to another woman: "I want to become related to you since the entire area loves your mother."[10] The way in which she would become related would be through the marriage of a male relative of hers to the other woman's daughter. The only qualification would be that the daughter ' be a girl and not a woman,"[11] that is, not married. The figure of the mother returns as a figure of power, this time not in her resistance to state sanctioned conflict but in her access to a prestigious web of social relations. The novelistic rendition suggests that power is not just about familial alliances or even about informal networks. It is also about the language used to negotiate and/or produce those affiliations. The line I have quoted belongs to a different discursive field because its interpretations remain inexhaustible. One would never call this discursive moment literature even as it relies on literary techniques. One would never say that this textual representation is less meaningful than the experience of Umm Tahir. This statement belongs to that experience. But because it remains the least self-conscious literary moment in the four essays in this section it offers the most compelling example of the falseness of the dichotomy between the real and the represented, identity formation and

the origins of social oppression. For it is Umm Tahir who reminds us
that there is only one way for a girl to become a woman.

REFERENCES

1. Peter Stallybrass and Allon White, *The Politics and Poetics of Transgression* (Ithaca: Cornell University Press, 1986), 5.
2. Toni Morrison, "Unspeakable Things Unspoken: The Afro-American Presence in American Literature," *Michigan Quarterly Review* 28:1 (Winter 1989), 1.
3. Anton Shammas, "Arab Male, Arab Female: The Lure of Metaphors," in Fatma Müge Göçek and Shiva Balaghi, eds., *Reconstructing Gender in the Middle East: Tradition, Identity, and Power* (New York, Columbia University Press, 1994), 167.
4. Miriam Cooke, "Arab Women, Arab Wars," in Fatma Müge Göçek and Shiva Balaghi, eds., *Reconstructing Gender in the Middle East: Tradition, Identity, and Power* (New York, Columbia University Press, 1994), 157.
5. Cooke, "Arab Women, Arab Wars," 162.
6. Cooke, "Arab Women, Arab Wars," 148.
7. Cooke, "Arab Women, Arab Wars," 159.
8. Shammas, "Arab Male, Arab Female," 170.
9. Elizabeth Bergmann, "Keeping it in the Family: Gender and Conflict in Moroccan Arabic Proverbs," in Fatma Müge Göçek and Shiva Balaghi, eds., *Reconstructing Gender in the Middle East: Tradition, Identity, and Power* (New York, Columbia University Press, 1994), 203.
10. Diane Singerman, "Where Has All the Power Gone? Women and Politics in the Popular Quarters in Cairo," in Fatma Müge Göçek and Shiva Balaghi, eds., *Reconstructing Gender in the Middle East: Tradition, Identity, and Power* (New York, Columbia University Press, 1994), 181.
11. Singerman, "Where Has All the Power Gone?," 181.

CHAPTER ELEVEN

Arab Women Arab Wars

Miriam Cooke

Venturing out into street for the first time alone, Cherifa adjusts her veil
so that the seeing eye should not be seen. Heedless of propriety, she
crosses the medina to warn her dissident husband that he is in danger
of his life. Meanwhile, Touma in a bar in the French quarter tries to
look casual in her strange new clothes and the even stranger environment. Family and friends condemn her as a prostitute.

Nuzha, the "prostitute," watches incredulously as the young men climb
the walls to their death. The Israelis are not going to run out of bullets.
Another way must be found to penetrate into their stronghold. She offers to lead the combatants into the compound through a secret underground passage that can be accessed through her kitchen.

In a paroxysm of pain, a woman tries to prevent her child from being
born, while her husband at the front tries to survive mortal wounds.
They are both struggling to keep the promise that he should be the first
to see their son. The dead infant is placed on the dead man's chest.

Three vignettes from three Arab wars: the Algerian Revolution, the
Intifada, the Iran-Iraq War. Glimpses snatched from stories women
wrote while their people were at war. Assia Djebar, Sahar Khalifa and

NOTE:
I would like to thank Evelyne Accad, Bruce Lawrence, Paul Vieille, and Jane
Tompkins for reading earlier drafts of this article and for their helpful suggestions.

Aliya Talib each recorded in fiction some of the roles women played in an event generally considered to be the preserve of men.

The way we talk about an event affects the way we will experience, or perceive our experience of a later analogous event. We all collaborate in this shaping of history. Some events like war are so existentially important for their communities that they demand a greater degree of collaboration in the construction of the narratives as of the counternarratives. Differences of perspective and in sociopolitical roles that are acceptable in normal times become intolerable in war time.

In *Writing and War* (1991), Lynne Hanley deplores the disputes that have so often arisen between those who have chosen to write about war and their critics. She says that a rigid distinction is drawn between the act of producing and the act of interpreting a literary work, and a battle ensues over which is the more essential enterprise. And because such battles for supremacy are premised on the validity of the categorical distinctions upon which they are based, the bellicose literary mind is always vexed by writing and writers who refuse to stay in their proper place.[1] She urges war writers and their critics to work together without striving to set up hierarchies of value and "truth." Her contribution to this cooperative project is a volume that alternates short stories and literary essays. Hanley's project is both creative and critical, and its januslike ambition has helped me to situate my own work: I do not see myself as simply criticizing or dispassionately describing and analyzing what Arab novelists and short story writers have penned on the wars they have experienced. I conceive of my work as part of a broader literary intervention: to explore possible causes, to expose probable effects and then to imagine alternatives.

The premise of this paper is that attention paid to literature that emerges out of the very entrails of war may change the ways in which we experience and express war. During the anger and chaos of war, many write; most will quickly be forgotten, if they are ever noted. Yet, many of these women and men who write, even those who are paid, do so because they hope, however forlornly, to intervene in the situation and thus make a difference. Such writing is an integral part of the war endeavor, and as such it has new and often surprising things to say. If we wish to approach the dynamic of war and not just to repeat canned tales of heroism and victimization, we should listen to these writers' words and make others listen. It is this literature, much more than that written out of the comfort and safety of postbellum panelled studies, that can teach us about war, about the ways in which people negotiate violence and about the construction of counternarratives.

These narratives cannot be invented *ex post facto*. They have meaning and power primarily when they participate in the action itself. To locate and recognize these oppositional stories, we must take seriously the immediately encoded war experience. Yet, few until recently have accorded such writing any worth. In general, the only war literature to be taken seriously was that which emerged after the passion of war had subsided. In *Wartime* (1989), Paul Fussell reiterates a commonplace of literary criticism when he condemns military men's recording of life at the World War II front, as gush, waffle, and cliche occasioned by high-mindedness, the impulse to sound portentous, and the slumbering of the critical spirit.[2]

However, in the 1990s there are two problems with such an attitude. First, debates about the literary canon have revealed that blanket statements about literary production enable a kind of knee-jerk censorship— don't bother to read any European war fiction published between 1939 and 1945 or any Iraqi war novels and short stories that came out during the Iran-Iraq War of 1980–88. They're all rubbish. With so much fiction published, the judicious reader will not open the maligned books. Thus, works important possibly for literary and certainly for political reasons will become effectively censured. A second problem is still more crucial. It concerns the interface between war and social values that fiction uniquely elicits. The unthinking rejection of fiction written during war makes it difficult to understand how war today is fought other than it was during and at any time before World War II. War today does not always feel like war. The front that had conveniently marked a space as other and appropriate for killing and dying has in may cases come home. As we in the West watch our world as knew it crumble, we recognize that the Cold War was cold in the West only. Hot war pervaded and continues to shape the lives of others. Now war as a condition of militarized alertness has become endemic to our daily lives. We realize that it is as hard to separate armed, organized conflict from unarmed, disorganized violence[3] as it is to distinguish between combat and non-combat. Yet, we have few guides to thinking anew about war. Fiction is one such guide. For writing which we had thought to be about peace time may also relate to war. In fact, it may not be so different and certainly not so easily separable from that which was once only written about an event clearly labelled war.

Since the outbreak of the Iran-Iraq war in 1980, Iraqi critics, such as Abd al-Sattar Nasir, Salah al-Ansari and Latif Nasir Husayn, have debated whether this war was the first to have produced what they have called War Literature[4]. They use the term to specify literature written during war which is not transparently propaganda. Of course, in the absolute sense of the term, this is not true—Homer himself was surely not the first to turn fighting into writing. But then again, these Iraqi critics may be at least partially right. It is only in the twentieth century, perhaps as Gareth Thomas suggests since the Spanish Civil War,[5] that war literature has been discussed and self-consciously produced as a constitutive part of a war effort. However, this literature in war, even when not rejected out of hand, remains at best controversial.

When I met the Lebanese male writer Taufiq Awwad in the summer of 1982, he told me that it was not yet time to write the *War and Peace* of the Lebanese Civil War nor to paint its Guernica. Time was needed, he assured me, to see the contours of this chaos more clearly. Yet, many women and some men in Lebanon had by that time written libraries of books and painted galleries of paintings, and what they had produced could not be so easily dismissed as mere journalese and photography, in other words a form of unreflective recording that can respond to the unexpected. Awwad was nostalgically calling for Wordsworthian reflection or what the Iraqi critic Basim Abd al-Hamid Hammudi in 1986 called *takhzin* (storage). However, Hammudi does not use this word as did Wordsworth and Awwad. He rejects such storage as damaging because it does not permit the authentic war text to be constructed. In his enthusiasm to tout the war writer's, and incidentally the critic's, importance, Hammudi goes beyond Hemingway's advocacy of the true transcription of the experience of great events[6] to assert that literary merit *derives* from the documentary function. In effect, he claims, glorious events spontaneously unfold into glorious texts.

Even if I do not agree completely with Hammudi, I *do* believe that the novel, poem, short story or painting that emerges directly out of the war experience (whether this be at the front or in a war-like situation analogous to civil war or to social anarchy) does have a unique and important story to tell. And not just about Iraqis, but about all present day communities at war. This a story that challenges the Homeric myth that divides itself between men fighting and women crying. These war texts may also have a unique and important role to play, because they not only reflect but they may sometimes interact with the events and mood of the conflict. By retaining and perpetuating the dynamism of the experience, they can project a space in which changes can be imagined. This envisioning is possible because the final form has not been fixed and now, thanks to such texts, might never be. The experience that is immediately encoded retains the play of the conflicting discourses of war time. In his poem War Poet, the British soldier Donald Bain captures the dynamic between a harrowing experience and its immediate narration:

> We in our haste can only see the small components of the scene;
> We cannot tell what incidents will focus on the final screen.
> A barrage of disruptive sound, a petal on a sleeping face,
> Both must be noted, both must have their place.
> It may be that our later selves or else our unborn sons
> Will search for meaning in the dust of long deserted guns.
> We only watch, and indicate, and make our scribbled pencil notes.
> We do not wish to moralize, only to ease our dusty throats.

In reply to Bain's wistful conjecture about future semanticists, Paul Fussell wryly comments: but what time seems to have shown our later selves is that perhaps there was less coherent meaning in the events of wartime than we had hoped.[7] Exactly so. Time should not be allowed to impose coherent meaning as though it inhered in the events themselves. Time creates an illusory coherence that does not substitute for, or negate the impressionistic notations of those who suffered war first-hand.

War is experienced in scattered fragments. What is the participant to make of these small components of the scene that are united only by the fact of a single experiencing subject? What is to be made of the barrage of disruptive sound and the petal on the sleeping face? They do not make any sense except if they fit into some larger sense, some framework, best of all a myth, a war myth. The war myths of many cultures, including those of the Arab world, designate appropriate spaces for specific kinds of actions and appoint protagonists for particular preconfigured roles. When the fighting is done and it demands to be described, understood and especially to be justified, then the war myth becomes the ultimate ordering principle.

But how is the myth evoked, and who invokes it? Whether the barrage of disruptive sound and the petal on the sleeping face are remembered depends on how the story is told, and who tells it. However, in most cultures' myths it is men who tell these stories, and they remember the components that add to the notion that war is an arena for the display of men's manliness and heroism. Thus, we see that details are not in themselves intrinsically important, they acquire long-term significance only if they find a context and a narrator to accommodate them. The ill-shaped components, e.g., the heroic women combatants, may tease for a while, may disturb apparently self-evident categorizations and classifications. However, if they are not given due heed within their own contexts and by multiple narrators, if they are not allowed to function outside the stranglehold of the mythic and too often male mold, they will soon be forgotten. I want these clumsy components, these heroic women combatants, to survive the manipulations of time.

The license to write the war experience at once defies the manipulations of time and destroys the neat and generally dichotomous categories that have shaped the western war narrative since Homer, and the Arab war story since the *Ayyam al-Arab*. It renders transparent the blatant falsifications inherent in other war narratives that continue to describe all war experience, however differentiated, in the same mythic terms. The old war story in the west as in the Arab world erases the experience by squeezing it into a bipolar mold. When critics like Fussell disdainfully dismiss as catharsis all war fiction unmediated by time, it seems to me that what they are actually dismissing is not so much the story as its impact: what they correctly perceive to be threatening signs of change in the story. So many loose ends, they may never be neatly tied. Such a situation is intolerable. In war, without closure, there is uncertain meaning. In war, without clear meaning, there is doubt about the war project. In war, where there is doubt there is a weakening of the will to fight. The specter of the *WIMP* the dreaded alter ego to the male hero looms large.

Lynne Hanley ascribes the reflexive male need for time and the dichotomous order it brings to a bellicose mentality which creates arbitrary categories that are presumed to be mutually exclusive and hostile (self/other, masculine/feminine, white/black, us/them), and of then insisting on the supremacy of one category over the other . . . Since the assertion of the supremacy of one category over another requires, above all, an inflexible definition of membership, the bellicose mind is always resistant to any erosion of its 'mystic boundaries.'[8]

Whether the insistence on these mystic boundaries in itself denotes bellicosity is debatable, but what I shall argue is that these boundaries do play an important part in constructing, justifying and enabling the easy and unchanging reiteration of war and its narration. It is not new that front and home front, combatant and civilian, friend and foe, defensive

and offensive actions, victory and defeat[9] are not so easily distinguish-
able; not new at all that combatants are not always male, nor that non-
combatants are not necessarily female or feminized. Yet, that is the frame
that has shaped and contained most cultures' war stories. It was the way
war was remembered until the late twentieth century, until perhaps
Vietnam and the postcolonial era.

What is new since the 1960s is that the mystic boundaries that staked
out a binary world have begun to be represented and discussed. This
representation and these discussions have revealed that the mystic
boundaries are at least in part responsible for the prosecution of war.
What has changed since Vietnam and in the postcolonial era is that
war is increasingly represented as spreading beyond its conventional
boundaries. It is a not a peaceful society but one that is at war that not
only tolerates but encourages the growth of a military-industrial complex. In this postcolonial period, war metaphors abound but I would
suggest that by their very abundance they cease to be metaphors. As the
sociolinguist George Lakoff tells us so starkly, metaphors can kill.[10] The
inner city drug wars, in late April 1992 climaxing in the Rodney King
riots in Los Angeles, the failed wars on poverty are all products of the
militarization of postmodern society. In *Pure War* (1983), Paul Virilio
has written that *volens nolens* we are civilian soldiers waging hi-tech Pure
War which isn't acted out in representation, but in infinite preparation
(which leads) toward a generalized non-development . . . of civilian
societies.[11] How can we substantiate such a grandiose claim? We cannot,
but we can pursue it as a thesis to see whether or not Virilio etches the
conditions of a world in which violence has increasingly become its own
justification.

Postcolonial wars, of which the Vietnam War and the Gulf War
are vivid examples, during their waging exploded binary oppositions,
overflowed all categories. In Vietnam, the confusion between warrior
and peasant, between South Vietnamese friend and Vietcong foe when
both looked alike, and between masculinity and femininity became a
commonplace of American filmic and literary representations. At times,
even the boundary between the war and its representation was erased, so
that performance could no longer be considered to be not reality but
rather part of it.Indeed, during the filming of *Apocalypse Now*, Coppola
and the Filipino army rotated military materiel according to need.

The merging of reality and performance that marked Vietnam can
be seen in other postcolonial wars; in Soweto as in the West Bank,
demonstrations and military reprisals merged with street theater perfor-

mances.[12] In the postcolonial period, war has been technologized to the extent that its representation has become implicated in its waging. As Simon During has written, the fusion of theater and war, war as theater, is a product of modern communications technology.[13] Sophisticated media interact with and sometimes supplant superguns. Television viewers, as Baudrillard noted, are becoming increasingly aware that the media closes the gap between the reality of war and its representation. Coverage of the Gulf War in America emblematized the conflation.[14] Many have discussed the erasure of the boundary between the lens of the bomber pilots and that of the American television viewers. Judith Butler writes that the visual record of this war is not a *reflection* on the war, but the enactment of this phantasmatic structure, indeed, part of the very means by which it is socially constituted and maintained as a war. The so-called smart bomb records its target as it moves in to destroy it—a bomb with a camera attached in front, a kind of optical phallus; it relays that film back to a command control and that film is reshown on television, effectively constituting the television screen and its viewer as the extended apparatus of the bomb itself. In this sense, by viewing we are bombing, identified with both bomber and bomb . . . and yet securely wedged in the couch of one's own living room.[15]

However, in the Gulf War the conflation of reality and representation in the media went beyond the collapse of the screen; it had above all something to do with the role of the media in the 100 Day War. A chronicle of the coverage of the war reveals that the media slipped constantly between reinforcing and undermining its differences from the reality lived in the Arabian desert. In its representative function, it seemed to maintain an independent perspective that allowed it to target and name what it willed: the line in the sand could be a metaphor for blurred boundaries between the two armies, just as it could conversely describe sharply demarcated zones. As participant, it lost this freedom to find itself constrained by its drive for power and influence.[16] Between August 1990 and March 1991, it was not always clear that it was General Norman Schwartzkopf who was briefing the TV newsanchor star Ted Koppel, it often seemed to be the reverse.

The liberty and sanction to narrate and represent directly the war experience captures these paradoxical moments. It does not attempt to resolve the paradox by eliminating inconvenient components; it allows contradictions to coexist. In so doing, it reveals that the disorganized, unarmed violence away from the epicenter of the theater of operations lies on a continuum with the organized whole that is called War. The recognition of this continuum disables automatic adjudication about who has the right to write when about what. In contemporary civil wars like Lebanon, Northern Ireland and Sri Lanka and increasingly in the American inner cities it is less and less clear when it is war or when it is peace.[17] By the same token, it may be equally unclear when a writer is writing about war and when about peace, especially when euphemisms like the events, the situation, collateral damage and neutralizing assets abound. Not only the war zone but the writers' guild collapses: the narration of postcolonial wars is no longer a male preserve. These war stories, although men's domain, may also be interpreted as being about peace,women's domain.

Before Vietnam, Lebanon and the Cold War, women were not supposed to write of war. Often, as in Cassandra's case, they were not even to *speak* of war. Margaret Higonnet has shown how the European literary establishment rejected women's writings on the two world wars. Their pretext was that women could not experience the war first hand, and that they, being denied the experience, should not presume to write of it.[18] But was it true that the women *had* not experienced these wars? Of course not. However, because they had not been written, or had not written themselves, into the war, it was, with time, easy to conclude that women had not been there. In the interval, the wars had been remembered, or, rather crafted anew to fit their culture's myths of how wars were thought to be fought. Ambiguities and inconsistencies were eliminated: men were warriors, women were watchers. Warriors talked about other warriors, women waited and listened.

The post-1948 wars in the Arab world demonstrate the transformation in the reality of war and its representation in the postcolonial era. This transformation is at once military and discursive. In what follows, I shall focus primarily on the literary impact of this change on women. There has not been a single way of representing their participation in combat, however defined; nor have there been uniform controls on their writings. During the Algerian Revolution as well as in pre-1967 Israel, Arab women fought, but they fought as men, and women's writings were subject to men's control and therefore often also to internal censorship. Although the waging and writing of war were on the cusp of change, pressure to conform to conventional notions of war telling was too great to be withstood. This has not been so much the case in the post-1967 Israeli-occupied territories or in Lebanon or even in Iraq.

The Algerian Revolution 1954-62 provides a paradox: it set a precedent for women's visibility in national struggle, yet it has come to be regarded as also the source of their ills in the patriarchal postcolonial society to which it gave birth. Several reasons may be adduced for women's failure to exploit their opportunities during the Algerian Revolution. Firstly, the years of French colonial domination had been marked by attempts to coopt Algerian women through education and acculturation. Algeria of 1962 remained resistant to new values and concepts such as women's rights because they were linked with the hated, now departed colonial overlord. Hence, Algerian women did not have a feminist context within which to situate their struggle. This latter point is significant from both a military and a literary perspective. The women did what the men wanted them to do. Even when they were in charge of operations,[19] they acted in place of men, never in ways that highlighted their otherness to the new role and the unprecedented nature of their visibility and behavior. Crossdressing demanded conformity to the rules regulating the role. With such an attitude, they could change neither the role nor their consciousness. Thinking as men, they anticipated that participation and self-sacrifice would produce their own rewards. They did not realize that they had to fight to be recognized and to be remembered. They did not understand that they should not allow themselves to be caught up in the war of symbols that always follows the war of weapons. They allowed their return to the home, to the domain of women's activity, to epitomize the return of peace. From then on, peace was conserved by eliminating ambiguity in the roles men and women played.

Algerian women did not recognize the importance of conserving the role ambiguity brought about by women acting in men's space, the advantages to be gained by confusing expectations of how men and women should behave. Unlike their sisters, students and spiritual heirs from Northern Ireland[20] to Palestine, they did not realize that to change *status quo* they had to: 1) emphasize their importance *as women* to Algerian success in the war; 2) continually affirm, particularly in writing, their presence and its importance so as not to be ignored or forcibly repressed; 3) articulate their experiences not as crossdressing but as transformative; 4) act in terms of the discourse they had thus created. Of course, many Algerian women *did* write, but later. It was not enough to write later. They should have written at once. Since they did not, it was the men's books that flooded the market. Consequently, the story we now have of the women in the Algerian Revolution is one that tells *what happened to the women* and not *what the women did*. Even Djamila

Boupacha's story is known primarily through the writing of Simone de
Beauvoir and Gisele Halimi.

My comparative readings of Algerian women's and men's war literature indicate that whereas the women themselves were not aware of their
importance, the men were and they overreacted. Their writings reflect
the post-World War I writings that Sandra Gilbert and Susan Gubar
have analyzed in *No Man's Land. The Place of the Woman Writer in the
Twentieth Century* (1988). Whereas the British women writers were
scarcely aware of the significance of women's new visibility and particularly of their participation in the Great War, the men were wracked with
anxiety. In Algeria, men like Muhammad Dib, Mouloud Feraoun and
Malek Haddad wrote on the one hand of Medusas and of monstrous
daughters, and on the other hand of paralyzed and impotent intellectual
men. Although women writers like Djamila Debeche and Assia Djebar
gradually came to write about the war, they were less concerned with
their just deserts than they were with the end of the war. The persistent
problem for women of biculturalism, i.e., European-style education en-
tailing certain expectations but marriage into non-European circumstances that made a mockery of such promises, was censored out of their
fiction as men demanded total attention to the nationalist struggle. In *Les
Enfants du Nouveau Monde* (1962), which was written and published in
the last year of the war, Assia Djebar did write of the new roles women
were playing, but without any sense of moment. Even the dramatic first
emergence out of the house and crossing of the city by the veiled Cherifa
is presented as intimidating rather than as empowering. Her heroines
seemed not to know that they might profit from their war experiences.
Even in the one realm in which women fought as women, donating their
bodies to the cause by alternately dressing as French women so that they
might place bombs in the nouvelle ville and then reveiling so that they
might hide the bombs they were moving around the medina, Djebar's
assessment is negative: Touma is clearly a prostitute. The fact that, like
women in the two world wars, the Algerian women had functioned
effectively in roles traditionally assigned to men did nothing to change
their self-image. They held on to the roles society had assigned to them.
Neither they nor the context were redefined to accomodate a new reality.
Women who for a period had done what men do went back to doing
women's things. *Status quo ante* became everyone's overriding goal: to
the men it represented a reaffirmation of control in the family; to the
women it meant that the war was over and the foreigners had been

expelled. The need for peace and self-governance after almost a century and a half of resistance and tutelage precluded the possibility of change. It was only considerably later that people began to understand the lessons of other twentieth century wars, and particularly the Spanish Civil War, in other words, that political wars are often inseparable from social revolutions.[21] In the absence of a concerted attempt on the women's part to change their situation, or even only to write of the war as transforming, Algerian men quickly imposed a neotraditional system that deprived the dreaded new of any voice. Literary evidence supports recent sociopolitical contentions by women like Marie-Aimee Helie-Lucas that Algerian women were not so much forced back into oppression as they were blocked from pursuing opportunities they had not at the time recognized.[22]

The transformation in the war narrative in the postcolonial period can be read in a single literature of the Arab world: Palestinian women's writings on two of their wars with the Israelis, the first in 1948 and the other the Intifada that broke out almost forty years later. Many, especially political scientists, would contest my classification of the Intifada as a war except in the purely metaphoric sense.[23] However, I contend that it is. As I shall argue below, the Intifada may not confront equivalent forces, but it does line up a nation against the army of a nation-state. Above all, it functions within the parameters of military constructs.

Both men's and women's writings of the early post-1948 period out of Israel reflect great ambivalence about the Israelis as well as about their own status and future. There is little of the later anger that marks the post-1967 writings by Palestinians worldwide. The major concerns of both men and women writers from within Israel are survival with dignity and the establishment of a just if patriarchal society. There is no hint that radical changes must be contemplated so as better to confront new challenges. To the contrary, traditional values and roles, particularly for women, are enforced and often by women like Najwa Qawar Farah.

Nineteen Sixty-Seven marks the beginning of a seismic shift. Wars in the Arab world which until then had been treated as discrete events, usually in connection with a colonial power, came to be regarded as systemic. The Palestinians' plight became a pan-Arab cause, if not always in reality then certainly in rhetoric. With this came a change in expectations of Palestinian women's behavior and, coincidentally, of their writing. Five years after the end of the Algerian Revolution,

Palestinians were invoking its lessons: the use of violence in the struggle
for independence; the indispensability of women to national liberation;
the importance for women of remaining vigilant on all fronts so as to be
able to withstand what the literary critic bell hooks has called inter-
locking systems of domination[24] that would force a repetition of Algerian
women's experience.[25] Palestinian women writers, in concert with their
Irish and South African counterparts, are claiming that not only are
women as actors playing out new as well as traditional roles vital to the
nationalist revolution but so is feminism as an ideology of radical social
change.

The poetry, autobiographies, novels and short stories of Fedwa Tu-
qan, Sahar Khalifa and Halima Jauhar already in the late 1960s and 1970s
draw the contours of the Intifada that actually broke out in 1987. This
popular uprising derived its name from the term the women had been
using for twenty years to describe their women-specific ways of resisting
Israeli aggression in Gaza and the West Bank. Their resistance draws
upon strategies women have begun to practice *worldwide*. The mothers
in South Africa and in Yugoslavia, the Women in Black in Israel, the
Madres of the Plaza de Mayo all have recognized the power of the
spectacle.[26] Women, and particularly in the guise of mothers, theatrical-
ize confrontations and the struggle to control public space and attention.
They are using the media against the guns.

This initiative and leadership by women *as women* in national struggle
is one of the most visible aspects of the change in postcolonial warfare.
In their struggle to control public space and attention, they refuse to
play men's roles. As never before, women are occupying what were
defined as male-specific arenas, but they do so as women, and particularly as mothers. The woman whose resistance as a woman succeeds
cannot be absorbed into a gender-neutral, or better, male movement.
Out of a space presumed to be closed to her, she has asserted her right
to launch action. Because the system is in crisis, normal policing proce-
dures are on hold. Not only is there access to that space but the fact of
access changes that space into a hyperspace. It is no longer the front,
that space that Cynthia Enloe tells us must always be redefined, relocated
so as to remain that place where women are not. It has become the
hyperspace of the home-front, what Doris Lessing calls a "habit of mind,
a structure of feeling, a cultural predisposition,"[27] that ambiguous place
that is neither home nor front because it has become both. And it houses
Paul Virilio's "civilian-soldiers" who are neither civilians nor soldiers
because they have become both.

Palestinian women writers are aware of the advantages of mixing roles and genders in the hyperspace, and they describe and thus inscribe the process. Their stories of women going out into the streets and, under the ever watchful eye of the international television cameras, confronting soldiers with their vulnerable women's and children's bodies demonstrate how all the familiar binaries that structure the Israelis' expectations of and training for war are thrown into confusion. Soon after the men took it over in December 1987, the women-specific nature of the Intifada changed. The sporadic, individual happenings were controlled and strategized. The use of arms was encouraged and young men wearing the national symbol of the *kuffiyeh,* or checkered scarf tied about the head in a distinctive manner, became soldiers it was legitimate to shoot.

In her 1990 novel *Bab al-Saha,* Sahar Khalifa explores women's attitudes to the organizing and centralizing of the resistance and to the mobilizing of young men. Nuzha, the prostitute heroine, compels the men who enter her life to acknowledge that women's ways, often domestic ways, including unarmed, disorganized, fragmented struggle by women and children was still the best way to achieve the kind of results they wanted. After seeing twenty men climb to their death as they try to get into an Israeli military headquarters, the prostitute offers an alternative access: through a trapdoor in her kitchen, to an underground passage and then up into the heart of the headquarters![28]

More than the Intifada, which blurred and challenged some of the binaries usual to war, yet had to acknowledge others, the Lebanese Civil War defied conventional categorizations. It confronted and undermined all the black and white distinctions that, once established, enable the tired repetition of the War Story, that reassuringly familiar skeleton we merely flesh out with new details. The Lebanese Civil War lent itself to multiple unorthodox narrations, especially by women.[29] It allowed the women to rewrite the violence so that, for example, passivity, endemic to many moments of war, could be written as activism. This discursive transformation can be read in women's evolving descriptions of waiting, that aspect of war that Paul Fussell describes as so debilitating,[30] probably because it is so feminizing. During the seven-year period that preceded the Israeli Invasion in June 1982, women like Emily Nasrallah wrote progressively of their staying in Lebanon and waiting as first "Doing Nothing," then as "Survival" and finally as "Resistance." With time, they described this staying in Lebanon, which had originally been unthinking, as though it were a need, a response to a maternal instinct. Lebanon was a child in pain, it had to be protected. If mothers—not, of course, biological mothers, but rather what Sara Ruddick calls "maternal thinkers"—did not care for Lebanon, who would?[31]

By the early 1980s, the women's writing became more assertive and self-consciously resistant. The tolerance of those who were leaving was fast disappearing. They were beginning to realize that whenever there was an opportunity to leave, it was generally the women who stayed and the men who departed. And when they stayed, the women remained vigilant against the war. As Evelyne Accad writes, whenever the demarcation line between the predominantly Christian East and the Muslim West Beirut closed, it was the women who organized, or, like Andree Chedid, wrote about organizing protest marches. They believed, despite all odds, in a possible reunification and to this end they were prepared to sacrifice their lives.[32] It was not that the men had no conscience and the women did, but rather that they had a different notion of responsibility. Whereas men, both writers and male protagonists in women's writings, pointed the finger of blame at others, particularly the fighters and every possible -ism, women constantly affirmed that responsibility is shared by all. Individual innocence, Ghada Samman insists, is not possible in a guilty society.[33] These women's writings articulate their transformed consciousness. Whereas they had originally stayed out of selflessness, they were now staying to resist Lebanon's total destruction. Above all, they were staying to achieve for themselves a sense of self, as women and as Lebanese citizens.

Despite apparent differences in the nature of the Intifada and the Lebanese Civil War, their writings are comparable. What is shared is exemplified in a comparison between men's and women's writings. For the women writers, these are wars in which binary structures are recognized to be artificial and unhelpful in trying to understand and resolve their conflicts. In this destabilized context, Lebanese and Palestinian women are the ones to take the initiative in the struggle and to forge a new relationship between the individual and the collective. This relationship is premised on care for each other and on the hope for survival for oneself and by extension for the society as a whole. Lebanese and Palestinian men's writings, mirroring women's literary assessments of men's political actions, tend to trivialize the women's new strategies and the realities they produce. At the same time they continue to advocate the pursuit of traditional organized, armed conflict, however suicidal and unsuccessful it may have proved itself to be. Thus do they seek to rehabilitate the familiar binarisms. Wars in such a world view seem to be necessary, the only solutions to apparently irresolvable conflicts.

The eight year Iran-Iraq War would seem to be quite different, yet my reading of its literature suggests changes in war representation comparable to those that have taken place during other postcolonial wars waged in the Arab world. Like its successor, the Gulf War, it was more a parody of conventional, or, better, Total War. In 1980, Saddam Hussein launched what he thought would be a blitzkrieg. It was to be a show of strength, a bid for the leadership of the Arab world. In anticipation of an easy, resounding victory, already in 1979 he was lining up artists and artisans—whom he thus implicated in the military venture—to construct before the event its happy outcome. To boost the significance of the expected victory, Saddam Hussein dipped randomly into history's grab bag and, with the help of artists and writers, pastiched together a glossy facade that included New Babylons, Sharifian descents and Qadisiyas.[34] The reality of the slaughter of little boys and old men in the mud was replaced by the reassurance of glorious monuments and victorious stories. Eight years later, exhausted and his army and arsenal depleted, Hussein declared a victory that allowed the fighting to stop.

Most of the Iraq-Iran war literature, like most of its cultural production, was state-commissioned and -published. Conferences and festivals were held to give a platform to this new literature. Only a few were able to overcome atomization and retain the sense of responsibility that many assumed all Iraqi writers and artists had perforce lost.[35] So closely did some artists collaborate with the government that their works came to shape reality; victory and martyr monuments were constructed before any victory was in sight, millennial literary series celebrating the war were conceived before the war had even started. Image-making replaced creative reflection and production.[36] Could this be art or was it pure propaganda? Can patronized but also terrorized writers question the validity of a patriotic war? How does one read such texts? One reads between the lines. Sometimes there is nothing there. Sometimes it turns out that there is *nothing on the line*, everything is in the "between."[37]

So, I have read between the lines of both women's and men's fiction on the Iran-Iraq War. Careful not to write of the front, women writers like Suhayla Salman, Aliya Talib and Lutfiya al-Dulaymi were bravely critical of the war. They alluded, even though necessarily obliquely, to the ways in which the state had coopted not only people's minds but also their bodies, especially women's bodies. Women, who had achieved considerable gains in access to educational and professional opportunities, including military service, and even in some cases to equal pay, were told during the war they should turn their bodies over to the state and produce at least five children, preferably boys.

Suhayla Salman's strong women disdainfully reject Patriotic Motherhood. Yet, ironically, it *is* as mothers, not Patriotic but rather Resisting Mothers, that they unmask a system that would turn their boys, the country's future, into dead heroes; they, like the Argentinian Madres and the Mothers of the Intifada, claim as each her own those non-kin men who are about to be wasted; they hold together a fragmenting society.

Aliya Talib's stories again and again satirize notions of heroic masculinity and passive femininity in times of war that produce nothing but corpses. In 1988, the apparently pro-Baathist woman Lutfiya al-Dulaymi published *Seeds of Fire*. Appropriately enough for a woman writer, it refers only tangentially to the war *does* refer to the war, it does so as though it were infinitely distant. This "homefront novel" revolves around Layla, a graphic artist working for an advertising agency while her husband is away at the mines. As in Lebanese and Palestinian *Künstlerromane* on their wars, the role of the woman artist narrator is crucial. Through her creative production, Layla is liberated from the constraints of her body so that she may enter the heretofore forbidden zone of male exchange. Her presence in the agency is doubly disruptive: it is repeated that she is the only woman employee; her artwork is so accomplished and increasingly radical that it threatens to ruin the business. How? Her male director fears that if she emphasizes the aesthetic aspect of her work, consumers will focus on the creator of the message rather than on the message alone. Prospective consumers will think before buying. The parallels between these marketing strategies and the production and dissemination of propaganda are striking. For when the people become aware that values they had thought to be essential are in fact packaged goods they are supposed to consume spontaneously, they will begin to doubt the imperatives of martyrdom and patriotism. *Seeds of Fire* seems to suggest during the war that the woman artist may find at the very heart of a totalitarian system the key to its undoing.

Although some of the men write of women warriors,[38] the women do not. This is surprising in view of the fact that in 1976 already women had begun to enlist into popular militia forces and by 1982 their numbers had swollen to 40,000.[39] Why? I would suggest that this is the case, because women soldiers, after all, are doing what the men are doing.

These Iraqi women write of what the women are doing *as women*. They write on and through the war, yet also against it. They write their protest into a war they are supposed to support. Like the post-1948 Palestinian literature out of Israel, men and women seem to be subject to similar pressures. Yet, in Iraq it is primarily the women who have found ways to write against the war. For the men, who were more assured of an audience, or, at least, of censorship, criticism was a more risky business.

My reading of Arab writers' fiction on their wars since 1948 suggests that attention to women, both as fighters and as writers, reveals a change in warfare and its representation over the past forty years. During precolonial and colonial wars, women's participation in national conflict is presented as a copy of men's ways of fighting; they are femmes soldats. Temporary and expedient gender role reversals do not lead to narratives of role transformations or even only ambiguities. In conventional war, women do not have the space to imagine another way to live or to fight. Like the Algerian women, they are temporarily transformed into something they know they do not wish to become. However, when writing out of postcolonial wars, many Arab women describe and extol women's agency as women in what used to be but thus ceases to be a male-only space. Their trespassing bodies break down the black and white distinctions that had shaped the war story and allow them to create countervisions of society and of war. In Lebanon, the women wrote of the need to reject the old norms of emigration and to stay, to adopt responsibility for the chaos and to work for the survival of the self, of others and of the country. Their message was stay and thus stop the war. Although in the wake of the war of 1967 the Palestinian women were agreed with the men on the need to resist the occupation, they did not agree on the means. They opposed the use of confrontational violence, which enabled the Israelis to fight as they had been trained to fight. They called for transformed social arrangements and gender relations and a valorization of women's ways of fighting so as to resist more effectively. The Iraqi women writers showed that their society's male-dominated values and the war they created were self-destructive. Since they could not with impunity criticize their leader, they directed themselves to their readers. Their writing creates citizens with a conscience who can see through the manipulation that mobilizes a whole nation to fight a foolish war.

In all of the Arab women's literature on postcolonial wars, images of motherhood have acquired centrality. The nurturing persona who in the literature of the colonial period seemed bent on molding her daughter into her own oppressed shape, has multiplied so as to be able to play numerous roles. These mothers are both aggressive and pacific, Patriotic and nationalist, desiring and destructive, martyr and prisoner. They may be all of these at once or at different times. Motherism as a multi-faceted strategy of resistance in postcolonial war and its literature is no longer a "mere" social fact, it has become a resisting act. As such it is constantly reconstructed to suit its challenges. No boundary is so resilient that it cannot bend.

Postcolonial wars have transformed the relationship between women's participation in war and its narration: the change in women's experience has found a necessary corollary in the change in discourse. Women are inscribing their experiences in war into the war story. They are thus countering others' naming of women's experiences as having not been in war. The delicate balancing act between experience and its recording must be maintained so that action and its recording will remain in tension. The political mother only retains efficacy if she is *written* as politically effective. Yet, at the same time, she will only continue to have a literary voice if she can hold on to political agency. The postcolonial war writer realizes that her writing—the struggle to reclaim language in such a way that it will empower and no longer suppress her—is critical to her understanding of the role she may play in the war theater. Out of postcolonial war, women write to transform themselves, their relationships with others and by extension the social context. Whereas Algerian women fought as men, Arab women after them have fought as women and often as mothers. Their participation cannot be forgotten or eliminated as women playing at men's roles, as cross-dressing, because it is written and will therefore be remembered as women fighting as women. These women writers have found a space in which to make their voices heard and their heard voices are changing that space.

I would like to conclude with the words of Hanan Ashrawi, the spokesperson for the Palestinian delegation at the 1990s Middle East Peace Talks who expresses eloquently and forcefully the difference women make in war: "And if we lose sight of the human substance then we lose sight of the basic essence of all our work . . . Men always choose the politics of domination and destruction . . . It is time to transcend the pain of the moment and to impose a woman's solution on the Palestinian-Israeli conflict, and the women's solution is based on equality, on non-discrimination, on the preservation of life and rights and on addressing the core issues of justice, freedom, with candor and with courage, not with weapons and power."[40]

REFERENCES

1. Lynne Hanley, *Writing War. Fiction, Gender and Memory* (Amherst: University of Massachusetts, 1991), 8.
2. Paul Fussell, *Wartime: Understanding and Behavior in the Second World War* (Oxford: Oxford University Press, 1989), 251.
3. In the wake of the Gulf War, Cynthia Enloe writes that "contemporary warfare made the conceptual divide between combat and non-combat irrelevant." Enloe, "The Gendered Gulf" in Cynthia Peters, ed., *Collateral Damage. The 'New World Order' at Home and Abroad* (Boston: South End Press, 1992), 107.
4. Basim Abd al-Hamid Hammudi, *Al-naqid wa qissat al-harb. Dirasa tahliliya* (The Critic and the War Story) (Baghdad: 1986), 95.
5. Gareth Thomas, *The Novel of the Spanish Civil War* (Cambridge: Cambridge University Press, 1990), 18–29.
6. "Hemingway has written that some events are of such magnitude that 'if a writer has participated in them his obligation is to write them truly rather than assume the presumption of altering them with invention.' " Preface to Regler's *The Great Crusade* (1940) in Thomas, 10. Ortega y Gasset, on the other hand, found "the reality of lived experience and aesthetic expression are incompatible in art." Thomas, 20.
7. Fussell, *Wartime*, 296.
8. Hanley, *Writing War*, 7.
9. In this connection, it is worth noting that Saddam Hussein celebrated the anniversary of his victory in the Gulf War, saying "We emerged triumphant from that war." Jim Hoagland, "Unfinished Business Muddies Impact," *The Denver Post*, January 12, 1992, 18A.
10. George Lakoff, "Metaphor and War: The Metaphor System Used to Justify War in the Gulf," *Journal of Urban and Cultural Studies*, 2/1 (1991): 59–72.
11. Paul Virilio, Pure War, *Semiotext*, 1983, 92–93.
12. Susan Slymovics, " 'To Put One's Fingers in the Bleeding Wound': Palestinian Theater under Israeli Censorship," *The Drama Review*, 35/2 (T130) (Summer 1991): 18–38.
13. Simon During, "Postmodernism or Post-colonialism Today" *Textual Practice*, 1/1 (1987): 37.
14. See for example, William Hoynes, "War as Video Game: Media, Activism, and the Gulf War" in Peters, *Collateral Damage*, 305–326.
15. Judith Butler, "The Imperialist Subject" *Journal of Urban and Cultural Studies*, 2/1 (1991): 75–76.

16. Claims that the Vietnam War had taught the American military to marginalize the press are daily being disproven.

17. Yasmine Gooneratne's poem on the Sri Lankan Civil War entitled "The Peace Game," she writes of children playing war and peace. She concludes:

> We called the entertainment "Peace"
> or "War"—I can't remember which . . .

In Miriam Cooke and Roshni Rustomji-Kerns, eds. *Blood into Ink: Middle Eastern and South Asian Women Write War*, (Boulder, CO: Westview, 1994).

18. Margaret Higonnet, "Not So Quiet in No Woman's Land," *Gendering War Talk*, Miriam Cooke and Angela Woollacott, eds., (Princeton: Princeton University Press, 1993). See also Virginia Woolf's *Three Guineas*, in which she claims that women have not been considered capable of writing about war.

19. Bouthaina Shaaban, *Both Right and Left Handed. Arab Women Talk about their Lives*, (London: Women's Press, 1988), 182–219.

20. Rita O'Hare, the head of the Sinn Fein Department of Women's Affairs, said at the Irish Women United conference in 1981 that: "Women in the Republican Movement have worked for, and welcomed, in recent years, the recognition by the Movement of the importance of building and developing a real policy on women's struggle and attempting to carry that out, just as it has realised the importance of developing the struggle in the labour movement, without which socialism cannot be built . . . In the aftermath of national liberation struggles around the world we have seen attempts made to force women who were active in those struggles alongside men back into subordinate roles in the new society. This danger cannot be overcome by standing on the sidelines. It can only be totally negated by the fullest possible involvement of determined women in the heart of that struggle." *Iris: The Republican Magazine*, 7 (November 1983): 22.

21. Thomas writes that this linkage is "A positive aspect which is lacking in the classical war novel. Man is not here a pawn of the possessing classes sent to fight a colonial war in the interests of capitalist exploitation, but a defender of rights by dint of collective political and syndical action." Thomas, *The Spanish Civil War*, 13.

22. Marie-Aimee Helie-Lucas, "Women, Nationalism, and Religion in the Algerian Struggle" *Opening the Gates. A Century of Arab Feminist Writing*, (Virago/Indiana University Press, 1990), 104–114.

23. Paul Vieille, in a reaction to this essay, wrote that the Intifada is "not war in the real meaning of the term, i.e., the confrontation of armies. It is rather a new form of opposition to a national domination, a non-military resistance to oppression by another. It is only war in the metaphoric sense." Letter from Paul Vieille, June 20, 1992.

24. bell hooks, *Talking Back* (Boston: South End Press, 1989), 175.

25. In her novel *Abbad al-shams*, Sahar Khalifa writes: "What happened to the Algerian women after independence? Women returned to the rule of the

harem and to covering their heads. They struggled, carried arms and were tortured in French prisons -Jamila, Aisha and Aishas. Then what? They went out into the light and the men left them in the dark. It was as though freedom was restricted to men alone. What about us? Where is our freedom and how can we get to it? They shall not deceive us! " (119).

26. Michael Rogin says that spectacles "In the postmodern view, define the historical rupture between industrial and post-industrial society-the one based on durable goods production, the other on information and service exchange. With the dissolution of individual subjectivities and differentiated autonomous spheres, not only does the connection between an object and its use become arbitrary. . . but skilled attention to display also deflects notice from the object to its hyperreal, reproducible representation. the society of the spectacle provides illusory unification and meaning, Guy Debord argues, distracting attention from producers and from classes in conflict. Simulacric games have entirely replaced the real, in Jean Baudrillard's formulation, and offer not even a counterfeit representation of anything outside themselves." Rogin, "Make My Day! Spectacle as Amnesia in Imperial Politics," *Representations* (Winter 1990): 106.

27. Hanley, *Writing War*, 7.

28. When I interviewed Sahar Khalifa in Nablus in June 1991, I asked her about the domestic symbolism evident in this her most recent novel. Her reaction was first confusion and then amusement. She had not chosen the kitchen site self-consciously, but now she was glad that she had.

29. Miriam Cooke, *War's Other Voices. Women Writers on the Lebanese Civil War* (Cambridge: Cambridge University Press, 1988).

30. Fussell, *Wartime*, 75–78.

31. Sara Ruddick, *Maternal Thinking. Toward a Politics of Peace* (Boston: Beacon Press, 1989).

32. Evelyne Accad, *Sexuality and War. Literary Masks of the Middle East* (New York: New York University Press, 1989), 78–90.

33. Ghada Samman, *Beirut Nightmares* (Beirut: Kawabis Bayrut, 1980), 14–15.

34. *Qadisiya* is the name of the first battle that the Arab Muslims won against non-Arabs, in fact Iranians, in 637 C.E.

35. At the Modern Arabic Literature conference held at the University of Nijmegen (Holland) in May 1992, Sabry Hafez ridiculed me for choosing to take Iraqi war literature seriously. Everybody, he assured me, knew that what these women and men wrote was rubbish. Of what possible value could such propaganda be? Samir al-Khalil seems to support such an attitude. He has attacked all artists who stayed in Iraq and continued to create: "The peculiarity of the Iraqi regime therefore is to have involved enormous numbers of people directly in its crimes over twenty years, while making the rest of the population at the very least complicit in their commission. Yet, everyone inside the country, including the opposition outside, denies all responsibility for what they know has been going on." *The Monument* (1991), 129.

36. "Substituting symbols for substance, these staged events (Grenada, Libya, etc.)

constitute the politics of postmodernism, so long as one remembers that symbols produced for consumption at home and abroad have all too much substance for the victims of those symbols, the participant-observers on the ground." Michael Rogin, " 'Make My Day!,' Spectacle as Amnesia in Imperial Politics" in *Representations*, 29, Winter 1990, 116.

37. Lev Loseff describes the same phenomenon in Russian literature. He analyzes what he refers to as "slavish" language which is "a systemic alteration of the text occasioned by the introduction of hints and circumlocutions." (6) For over 100 years Russians have themselves been using the term Aesopian to describe such techniques. He argues that it emerges in response to state-imposed censorship and chronicles over two centuries of writing that had to find ways to express itself in spite of wary censors. See Lev Loseff, *On the Beneficence of Censorship [through] Aesopian Language in Modern Russian Literature* (Munich: Otto Sagner, 1984).

38. Salah al-Ansari writes of Tiswahun, who took up her husband's rifle when he was killed. Carrying her baby daughter on her back she forayed into the battlefield and killed many soldiers. *Alphabet of War and Love*, [Fi Al-Thaqafa Waal-Harb: Baghdad, 1988], 39).

39. Samir al-Khalil, *Republic of Fear*, 92. Interview with Gamal al-Ghitani, Egyptian author who covered Iran-Iraq War. Nijmegen, Holland, April 24, 1992.

40. Hanan Ashrawi. "Address to the Twenty-fifth Anniversary Conference of the National Organization of Women, January 1992," *Episcopal Life*, (March 1992) 1.

CHAPTER TWELVE

Arab Male, Hebrew Female:
The Lure of Metaphors

Anton Shammas

In June 1987, some five months before the Intifada, the Israeli Hebrew daily *Yedi'ot Aharonot,* whose reports carry, more often than not, a whiff of sensationalism, ran the following story: Jewish prostitutes were brought every night to a public park in Gaza, by their Jewish pimps, and there they changed their professional attire into army uniform, and sometimes even decorated their shoulder loops with fancy insignia of high ranking officers. The clients, local Gazans, would line up in Indian files—pun not intended—with ostentatious pride, as the reporter wrote, in order "to give it to the Israeli occupation," and then go out the next morning and brag about it the whole day long in the market place.

A smiling client, who was asked whether he was sure those were Israeli women soldiers, said, "But of course, they are women soldiers all right, with army IDs." Has he seen the IDs? "No," he said, "But the women said they had them." Which means, and this is *my* wisecrack, that sometimes you have to make do with the signified, and only imagine that the signifier is out there somewhere.

But seriously, "If you leave out sex," Mark Twain would have commented, "and just consider the business facts," as readers of subversive texts you might have thought immediately of the famous brothel scene in Salman Rushdie's *The Satanic Verses,* in which the whores of The Curtain, as the brothel is called, each assumes the identity of one of Mahound's wives. And then, as devout students of Gender, Race and Class, you might as well find the Gazan Brothel-in-the-Park a perfect manifestation of the golden rule: That gender is a matter of ideology, ideology being its original impulse and not biology.

However, the reason *I* started off with this manipulative anecdote—

and a manipulative anecdote it is—is, first, to show you, up front, as if you needed the proof, how powerful metaphors are in their "chaste compactness" (to use a Benjaminian phrase), creating a concise, hard core reality, instead of the fragmented, loosely coherent one lying outside the text; and second, a long shot as it is, I am shamelessly using this anecdote as a *safe* (I hope) metaphor for the subversive things that I plan to say about the dangers of gender in modern Hebrew literature.

To my mind, the only achievement of the Jewish National Movement/Zionism was the desire, and later the power, to reterritorialize the Hebrew language. The rest, again, to my mind, is a moot question. Subsequently, modern Hebrew literature, as a major component of the national Jewish Renaissance, took upon itself, since the turn of the century, to turn the dead language of text into a normal, live language of con–text, territorially and otherwise.

The Palestinians, in 1948, were de-territorialized, and their language, their Palestinian vernacular, became just another dialect. For them, on more fronts than they would admit, the prevalence of Hebrew discourse was, and still is, a perpetual testimony to their defeat and their shame. In this context, nothing is more illustrative of their bereavement than a Palestinian Arab character in a Hebrew novel, who is being constructed in the very language that had caused her/his de-construction.

Along these lines, imagine, if you will, the Gazans in that park finding out that they have been taken in by a Rushdian shrewd pimp of sorts, and that the prostitutes wearing the IDF uniforms were actually local Arab ladies whose tongue is theirs, so to speak. The whole episode could be set off balance, and the ladies could be accused of lethal, double-crossing: not only did they play the enemy, but they also didn't speak the *right* tongue. Which means that for those who had lined up, the actual attraction was the knowledge that the ladies actually spoke the language of their deterritorialization, which was committed some forty years earlier, by people of a—as it were—higher class and race, wearing the very same uniform. So for them, this is now, albeit a sham, the perfect revenge; biology is being sublimated into ideology through a special type of cross-dressing.

In recent years, some Israeli writers have become fond of the following genderized metaphor: the Hebrew language, a lady at the turn of the century, whom writers treated with utter respect and awe, has become a coquettish broad, best treated with frolic and hanky-panky. They were not speaking disparagingly of Hebrew; rather, they meant to suggest that the Holy Script was finally "normalized."

In the wake of the Gaza story, I am fully aware that the above metaphor sounds utterly contrived, which it is not, but I still would be interested in creating a contrived metaphor that, in a Borgesian convoluted way, would eventually make the point that I'm driving at.

The Hebrew language, which the Kabbalists believed was the language of creation, and Dante believed was the language of Grace, and in which truly remarkable texts were written in the last hundred years or so, has for some twenty-seven years now become the language of occupation. The same language of Creation, of Making, has been used for twenty-seven years to order the demolition of a house, and the unmaking of a body. But one should hasten to add, that this plight has not befallen only the Hebrew language; the twentieth century, if nothing else, has tainted many languages, and Hebrew should not be singled out. However, for me as a devout and admiring reader of Hebrew literature, albeit a politically motivated one, I find that a very crucial thing is missing. Except for two or three works of literature, twenty-seven years of bloody occupation have left no trace, neither in the language, nor in the literature written in it.

Generations of students in Israel, interested in the image of the Arab and the reflection of the Arab–Israeli conflict in Hebrew literature, have been brought up on three short stories (two by S. Yizhar, and one by B. Tammuz, written between 1948 and 1953),[1] each a remarkable achievement on its merits. These stories, especially the two stories by Yizhar, depicted a group of Israeli soldiers, ethically wading their way out of a moral dilemma. These stories, alongside the official histories of the newborn state, created an immaculate picture of a fighting Jewish soldier in the war of 1948. Juxtaposed with the usually immoral and the bloodthirsty Arab, the Israeli soldier did not only win the war, but also managed to keep the upper moral hand.

Now that the revisionist and oppositional histories are being written by young Israeli historians, demythologizing many aspects of the 1948 war and painfully probing into some of its consequences, these same stories are read with different eyes. But it seems that the metaphor created by them cannot be tarnished: most Israelis truly believe that their War of Independence was fought by Yizhar's soldiers, a group of reflective Prosperos against red-handed Calibans; and more importantly, that literature is a true reflection of the reality against which it was written. This might explain to some extent why the average Israeli is deeply convinced that insofar as the Jewish–Arab relationships are concerned, the Israelis, all along, have been the righteous side. In this sense, Hebrew literature managed to create, in a very impressive manner, a retroactively alternative reality, a seemingly "normalized" state, an imaginary Jewish state of the mind.

The reason I'm unpacking these rather crude ideas in such a clumsy manner is that a very similar thing has happened to the genderization of the Arab/Palestinian presence in Hebrew literature. The image of the Arab in Hebrew literature is a wildly researched topic, and some of the literature on the subject is quite impressive.[2] However, I'm not aware of any attempt by this literature to conduct a comparative reading of the related material, i.e., read it against the Israeli *social* reality. What interests me here is the literature written by male writers since the early sixties, and let me say up front that I am fully aware of the fact that a comparative reading of the Other's theme in Arabic and Hebrew literatures can easily show that the latter is incomparable in point of scope, treatment and depth of interest. (Books like A. B. Yehoshua's *The Lover*, for instance, I believe could not have been written in Arabic, for various reasons that do not concern us right now.) So in a certain way, it won't be easy to play the party pooper.

Now, as in every minority–majority discourse, most of the engendered, inter–racial encounters in this literature take place between an Arab man and a Jewish woman, mostly in the fringe of an impacted reality. In *The Lover* it's between two adolescents. But one of the most quoted passages in this context comes from Amos Oz's *My Michael* (1968): the sequence in which Hannah Gonen, the first person narrator of the book, finds herself, two nights before her wedding, in a dream with the two Arab twins, Aziz and Khalil, whose family used to live near hers before they became refugees in 1948. In a certain way, this sequence reads today as it if was written by a special request, or by the book. The twins, Aziz and Khalil, despite their short performance, have long become the two most famous Arab characters in modern Hebrew literature, so much so that any Arab character that was introduced in their wake fell under their shadow and was read against their two powerful images. And here's the dream sequence:

> One of the last nights, two days before the wedding, I had a frightening dream. Michael and I were in Jericho. We were shipping in the market, between rows of low mud huts. (My father, my brother, and I had been on an outing together to Jericho in 1938. It was during the Feast of Succot. We went on an Arab bus. I was eight. I have not forgotten. My birthday is during Succot.)

Michael and I bought a rug, some pouffes, an ornate sofa. Michael didn't want to buy these things. I chose them and he paid up quietly. The *suk* in Jericho was noisy and colorful. People were shouting wildly. I walked through the crowd calmly, wearing a casual skirt. There was a terrible, savage sun in the sky, such as I have seen in paintings by Van Gogh. Then an army jeep pulled up near us. A short, dapper British officer leaped out and tapped Michael on the shoulder. Michael suddenly turned and dashed off like a man possessed, upsetting stalls as he ran till he was swallowed up in the crowd. I was alone. Women screamed. Two men appeared and carried me off in their arms. They were hidden in their flowing robes. Only their eyes showed, glinting. Their grasp was rough and painful. They dragged me down winding roads to the outskirts of the town. The place looked like the steep alleys behind the Street of the Abyssinians in the east of new Jerusalem. I was pushed down a long flight of stairs into a cellar lit by a dirty paraffin lamp. The cellar was black. I was thrown to the ground. I could feel the damp. The air was fetid. Outside I could hear muffled, crazed barking. Suddenly the twins threw off their robes. We were all three the same age. Their house stood opposite ours, across a patch of wasteland, between Katamon and Kiryat Shmuel. They had a courtyard surrounded on all sides. The house was built round the yard. Vines grew up the walls of the villa. The walls were built of the reddish stone which was popular among the richer Arabs in the southern suburbs of Jerusalem.

I was afraid of the twins. They made fun of me. Their teeth were very white. They were dark and lithe. A pair of strong gray wolves. "Michael, Michael," I screamed, but my voice was taken from me. I was dumb. A darkness washed over me. The darkness wanted Michael to come and rescue me only at the end of the pain and the pleasure. If the twins remembered our childhood days, they gave no sign of it. Except their laughter. They leaped up and down on the floor of the cellar as if they were freezing cold. But the air was not cold. They leaped and bounced with seething energy. They effervesced. I couldn't contain my nervous, ugly laughter. Aziz was a little taller than his brother and slightly darker. He ran past me and opened a door I had not noticed. He pointed to the door and bowed a waiter's bow. I was free. I could leave. It was an awful moment. I could have left but I didn't. Then Halil uttered a low, trembling groan and closed and bolted the door. Aziz drew out of the folds of his robe a long, glinting knife. There was a gleam in his eyes. He sank down on all fours. His eyes were blazing. The whites of his eyes were dirty and bloodshot. I retreated and pressed my back against the cellar wall. The wall was filthy. A sticky, putrid moisture soaked through my clothes and touched my skin. With my last strength I screamed.[3]

I'm sure that any dream interpreter, Freudian or otherwise, would find it fascinating to analyze this text, line by line and image by image, in the light of the Trinity: Race, Class, and the Holy Gender, but I'd like to draw your attention only to a couple of things.

Note that there is a British soldier, and he leaves the female dreamer alone, chasing her Jewish "owner," (literal meaning of "husband" in Hebrew) and then she's kidnapped by two Arabs into a dark cellar, and she is completely under their spell, and though offered a way out, she does not want her Jewish "owner" to come and secure her until the end of "pain and pleasure." In a certain sense, Oz's dream is the first attempt to see the S&M component in the Arab–Israeli conflict. A dirty mind like mine would also notice the fact that, unlike the ladies of Gaza, she is wearing a skirt, and not an army uniform, which would have really been a heavy–handed touch on the part of Oz.

What I have been trying to suggest—and I'll leave it here as an open-ended suggestion—through reading some of the contemporary male Israeli writers (Oz, Yehoshua, and Sami Mikhael in particular), is that the sexual presence of the Arab/Palestinian male in modern Hebrew fiction, and the way this presence/threat is literarily dealt with and (textually) defused, "if you leave out sex and just consider the business facts," that is, gives the metaphor a luring power: literature becomes an alibi, completely detached from, and oblivious of, the alarming reality which lurks outside the text. The text, pretending to represent reality, permeates the minds of its readers with the soothing belief that reality, harsh and alarming as it is, has been confronted and its ticking sound taken care of.

There's nothing wrong about that, you might say; after all this is what literature usually does. But I'm afraid that modern Hebrew literature is overdoing it.

REFERENCES

1. S. Yizhar, "The Prisoner,"; S. Yizhar, "Khirbet Khaz'ah,"; Benhamin Tammuz, "Swimming Contest."
2. The reader is referred to the following, selected bibliography of English language works: Risa Domb, *The Arab in Hebrew Prose, 1911–1948*, (London, Totowa: Vallentine and Mitchel, 1982); Gilah Ramraz–Raukh, *The Arab in Israeli Literature*, (Bloomington: Indiana University Press; London, I.B. Tauris,

1989); Robert Alter, "Images of the Arab in Israeli Fiction," *Hebrew Studies* 18 (1977): 61–65; Warren Bargad, "The Image of the Arab in Israeli Literature," *Hebrew Annual Review* 1 (1977): 53–59; Edna Amir Coffin, "The Image of the Arab in Modern Hebrew Literature," *Michigan Quarterly Review* (Spring 1982): 326–330; Gilead Morahg, "New Images of Arabs in Israeli Fiction," *Prooftexts*, 6 (1986): 147–162.

3. Amos Oz, *My Michael*, translated by N. de Lange (New York: Knopf, 1982), 45–47.

CHAPTER THIRTEEN

Where Has All the Power Gone? Women and Politics in Popular Quarters of Cairo

Diane Singerman

Despite a recent proliferation of research on women in Egypt and their participation in political and economic life, the macroanalysis of "high" politics remains androcentric and gender-blind.[1] Paradoxically, anthropologists demonstrated that Middle Eastern women play a central role in their communities, as they exert influence over the management of the household and wider social networks. Yet women are still treated as largely irrelevant to so-called "real" politics by political scientists.[2] The classic works on Egyptian politics and political economy barely allude to their influence or control over public and private resources. Most of these works cannot articulate women's political participation because they analyze interest groups, political institutions, elite politics, and bureaucratic hierarchies in which Egyptian women are only marginally represented. I therefore base my research on a particular *sha'bi* or "popular" community, located in one of central Cairo's most densely-populated areas. I situated the locus of my study within the household,

―――――――
NOTE:

My interpretation of this community is no doubt colored by my intellectual, political, and personal baggage, but I hope to convey my deep admiration, respect, and gratitude for the people who opened up their homes and lives to me. During my research I received vital support from Nawal Hassan, the Director of The Centre for the Study of Egyptian Civilization. Her colleagues at the Centre were tremendously helpful when I was formulating my ideas and completing my research. This research was funded by the Social Science Research Council, the Fulbright Commission and the Council on Regional Studies and the Center for International Studies at Princeton University.

where the actions and decisions of both men and women unfold together.[3]

The *sha'b* describes a collective "people." It refers to the Egyptian masses who remain tied to indigenous culture, social norms, and patterns of living. The indigenous nature of *sha'bi* characteristics is key to an understanding of its meaning among Egyptians. Upper class and more westernized Egyptians would never use this term to describe their way of life, since it is associated with the more popular, lower class, "common" mainstream. A similar but distinct adjective, *baladi,* refers more to one's place of origin and the lifestyles or practices associated with it. Egyptians use *al-balad* to mean country and nation, but the same word also means village or town. An *ibn al-balad* is a son of the soil, the Egyptian salt of the earth with the best of positive connotations.[4] In several ways, *baladi* has more of a provincial connotation to it: the term carries suggestions of the countryside and its peasantry. Yet many *baladi* customs and values are shared by urban residents who have lived in urban areas for generations. In Egypt, the *sha'b* are similar to the *pueblo* or *lo popular* in Latin America in that they share collective identities that may stand above class cleavages as middle class and even wealthy families often reside in popular neighborhoods, despite their upward mobility.

Between 1985 and 1986 I lived with a family in central Cairo to try to understand the everyday activities of lower class women (and men) by tracing the consequences of their actions on wider associations embedded in the community and the polity.[5] As a woman, I was allowed to enter domains that are off-limits to many male observers of Egyptian society. Through a methodology of participant/observer and informal interviewing I was able to recognize and appreciate the political implications of women's day-to-day lives. The following discussion makes use of this experience and thus weaves stories, empirical data, and theoretical reflection together. My methodology and conclusions aim to break down the intellectual barriers that have separated political science from sociology and anthropology.

I focus on the political component in two spheres of women's activities. First, I examine women's participation in informal networks and the political aspects of these informal institutions. These networks secure jobs, produce manufactured goods, procure basic goods and services (both private and public goods), arbitrate conflicts, cope with bureaucratic processes, save money, and educate children. Networks are traditionally considered social, but I argue that informal networks constitute a collective institution for *sha'bi* women and have an explicitly political component, because they are vehicles to power. Second, I analyze women's participation in the labor force, the informal economy, and familial enterprises. There are two implications for the growing role of women in the economy. Through the creation of economic institutions such as informal savings associations, women acquire financial autonomy to pursue their individual interests, and their enhanced financial status enables them to pursue their collective and political interests.

The everyday activities of women, although undertaken in the household and community, are not simply concerned with "domestic" affairs; rather, they are involved in wider matters of power. There is the sense among the *sha'b* that they represent "the people," and a majority of the urban population. Collective identities, under specific political circumstances, can be the basis for significant political mobilization and the emergence of social movements as common people demand to be treated as citizens. The history of the popular sector has received far more attention in Latin America than in the Middle East due to its prominent role in populist projects, labor movements, revolutionary movements, and much more recently, in urban social movements, liberation theology and redemocratization campaigns that brought civilians back to power throughout Latin America. The popular sector seeks additional power and its fair share of public resources, because it is still economically oppressed or disadvantaged, unlike the middle and upper classes who have prospered through dependent development and the growth of the state.

The *sha'b*, *lo popular* and the *pueblo* all connote "a 'we' that is a carrier of demands for substantive justice that form the basis for the obligations of the state toward the less favored segments [and majority] of the population."[6] One sees this phenomenon in the *sha'b*'s persistence in building collective institutions to further their interests. More specifically, women among the lower and middle classes participate in the labor force, informal networks, the informal economy and familial enterprises. (Abdel-Fadil defines the informal economy as "economic activities which largely escape recognition, enumeration and regulation by the government.")[7] These arenas are not merely private in nature and unconcerned with the distribution of public resources. Rather they are embedded in networks of association that tie them to, or implicate them in, the formal, official domains of government and public life. In short, women's activities shape the character of communal experience at both the local level and in the larger sphere of the Egyptian polity and economy.

Formal and Informal Networks

In Egypt, it is illegal to hold a meeting with a group that is not registered by the Ministry of Information. Every mechanism used to further collective interests, such as unions, political parties, newspapers, voluntary associations, interest groups, demonstrations, books, radio, and television are controlled and regulated by the state.[8] While Egyptian politicians have clearly tried to exclude people from political activity and narrow the venues of political participation, it is less clear why political scientists typically accept elitist portrayals of national politics. Political scientists must agree upon definitions of politics and participation that capture the political preferences and activities of a wide range of constituencies-including women and men from the lower classes.[9] Otherwise, these groups' oppression will be compounded by their depoliticization and dismissal by academia's reigning typologies of political activities. Scholars must be more sensitive to the interests and experiences of communities living under authoritarian rule. Narrowly-based regimes' success at controlling political participation should not blind scholars to the strength of people's ability to adapt, resist, and even prevail. If opposition to a regime is too risky and is not publicly articulated, it does not mean that political activity has disappeared, or that the people are apathetic or apolitical.[10] Rather, scholars are challenged to look harder, and certainly to look outside of conventional political venues. While the state, the dominant party, or the elite may try to deny subordinate groups a voice or freedom of association, they are not always successful. The constant negotiation over power, resources, and authority which lies at the crux of politics, deserves far more attention from scholars.

Political science suffers from a classic case of methodological bias: where one looks determines what one finds. For example, when one suffers from this type of myopia, one assumes that if women are rarely visible in the upper echelon of the state bureaucracy, the military, or among the elites, then they must not be engaged in politics. However, if one investigates politics at the level of the household and community, women are obviously engaged in decision-making processes, distributional activities, and in informal institutions. In the same vein, lower-class men are also intricately involved in informal institutions and decision-making processes within their community. At the level of the household it becomes possible to integrate both men and women into analyses of Egyptian politics.

Although women are represented in high politics in Egypt, (though as Sullivan points out, this pattern is no different than similar ratios in many Western democracies as well) it must be remembered that even though men participate at the elite level, their influence and power is carefully moderated by the regime's methods of control and co-optation.[11] Explicit political activity is dangerous for both men and women. In Egypt, the government, through legal and illegal means, curtails political opposition, freedom of association, and freedom of expression. People are routinely arrested or harassed for their views and activities. Haniff suggests that when Western feminists and social scientists highlight the repression and subjugation of women in the Third World, they should remember that most men in Third World nations also are excluded from conventional spheres of political life.[12] This caveat does not legitimize the exclusion of women, but places this issue in a larger structural context, where political exclusion is systematically perpetuated by those who rule.

Yet formal and informal networks permeate daily life and are critical (though ambiguous and concealed) arenas of Egyptian politics. Though informal networks lack formal, juridical recognition, they receive the sanction of the community and are therefore legitimate. For their constituents, "communal sanction is as definitive for informal associations as legal recognition is for formal ones."[13] The norms and values of the community are reflected in what I have called the *familial ethos*. The *sha'b* share a common world view of the rights and responsibilities of individuals within the household and of the proper boundaries of family authority, morality, and power within the larger community. People constantly articulate and defend the importance of family within the community and within the nation. Ideal notions of family relations and authority pepper conversation in homes, on the streets, and at work.[14] Families seek to maintain the integrity of the household unit despite personal differences or external threats. The accepted wisdom of the community, articulated in the familial ethos, enhances this objective. In times of crisis, when the integrity of the household or the family is threatened, members of the extended family, trusted neighbors, or colleagues are asked to arbitrate disputes. They work to preserve the family, while accommodating individual feelings and interests. Although conflicts within families are very common, the accepted protocols of the familial ethos are used to resolve them. Women are more involved than men in shaping and enforcing these ideological norms of the community.

The familial ethos, however, does far more than form the groundwork for conflict resolution. People's values, their opinions, interests, and goals resonate throughout the community, the economy, and the nation. Interests that are important to maintaining the family are pursued within the larger community. People judge local bureaucrats and politicians by the principles of the familial ethos.

Egyptians who support the familial ethos or organize informal networks and familial institutions are clearly engaging in "adaptation through opposition,"

> 'Adaptation through opposition' is a way of maintaining the collective identity of a nation. . . Its main features . . . consist [of] preserving, elaborating and cherishing values, attitudes and opinions contradictory to or different from those officially imposed and practiced; tacitly rejecting the imposed system and/or its important constituent aspects and institutions; at the same time adapting to the exigencies of life under. . . [the status quo]. . . ; supporting existing state institutions on the behavioral level; at the same time taking advantage of them and displacing their goals by trying to achieve private goals at the expense of official ones; cheating and trying to outwit distrusted authorities.[15]

As Migdal argues, the struggle over setting the rules of the game is one of the foremost sources of political tension in Egypt, as it is in any polity.[16] Within *sha'bi* communities, the principles of the familial ethos order and regulate behavior, opinions, and actions. Because the *sha'b* not only retain and promote their rules of the game, but also control the resources and institutions that support their rules, they constitute a political force in Egypt.

At the same time, this does not mean that the familial ethos, informal networks, and state policies operate in separate realms. Informal networks are intertwined with public institutions. State policies, distribution networks, and bureaucratic regulations affect the daily lives of most Egyptians, and they strive to understand and manipulate these policies. Networks have proliferated at all levels of the bureaucracy; these networks begin in the household and community, and women routinely participate in them. The complexity of these relationships suggests that the distinction between "private affairs" and "public life" needs to be rethought. Political scientists, Egyptian analysts, and opposition groups concentrate their attention on Parliament, elite decision-makers, bureaucrats, the military, or interest groups, yet these formal realms of politics, which the regime strives to control, are manipulated and at times, subverted by informal politics.

Rassam argues:

> Ethnographic studies of Middle Eastern societies usually acknowledge the existence of two separate and sharply differentiated social worlds. Implicit in this dichotomy of public/male, private/female is the assumption that power, viewed as belonging to the public-political domain, is a male monopoly and that women, confined to the domestic sphere, are power-less. . . . To begin a study on Arab women by accepting the public/private assumption as a basic premise is . . . to run the risk of distorting the facts.[17]

Rassam also suggests that "the family/household is not merely 'women's territory': in the Middle East it is the basic socioeconomic unit and the area where the public/private dichotomy breaks down."[18] The household is not the only arena in which the public/private dichotomy breaks down, however. Informal networks implode this dichotomy up the entire hierarchy of Egyptian political structures. Because women are deeply involved in designing and maintaining these networks, their political participation and power is significant.

Notwithstanding this insight, informal networks do not have the authority (many of the activities are illegal) or resources that are available to elected officials, administrators, party leaders, or military officers. Elite politics in Egypt are not insignificant; the power of the state is clearly extraordinary. Nonetheless, elite politics do not exhaust the political field. Although they are not *visible* decision makers, the *sha'b* pursue their interests through informal networks and influence the creation and distribution of public goods, and shape prevailing ideological norms. Thus, they intentionally and unintentionally influence the success of various government policies. It is politics from below as well as policies from above which shape political struggles in Egypt. As the present government of Hosni Mubarak continues on a cautious path of political and economic liberalization and more political space is opened up for the participation of a wider array of interests, the *sha'b,* already organized along informal lines, will be in a strong position to exploit those opportunities. The growing participation of women in the labor force and the growth of an informal economy described below suggest that men and women may be in a better financial position to support their political interests.

Women and the Politics of Informal Networks

One afternoon, an elderly woman, Umm Tahir, dressed in the traditional black of a widow, entered the local branch of a women's association with her four-year-old grandson. Umm Tahir had assumed responsibility for her grandson after the untimely death of her daughter-in-law, while her son provided financial and paternal support.[19] That day, she visited the local daycare center's administrator in order to pay her grandson's entrance fees. The young *muhaggaba* (veiled) daughter of the administrator was sitting in the office, and Umm Tahir complimented her on her manners and beauty.[20] She asked the young woman if she was a girl or a woman, *bint wala sitt?*[21] The woman responded: "I have two children and am married." Umm Tahir's disappointment was evident, but before she said anything, the young woman quickly responded, "but I have a younger sister who is still at home." "Is she as beautiful and well-mannered as you?" "Of course," was the reply.

Both women immediately understood that the subject of their conversation was marriage, and that Umm Tahir was seeking a match for a particular young man, most likely a relative. She continued: "I want to become related to you (*'anaasib-ik*) because the entire area loves your mother." This candid public comment was more than a compliment: it was a testament to the political power and standing of the administrator's family in the neighborhood. Becoming related to such a woman would offer Umm Tahir's family greater access to the power this woman and her family commanded. Ultimately, the source of the administrator's power was the web of networks that she had slowly cultivated in the neighborhood. The marriage of Umm Tahir's son to a well-connected family would connect his family to that network, or at least to parts of it.

The administrator's networks influenced the local distribution of education, housing, charity, subsidized food, credit, and community child care services. Her networks also organized the exchange and distribution of information and assistance, at times providing material and political support for individuals and groups. In order to enhance her networks' utility, she deliberately involved a variety of members of the local community. She drew on every group, from unemployed single mothers to local bureaucrats, merchants, and skilled workers. When possible, she even included members of Parliament. While the majority of her networks were centered in her immediate neighborhood, they extended to other areas of Cairo where her relatives, colleagues, and friends lived and worked. Many women and men in *shaʿbi* communities rely on a similar system of networks to fulfill their needs and promote their interests.

This woman's networks represent an important avenue of political participation for the *shaʿb*. Networks are the political lifeline of the community, allowing individuals and groups to cooperate with other members of the community to achieve individual and collective goals. Informal networks *aggregate* the interests of the *shaʿb*. They provide a mechanism for individuals and households to influence the allocation and distribution of public and private goods in their community and in their nation. Public goods are "a special type of collective goods provided by governments or by communities through governmental or community expenditure."[22] Throughout Third World nations, communities, as well as governments, produce public goods such as streets, security, schools, and cooperatives. While some of the *shaʿb*'s communally-produced public goods are not distributed to absolutely everyone in the community, many governments also discriminate in the distribution of their public goods and services. For example, while public transportation, public health care, or subsidized commodities are all public goods, the Egyptian government distributes them to the disadvantage of densely populated, low income areas.

Education is a case in point. Universal, public education is an integral part of Egypt's development plan, and has been since the Free Officers' Revolution in 1952. While the percentage of illiterates in Egypt still remains high, the state provides free primary school education, despite the ever-growing number of children.[23] Although most children in *shaʿbi* communities enter school at an early age, some leave because their families cannot afford even the modest expenses for books, uniforms, and meals. Others drop out in order to work, despite the legal obligation to remain in school until age fifteen.[24] Most parents want their children to remain in school, and constantly urge them to study and work hard to pass the national exams that determine their futures. Families value education because they respect knowledge and learned people. They believe that higher education will improve their children's career options, enhance their social status, and perhaps entitle them to higher incomes.

The resources of the public educational system in Egypt cannot keep pace with the demand from a population that values education, however. Although every government since 1952 has attempted to extend the reach of the public education system, the state has not, and perhaps cannot, invest sufficient resources for universally available high quality education. Because teachers represent such a large share of employment in government services, the government has been extremely reluctant to grant salary increases. The salaries of public school teachers have not increased with the rate of inflation or the rising standard of living. The *sha°b*'s answer to a deteriorating public educational system is another example of their use of informal mechanisms to achieve an important objective. In communities throughout Egypt, teachers and other educated members of the community are paid to provide afternoon and evening lessons to augment public instruction. Although private lessons are not a new phenomenon in Egypt, during the past decade they have become extremely common. A consequence of positive and negative trends in Egypt, private lessons have become a parallel educational system for children and adolescents from a wide cross-section of the population (both urban and rural).

Although teachers are technically forbidden from offering private lessons to their students, these lessons have provided a lucrative secondary source of income, as the case of an elementary school vice-principal in a *sha°bi* community demonstrates. The vice-principal earned a monthly salary of £E170, but supplemented this income with £E1,000 per month from private lessons ($119 and $700 based on a 1985 estimate of £E1 = $.70).[25] A teacher at a commercial girls' high school earned £E55 per month, but received another £E60 a month from only one of the groups of students he tutored twice a week.

Remuneration for private lessons increases as one progresses through the educational system. In this community, parents had begun to arrange private lessons for first graders, although these lessons were relatively inexpensive (£E2-£E5 per month). At university, private lessons are almost more important than formal instruction because students often take huge lecture courses where they have almost no opportunity to interact with professors. In one case, a prosperous merchant in the community from an upwardly mobile family paid £E1,500 for private lessons to his nephew's chemistry professor for a one semester course. The professor received another £E4,500 from the other three members of the study group; it should be noted that this was only one of the many groups he tutored. The previous year, the merchant paid another professor £E500 for private lessons.

The phenomenon of private lessons is more remarkable because students in *sha°bi* communities are not the super-achievers of middle and upper class families who will enter the most prestigious universities. They are students from working-class or lower middle-class backgrounds who will most likely fill the lower strata of the government bureaucracy, become merchants, or learn a skilled trade. Even so, their families are prepared to invest a significant proportion of their income on private lessons. For example, a widow spent £E35 per month on private lessons for her two children in secondary school, although she only earned £E80 per month. In families with several school-age children, routine monthly expenditures of £E30-£E50 for private lessons were not uncommon. The investment represents a sacrifice for many people, but an education provides opportunities they value and encourage. However, there are families that cannot provide private lessons for their children, or even pay the incidental costs of an education. Many students complain that their teachers provide hardly any instruction in the classroom, forcing them to pay for private lessons after school. While some private tutors accept reduced fees from poor students, others refuse to begin a lesson without first receiving payment. Other teachers in the public school system refuse to offer private lessons; either they do not believe in the ethics of private tutoring, or they are not attracted by the remuneration.[26]

Although parents willingly invest in private lessons for their children, they also exploit informal networks that incorporate teachers, administrators, and educational bureaucrats. The parents do their best to assure their children's success on the all-important primary and secondary school exams. These exams determine the type of secondary school and university (vocational, commercial, academic-public or private) a student will have the right to enter.

The public educational system in Egypt is clearly over-extended, yet education remains a high priority for a majority of the population. Instead of denying universal education to its population, the present system creates a series of obstacles for the aspiring student. Students face competitive examinations, over-crowded classrooms, frustrated, under-paid teachers and a poorly equipped school system. The *sha'b* rely upon a private parallel educational system and informal networks to claim their fair share of a public good: education.

In *sha'bi* communities, public goods created and organized by informal networks represent an increasingly important vehicle of distribution and redistribution. This is particularly true for lower-income groups. In Cairo, informal systems of distribution replicate some of the basic functions of government. Recently, opposition forces have recognized the importance of offering goods and services to gain supporters. Both legal and illegal religious organizations and political parties offer health care, education, legal assistance, tutoring, housing, and day care. Although people use these services without necessarily supporting the groups, it is easy to understand why the beneficiaries of such services might become active supporters of their benefactors. While opposition groups have small resources in comparison to the state or the National Democratic Party (the government party), charity and outreach programs have become very popular and appreciated in communities with unmet needs.

Scholars who study revolutions argue that one of the most efficient methods for guerrillas or political activists to gain popular support and the strength to mount direct armed resistance to the state, is through the provision of collective goods such as public education, health services or public security.[27] Once these services are provided to local populations, revolutionary organizations gain greater support and a larger resource base which they can rely upon once they are strong enough to embark on more direct, confrontational opposition to the state or economic elites. Whether or not opposition movements are successful in exploiting the provision of goods and services to further their aims, the *sha'b* spend a great deal of time and resources to ensure that informal networks further their interests.

Networks are a concrete manifestation of extra-systemic political participation and are not controlled by formal political institutions or the political elite. Neither the state nor the elite dominate informal networks, although women and men consciously strive to incorporate local state bureaucrats and political elites into their networks, in order to facilitate access to public goods controlled by the state. Informal networks are effective, efficient, flexible, and encompass a diverse membership. They fill a political need in the community by representing and furthering the interests of the *sha'b*, who have little access to, or influence over the formal political system.

Women and the Political Economy of the *Sha'b*

In a critique of conventional economics, Peattie and Rein argue that "the primary pattern of distribution is to be understood not as following invariant laws, but as following particular institutional processes. We see the primary pattern as the outcome of a social process of claims in which institutions have historically accommodated to internal and external pressures."[28] In *sha'bi* communities, the family is the most important institution: it meets social, political, and affective needs, and provides employment and wealth for family members. The family, its concerns, and interests lie at the center of the political economy of the *shaʿb*. Many businesses in the community I studied still remain within family hands and both men and women are employed by these enterprises.

Familial enterprises, like enterprises in the public sector, are organized to meet market and non-market objectives. The government depends on the public sector to meet its commitments to employ educated Egyptians, particularly the young, to control certain strategic sectors of the economy, and to fulfill the regime's plans for economic growth and development. Family enterprises are similarly designed to provide employment for family members, to increase and maintain control over the family's financial resources and to enhance the economic and political prestige and power of a family in its community. Market pressures and rapid economic changes are cushioned if the *shaʿb* can rely on family enterprises.

In the community under study, family enterprises accounted for 19 percent of the primary sources of income of the economically active sample and 14 percent of secondary incomes.[29] Within private sector employment (private enterprises, family enterprises, and self-employment), family enterprises accounted for 45 percent of all primary economic activity and 32 percent of all secondary activity.[30] These stores, workshops, factories, and restaurants provided employment and profit for members of the community who might not work in the formal economy (although some family enterprises are part of the formal economy). Women, were owners, partners, and workers in family enterprises such as clothing factories, bakeries, trading establishments, video shops, machine shops, and fast food stands.

Participant-observation and research in households and workplaces revealed many economic activities of women (and men) that are not typically captured by labor force statistics. According to the 1986 Population Census, female participation in overall urban employment is only 16 percent and rural employment is 4 percent.[31] The World Fertility Survey reports that 75 percent of "ever-married women" between the ages of fifteen and forty-nine had never worked.[32] In my own study, there were far greater numbers of working women. Fifty-six percent of the women among the economically active were engaged in a primary economic activity, twenty-seven percent were engaged in a secondary economic activity and *seventy-one* percent of the women in the sample earned income (in cash or kind) from either a primary, secondary, or tertiary economic activity.[33]

The much higher rates of participation can be explained by my familiarity with the economic activities of women in the community, repeated visits to many of their households, and knowledge of their financial affairs. Many of the women who were seamstresses, leaders of savings associations, or involved in the black market would not describe their activity as an occupation/profession (*mihna*), job (*waẓifa*), or as work (*shughl*) to an unknown government official, such as a census enumerator. To administer the Egyptian Fertility Survey, census enumerators were instructed to ask women whether they sold things, held jobs, worked on a family farm, or were self-employed.[34] From my experience in Cairo, many women (and perhaps men)[35] who were economically active would respond negatively to these questions, despite the fact that their activities fell under the definition of work.[36] Some people do not trust any government official and would not reveal information that could possibly be used against them. Others, particularly women in the presence of their husbands or male relatives, might be embarrassed by their contribution to the family's income, because it is customarily and legally the responsibility of the male head of the household. In other cases, both men and women might not reveal their financial resources to an outsider as a strategy to maintain the secrecy of their financial resources from other family members. However, the higher percentage of economically active women and men in this sample is most likely not a reflection of an unrepresentative or particularly industrious sample, but of a methodology that accurately counted primary, secondary, and tertiary economic activities.

Although household labor is not considered part of the economy by any prevailing classification schemes, in Egypt, due to the constant effort needed to purchase subsidized food at very crowded cooperatives and to cook, clean and care for household members, the duties of a housewife are critical to the economic viability of a household. Although the household cannot technically be labeled a family enterprise, women produce many goods and services within the household that otherwise would have to be purchased at market value. Although these activities exist outside of the production boundary that is generally used to define work, these contributions allow other family members to work for cash in one, two, or even three jobs.[37]

Because of the unpaid domestic labor of women, men are able to work as paid labor. However, the double burden of housework and paid employment places great pressures on women, and several recent studies of female employment in Egypt have noted that a number of women are choosing to quit their jobs (or not pursue employment) because government salaries are not lucrative enough to outweigh the pressures of work outside and inside the home.[38] Approximately twenty-seven women in the economically active sample suffered from this double burden while they juggled their duties as housewives and employees.

One of the financial barriers to greater participation in the economy for women everywhere has been the lack of affordable and accessible credit. In Egypt, however, an informal savings and credit system rivals the resources of institutionalized banking. In these associations, a small group of friends, relatives, neighbors, or colleagues contribute a fixed sum at regular intervals (daily, weekly, and most commonly, monthly). The association leader collects the money and immediately gives the total sum to one participant. The payment schedule is negotiated ahead of time by the members, and is organized according to their needs. In a financial emergency or when a business opportunity suddenly arises, a friend or relative will organize an association and arrange to give the person in need the first lump sum payment. There is no fee or interest charged to any participant.

Women are the unrecognized bankers of Egypt, particularly within *sha'bi* communities. Typically, the leaders of informal savings associations, or *gama'iyya,* are trusted women in the community, unless the association is based on male occupational networks, such as gold merchants or machinists concentrated in industrial alleyways. Women are so involved because they spend far more time than men encouraging and organizing networks and keeping track of the reputations and creditworthiness of their relatives and neighbors. Some women sponsor several associations simultaneously. Several of these women are teachers, clerks, or storekeepers; others do not "work" but have well-established reputations in the community for knowing everyone and seeing everything outside their windows. For example, one of these women usually sat near her window, and greeted most passersby. She was a well-known leader of many savings associations and proudly claimed that she was responsible for all the new marriages in the neighborhood. Because she ran several associations, she had access to cash and gave short-term loans to those in need.

If members have moved across Cairo, many women will travel across the city to maintain their savings associations. Very shrewd women contribute a fraction of one membership to several savings associations in order to enhance their credit line. Many Egyptians have an impressive capacity to save money, yet their pervasive savings ethic has gone unheralded by scholars and government officials because it is accomplished through informal savings associations.

Many of these savings associations are established to finance one of the most expensive and common Egyptian institutions: marriage. Before we understand the political behavior and preferences of a constituency we must first investigate its basic economic and social fault lines. Reproducing the family is one of the *sha'b*'s most basic struggles. While this goal might not seem to be political, to most Egyptians, the effort to marry off the younger generation is the largest economic struggle in their lifetimes. While marriage does not compete with screaming headlines on new economic projects, Palestinian autonomy, regional political alliances or "high politics" it is one of the most important issues around which "low politics" is centered. Reproducing the family is, to some extent, the key to understanding many other issues and the ways in which people react to domestic and international policy changes. If one ignores the struggle to reproduce the family, it becomes difficult to understand why gender and sexual relations are so sensitive in Egypt, why housing costs are so high, why migration is so critical to younger Egyptians, and why people riot over increases in the cost of living. A bread riot is not only a protest over prices or a government, but against a threat to the reproduction of the family. Raising the price of bread affects the speed at which people can save money toward the cost of marriage. Marriage is a deeply held normative preference in Egypt, as equality or individual rights might be in other societies, and it allows young people to engage in affective and sexual relations after a closely supervised adolescence. Through marriage, one generation transfers its assets to another and a couple gains some autonomy by creating a new household. In Joseph Gusfield's terminology, marriage is a "deep structure" that influences and is influenced by many different facets of Egyptian life.[39]

A typical *sha'bi* marriage can cost approximately £E15,000 ($10,500 in 1985 prices). In recent years, the cost has kept up with the pace of inflation. This sum includes the costs of a completely furnished apartment (down to the curtains, spices in the kitchen and appliances), a trousseau for the bride, new clothes for the groom, a dowry, jewelry, and the engagement and marriage celebrations. Each of the financial requisites of marriage are paid by either the bride, the groom, or their families, in a well-known system of shared responsibility. The groom and his family contribute approximately two-thirds of the expenses and the bride and her family a third.

Due to the expense of marriage, people utilize informal savings associations or *gam'iyyaa* to facilitate the accumulation of cash.[40] While these associations serve this particular need very well, people use them to finance other major expenses such as labor migration abroad, building a new house or a second story, buying a taxicab or expanding a small business. Considerable amounts of money are invested in these associations. The following table contains estimates of the resources circulating in *gam'iyyaat*. Because people throughout Egypt use them to save for marriage expenses, three different estimates are used to arrive at a national total of the funds circulating in informal savings associations.[41] These estimates are very conservative, because *gam'iyyaat* are also used for other needs and the cost of marriage within *sha'bi* communities is far less expensive than among the middle and upper classes (in these circles, housing costs, dowries, appliances, furniture, and jewelry would be far more expensive). The first estimate (A) uses the figure of £E15,000, which was the average total cost of a marriage within the *sha'bi* community under study. The second figure (B), £E7,500, is half of the previous estimate and recognizes that a significant portion of marriage expenses may not be saved through *gam'iyyaat*. The third figure (C) of £E4,000 purposefully reduces the average cost of marriage, to account for many rural or poor urban families in Egypt who do not spend as much on marriage as the *sha'b*. Even if the assets of *gam'iyyaat* approach the lowest estimate (C), these savings still represent 35 percent of gross domestic savings.

Gam'iyyaat offer credit to individuals who do not typically have the collateral to qualify for bank loans. Although Egyptians from all segments of society participate in these associations, the *sha'b*, who live with financial insecurity, are particularly drawn to *gam'iyyaat* because they are a source of interest-free loans. Many of these people also cannot fulfill a bank's requirement for collateral or a long-standing institutional credit record. These associations are also popular because they embody the principles of Islamic law (which forbids the collection of interest) and because they support the financial needs of the community.

The pervasiveness and efficacy of *gam'iyyat* suggest that some institutions are able to remain autonomous from government regulation and control, yet meet critical needs for communities. These savings associations represent a public good which benefits individuals and their com-

TABLE 1:
THREE ESTIMATES OF THE ASSETS OF *GAM'IYYAAT*
THROUGHOUT EGYPT

Year: 1986	Estimate A: £E15,000	Estimate B: £E7,500	Estimate C: £E4,000
Total Sum	£E6.9 billion	£E3.4 billion	£E1.8 billion
% Gross Domestic Savings (£E5.3 billion in 1986)	131 percent	65 percent	35 percent
% Gross National Savings (£E3.8 billion in 1986)	164 percent	91 percent	48 percent
% Gross Domestic Product (£E38.36 billion in 1986)	18 percent	9 percent	4.8 percent

munities, without costs. The foundation of a *gama'iyya* is explicit trust and cooperation. The familial ethos encourages these characteristics among *gama'iyya* members; in addition to its other effects, the familial ethos has a positive impact on the economic dynamism of *sha'bi* communities. Women in particular perform a vital and under-appreciated role in building and maintaining a system of credit that facilitates the physical reproduction of society and investment in the community.[42]

The goal of reproducing the family has a very privileged position among the *sha'b*. It is a priority, not only in a Darwinian sense, but because one generation transfers its material assets to the next through marriage, and as children reach adolescence (and even before) each family must commit its financial resources to marriage.[43] It is not surprising, therefore, that women lead so many savings associations and use their networks to find affordable housing, job opportunities, decent education, or inexpensive furnishings for their relatives of marriageable age. But what this also means is that the burden of saving money and of shrewd financial planning rests as much on women's shoulders as it does on men's.

While many women are very resourceful at saving money, in order to meet the weekly or monthly requirements of the *gam'iyya*, it means that they must keep their daily cash expenditures to an absolute minimum. They spend long hours on line to purchase subsidized food, or travel to other neighborhoods in search of cheaper goods. Some of these households do not eat very well because they are saving money. Marriages demand a high savings rate for a number of years, and sometimes decades, and thus rapid changes in the economy, the loss of migration opportunities or reductions in government subsidies of goods and services wreak havoc in household budgets and long-held financial plans. When governments enact unpopular economic policies or when recessions hit, it is not only men who suffer. Women join in mass demonstrations, lose their jobs, delay their marriages or drop out of school. The latest government price changes or policies of distributing subsidized food are frequent topics of conversations and most women can recite the prices of important food items over decades. Some might even argue that women are more aware than men of subtle economic changes, due to their constant struggle to feed their families and save money for marriage and other expenses.

Egyptian women are rarely naive about the importance of economic resources and are not easily exploited. The control of economic resources and assets is the focus of many arguments in these communities and it is not uncommon for women to fight for their fair share of resources, whether that means taking on their mothers, husbands, brothers, fathers or uncles. They do not always win their arguments, but few easily give up their legal or customary rights to property and assets.

As they become more active in the economy, women also become more vulnerable to its temper. Women therefore, become attuned to debates over economic and political policies. Most female high school and college graduates are sensitive to the government's policies of public sector employment, and most women who sell newspapers on the street are aware of the regulations for street vendors. Female bakers and store owners keep abreast of the price of subsidized goods and official pricing policies and female black marketeers are intimately and shrewdly aware of the government's food cooperative system and the police. Every woman of marriageable age understands that war or inter-Arab tensions affects migration opportunities. As women gain greater economic resources they will be more sensitive to, and critical of government policies that affect the economy and their lives.

The growing contribution of women to the economic life of the community solves certain problems and complicates others. It would be too simplistic to argue that because women work, they are more independent, autonomous or empowered. More data is necessary. It can be argued, however, that the role of women in the political economy of urban Egypt has been underreported and underestimated and deserves far more serious, systematic analysis.

The *sha'bi* women in popular quarters of Cairo are intricately engaged in forging, designing, establishing, and maintaining informal networks. These collective institutions pervade all aspects of community life and provide them with political capital. Individuals utilize networks to accomplish daily tasks, to build political alliances with powerful members of the community, and to organize and strengthen communal norms. Because the community directs and controls these networks they are sensitive and responsive both to their changing needs and policy changes by the government. Networks are political because they organize individual consumers and households into a more powerful, collective body. They break down some of the barriers between private and public domains, despite the visible appearance of gender segregation in some public places. In addition, informal networks increase the community's access to and influence over the distribution and allocation of public goods. As argued earlier, informal networks facilitate the creation of public goods and collective institutions within the community.

As members of *sha'bi* communities repeat over and over, one must master the formal *and* the informal faces of any problem. Certainly, some problems are best resolved through formal means; others are best left to informal brokers. The woman who knows whom to approach possesses critically important skills that are respected and valued by the community. These skills infuse the community with energy and creativity. This vitality, which is overlooked if one concentrates primarily on formal political organizations and state-centered political action, suggests that women are indeed politically active in their communities and, through geographically disparate networks, larger areas within Cairo. Not every association between three or more people need be an indication of political activity, but if extensive networks coordinate masses of people to achieve particular goals, they clearly serve as a political institution for this particular constituency.

The growing economic activity of *sha'bi* women—in both the formal and informal economy—adds another dimension to their involvement with informal networks. As their economic assets and skills increase, they can widen their networks and use them to pursue riskier objectives. Again, it is too simplistic to argue that greater economic power will result in enhanced political power, but economic resources *can* support collective activities. In the 1990s, when the Egyptian government continues on a cautious path of economic and political liberalization, the organization of networks, the experience of maintaining them, and the capability of financing community objectives, suggests that women (and men) will be in a stronger position to exploit any "political space" that becomes available. At the same time, regardless of state policies, the organization and maintenance of informal networks can continue to protect the individual and collective interests of the *sha'b*.

REFERENCES

1. This study is indebted to the rich tradition and scholarship of anthropological studies on women, family, and communities in urban Egypt. For more recent anthropological, historical, and sociological studies of women in Egypt see Homa Hoodfar, "Survival Strategies in Low Income Households in Cairo," *Journal of South Asian and Middle Eastern Studies* 13 (Summer 1990): 22–41; and her "Household Budgeting and Financial Management in a Lower-income Cairo Neighborhood," in Daisy Dwyer and Judith Bruce, eds., *A Home Divided: Women and Income in the Third World* (Stanford: Stanford University Press, 1988); Leila Abu-Lughod, *Veiled Sentiments: Honor and Poetry in a Bedouin Society* (Berkeley: University of California Press, 1986); Judith E. Tucker, *Women in Nineteenth-Century Egypt* (Cambridge: Cambridge University Press, 1985); Kathryn Kamphoefner, "Voices from the Bottom: Women of Cairo View Literacy," Ph.D. diss., Northwestern University, 1991; Evelyn A. Early, *Baladi Women of Cairo: Playing with an Egg and a Stone* (Boulder, CO: Lynne Rienner Publishers, 1993); Helen Watson, *Women in the City of the Dead* (Trenton, NJ: Africa World Press, 1992); and Mona Abaza, "Feminist Debates and 'Traditional Feminism' of the Fellaha in Rural Egypt," Working Paper No. 93, Sociology of Development Research Centre, University of Bielefeld, 1987; Judith E. Tucker, ed. *Arab Women: Old Boundaries, New Frontiers* (Bloomington: Indiana University Press, 1993). On the political life of women and the role of gender in Egyptian politics see Arlene Macleod, *Accommodating Protest: Working Women, the New Veiling, and Change in Cairo* (New York: Columbia University Press, 1991); Cynthia Nelson, "Public and Private Politics: Women in the Middle Eastern World," *American Ethnologist* 1 (1974): 555–564; Ann Mosely Lesch and Earl L. Sullivan, "Women in Egypt: New Roles and Realities," *UFSI Reports*, No. 22, 1986; Mervat Hatem, "The Enduring Alliance of Nationalism and Patriarchy in Muslim Personal Status Laws: The Case of Modern Egypt," *Feminist Studies* (Spring 1986): 19–43; and her "Egypt's Middle Class in Crisis: The Sexual Division of Labor," *Middle East Journal* 43 (Summer 1988): 407–22. Several studies of elite women and women's organizations have recently been published and add important new details and analysis of their role in Egyptian politics. See Earl L. Sullivan, *Women in Egyptian Political Life* (Syracuse: Syracuse University Press, 1986); Huda Shaarawi, *Harem Years: The Memoirs of an Egyptian Feminist*, ed., trans. Margot Badran, (New York: The Feminist Press, 1987); Kathleen Howard-Merriam, "Egypt's Other Political Elite," *Western Political Quarterly* 34 (March

1981): 174–187; and Cynthia Nelson, "Biography and Women's History: On Interpreting Doria Shafik," in Nikki R. Keddie and Beth Baron eds., *Women in Middle Eastern History: Shifting Boundaries in Sex and Gender* (New Haven: Yale University Press, 1991).

2. This study is indebted to the rich tradition and scholarship of anthropological studies on women, family, and communities in urban Egypt. My questions and the initial direction of this study emerged out of the important work of Nawal al-Messiri Nadim, "Family Relationships in a 'Harah' in Cairo," in Nicholas S. Hopkins and Saad Eddin Ibrahim, eds., *Arab Society: Social Science Perspectives* (Cairo: American University in Cairo Press, 1985): 212–222; Sawsan al-Messiri, "The Changing Role of the Futuwa in the Social Structure of Cairo," in Ernest Gellner and John Waterbury, eds., *Patrons and Clients in the Mediterranean Societies* (London: Duckworth Press, 1977) and her *Ibn al-Balad: A Concept of Egyptian Identity* (London: E.J. Brill, 1978); Unni Wikan, *Life Among the Poor in Cairo*, trans. Ann Henning (London: Tavistock Publications, 1980) and her "Living Conditions Among Cairo's Poor—A View from Below," *Middle East Journal* 39 (Winter 1985): 7–26; Andrea Rugh, *The Family in Contemporary Egypt* (Syracuse: Syracuse University Press, 1983); and Nayra Atiya, *Khul-Khaal: Five Egyptian Women Tell Their Stories* (Syracuse University Press, 1982).

3. This community remains anonymous in order to protect the confidences of people who so graciously shared their ideas and stories with me. The study was not geographically-focused and I did not systematically study the spatial organization, residents or workers of a particular community. Rather, the associations and networks of early informants defined the boundaries of my "sample." I visited homes or workplaces in twenty-three different neighborhoods, and concentrated largely in ten contiguous neighborhoods. I found that geography had little influence in respondents' answers about the political participation of the *sha'b*. Rather, those neighborhoods that shared a similar socioeconomic profile used the same strategies and institutions to pursue their objectives. If I had used a more middle-class, slightly suburban area in the study (such as Dokki or Muhandissin) one could expect greater internal variation by geography. For further information on the methodology of this study see Diane Singerman, *Avenues of Participation: Family, Politics, and Networks in Urban Quarters of Cairo*, (Princeton: Princeton University Press, 1995).

4. S. al-Messiri, *Ibn al-Balad*.

5. Because the research was conducted during a single year, 1985–1986, it suffers from a lack of historical context. Throughout the paper, when I argue general points, I hope the reader will bear in mind that this is a study of a specific community and although it is representative of many others, I am usually referring to characteristics of a single community during the mid-1980s. See Janet Abu Lughod's classic comprehensive work on the historical, administrative, and socioeconomic evolution of Cairo for further details. Janet L. Abu-Lughod, *Cairo: 1001 Years of the City Victorious* (Princeton: Princeton Univer-

sity Press, 1971). For a demographic analysis of the more recent sprawling
urban growth of Cairo see Frederic Shorter, "Cairo's Leap Forward: People,
Households, and Dwelling Space," *Cairo Papers in Social Science* 12:1 (Spring
1989); and Huda Zurayk and Frederic Shorter, "The Social Composition of
Households in Arab Cities and Settlements: Cairo, Beirut, Amman," *Regional
Papers* (Cairo: The Population Council, 1988)

6. Guillermo O'Donnell, "Tensions in the Bureaucratic-Authoritarian State," in
   David Collier, ed., *The New Authoritarianism in Latin America* (Princeton:
   Princeton University Press, 1979), 289.

7. Mahmoud Abdel-Fadil, "Informal Sector Employment in Egypt," *Series on
   Employment Opportunities and Equity in Egypt*, no. 1 (Geneva: International
   Labour Office, 1980), 15. More recent scholarship has argued that the informal
   economy is not only a "specific form of relations of production," but may refer
   to the status of labor, the conditions of work, and the form of management of
   some firms. Manuel Castells and Alejandro Portes, "World Underneath: The
   Origins, Dynamics, and Effects of the Informal Economy," in Alejandro
   Portes, Manuel Castells, and Lauren A. Benton, eds., *The Informal Economy:
   Studies in Advanced and Less Developed Countries*, (Baltimore: The Johns
   Hopkins University Press, 1989), 12–13.

8. The record of "politics without participation" in Egypt has been documented
   and analyzed extensively and will not be reiterated here. See John Waterbury,
   The Egypt of Nasser and Sadat: The Political Economy of Two Regimes
   (Princeton: Princeton University Press, 1983): 307–390. One of the most
   recent examples of these policies was the government's decision to dissolve the
   Arab Women's Solidarity Committee (AWSA) in Egypt and to hand over its
   property to the Society of Women in Islam. The 1964 Law of Associations,
   which regulates all private voluntary organizations in Egypt, forbids associations from discussing anything related to politics or religion, and it was on the
   basis of this law that the government justified its action. It accused the AWSA
   of convening a conference on women's journalism and differing publicly with
   the government's official position on the Iraqi invasion of Kuwait. The second
   offense was their decision to publish a magazine and bulletin without the
   permission of the Egyptian Higher Press Council. "Update: Dissolution of the
   Arab Women's Solidarity Association," *Middle East Watch* 3 (December
   1991).

9. Leftwich's notion of politics is rather broad but allows one to recognize the
   politics of the powerful as well as those in subordinate positions. "Politics
   consists of all the activities of cooperation and conflict, within and between
   societies, whereby the human species goes about obtaining, using, producing
   and distributing resources in the course of the production and reproduction of
   its social and biological life. . ." Adrian Leftwich, *Redefining Politics: People,
   Resources and Power* (London: Methuen, 1983), 11.

10. The invisibility of women from the study of politics is not at all limited to the
    Middle East. Liberal notions of the public and private have long excluded most
    women, lower class men and minorities from the political realm (outside of the

few elite women who made it into the system through wealth, marriage or sheer determination). Carole Pateman has argued persuasively that political scientists who claimed to be studying participation were usually only capturing the activities of white males with high socioeconomic status. She argued that liberal democracies rested upon the non-participation of their citizens and indirectly encouraged a "non-participation syndrome" for those left out of the system. Carole Pateman, "The Civic Culture: A Philosophic Critique," in Gabriel A. Almond and Sidney Verba, eds., *The Civic Culture Revisited*, (Boston: Little, Brown & Co., 1980), 60. For a further critique of elitist notions of politics and participation see Singerman, *Avenues of Participation*.

11. See Sullivan, *Women in Egyptian Political Life*.

12. Nesha Hanniff, "Western Feminism and Colonialism." Paper delivered at the Conference on Gender and Society in the Middle East, The University of Michigan, September 21, 1991.

13. Kathryn S. March and Rachelle L. Taqqu, *Women's Informal Associations in Developing Countries: Catalysts for Change?* (Boulder: Westview Press, 1986), 5.

14. As in any ideal notion, there were many examples of people who upheld the familial ethos in word but not action. The community I studied tolerated a much wider range of behavior than was articulated in the constant discourse on morality, propriety, and family. I found that strict gender and age hierarchies were not prevalent in this community. Women fought with men, and younger women fought older brothers, fathers, and other males.

15. Janina Frentzel-Zagorska, "Civil Society in Poland and Hungary," *Soviet Studies* 42 (1990), 761.

16. See Joel Migdal, "Strong States, Weak States: Power and Accommodation" in Myron Weiner, Samuel Huntington, and Gabriel Almond, eds., *Understanding Political Development: A Analytic Study.* (Boston: Little Brown, 1987), 391–434.

17. Amal Rassam, "Toward a Theoretical Framework for the Study of Women in the Arab World," in "Expert Meeting on Multidisciplinary Research on Women in the Arab World," UNESCO Final Report, Paris, 10 February 1983, 13.

18. Rassam, *A Theoretical Framework*, 14.

19. In the case of a mother's death, it is common for the father's family, rather than the father himself, to assume daily responsibility for the child.

20. The term, *muhaggaba*, refers to a wide assortment of modest dress, which signifies piety and religious observance in Cairo. Most women who wear Islamic dress, or *zayy al-Islami* conceal their hair in a scarf and wear long-sleeved blouses with floor-length skirts. Some women only wear a scarf and modest, but Westernized dress, while others completely veil their face and hands. In popular quarters of Cairo, women have traditionally covered their dress and head with a single piece of black fabric, a *milaaya*, to protect their modesty as well as their clothes from the dusty environment.

21. A girl, *bint*, in local parlance, refers to all unmarried girls and women who are

assumed to be virgins. A woman, *sitt*, refers specifically to married women (non-virgins).

22. John A. Booth and Mitchell A. Seligson, "Images of Political Participation in Latin America," in John A. Booth and Mitchell A. Seligson, eds., *Citizen and State*. vol. 1 of Mitchell A. Seligson and John A. Booth, eds., *Political Participation in Latin America* (New York: Holmes and Meier Publishers, 1978), 6.

23. According to the most recent population census, 49 percent of the total population over 10 years of age is illiterate, 24 percent can read and write, 22 percent have qualifications less than a university degree, and 4 percent have obtained university degrees and above (post-graduate degrees). The discrepancy between the educational qualifications of men and women is largest in figures for Egypt as a whole: 38 percent of men are illiterate in comparison to 62 percent of women (30 percent of men can read and write, 18 percent of women). However, in Cairo the educational gap between men and women narrows: 23 percent of men and 39 percent of women are illiterate; 28 percent of men and 22 percent of women can read and write; 35 percent of men and 31 percent of women have less than university qualifications; and 13 percent of men and 7 percent of women have obtained at least a university degree. CAPMAS, "Preliminary Results of the Population Census of 1986," 52–55.

24. Technically, it is illegal for children under the age of fifteen to work, although common labor practices routinely employ underage children.

25. This figure represents the black market value of the Egyptian pound, which was far closer to its "real" value than the protected official currency rates posted by the government. The official exchange rate for the pound remained at £E1 = $1.20 until 1986. See The Economist Intelligence Unit, "Egypt," *Country Profile Reports* (1986–1987), 8–9 and The Economist Intelligence Unit, "Egypt," *Country Profile Reports* 4 (1988), Appendix.

26. Female teachers with families do not usually have the time or the energy to accept private students. Unless they are a single parent, they are not the primary breadwinner of the family. Male school teachers, on the other hand, cannot support their family from an official salary alone and either offer private lessons or earn money from another occupation.

27. Jeff Goodwin and Theda Skocpol, "Explaining Revolutions in the Contemporary Third World," *Politics and Society* 17 (1989), 493.

28. Lisa Peattie and Martin Rein, *Women's Claims: A Study in Political Economy* (New York: Oxford University Press, 1983), vi.

29. In order to capture the industrious character of this community, I recorded their primary, secondary, and tertiary sources of income. The primary source of income referred to each person's official position of employment (which was registered with various government agencies), or the occupation or income-generating activity in the informal economy which supported them. Secondary sources of income usually referred to part-time jobs and semi-regular employment or income-generating activities. Tertiary sources of income were rarer and included in-kind exchange and skills of the self-employed as well as typical

sorts of jobs. In a further analysis of *informal* sector employment in the *shabʿi* community under study, family enterprises accounted for 48 percent of all primary economic activity and 19 percent of all secondary economic activity.

30. Secondary sources of employment were widespread (47 percent of the sample had a secondary source of income). The rate rose to 63 percent among public sector employees, because of the rising cost of living, inflation, and the declining value of public sector wages.

31. Heba Handoussa, *The Burden of Public Service Employment and Remuneration: A Case Study of Egypt* (Geneva: International Labour Office, September 1988), 49–50, 79.

32. CAPMAS, *Egyptian Fertility Survey 1980.* 4 vols. Cairo: 1983. vol. 2: *Fertility and Family Planning*, 9.

33. Many of the women who were primarily housewives earned additional income through activities such as leading a savings association, sewing, raising poultry, or organizing black market activities (largely in re-distributing food that they had acquired or stolen from government food cooperatives). These activities were not occasional activities, because women devoted significant and consistent amounts of time to them.

34. *Egyptian Fertility Survey*, vol. 1, 92–93.

35. Men in this sample also participated far more extensively in the labor force than national indicators suggest. Eighty-six percent of the men in the economically active population participated in the labor force as a primary economic activity, sixty-one percent as a secondary activity, and ninety-eight percent of the men as either primary or secondary activity.

36. The definition of work used in the World Fertility Survey was: "Occupation apart from ordinary household duties, whether paid in cash or in kind or unpaid, whether own-account or family member or for someone else, whether done at home or away from home." CAPMAS, *Fertility and Family Planning*, vol. 2, 10.

37. Huda Zurayk, "Women's Economic Participation," in *Population Factors in Development Planning in the Middle East*, eds. Frederic C. Shorter and Huda Zurayk (New York: The Population Council, 1985), 43. See also Hoodfar's discussion of the importance of the non-market activities in the calculation of a household's livelihood. Homa Hoodfar, "Survival Strategies in Low Income Households in Cairo, *Journal of South Asian and Middle Eastern Studies* 13 (Summer 1990): 22–41.

38. See in particular, Macleod's discussion of the double bind. *Accommodating Protest*, 90–91.

39. Joseph Gusfield, "Social Movements and Social Change: Perspectives of Linearity and Fluidity," *Research in Social Movements, Conflict and Change*, Volume 4, (JAI Press, 1981), 336.

40. Marital expenses usually take years to accumulate, considering typical lower-level government salaries of £E60–£E100 per month and private sector salaries (of skilled, blue-collar workers and merchants) of £E100–£E250 per month.

41. In order to estimate the sums circulating in savings associations, I used the

marriage rate, averaged for the previous five years, to estimate the number of marriage contracts signed in 1986 based upon preliminary figures of the 1986 Population Census. See CAPMAS, *Statistics on Marriage and Divorce, 1979* (Cairo: 1981), 8 and CAPMAS, "Preliminary Results of the Population, Housing and Establishment Census of 1986," (Cairo: 1987), 2.

42. The significant contribution of women to the labor force and their role in savings and investment represents the bright side of the picture, but many women still remain financially dependent on their male relatives. Even though it is customary for women in *sha'bi* communities to control the household's finances (and their skill in doing so is publicly lauded) many husbands do not give their wives sufficient resources. Others do not reveal their salaries and income to their wives. While insufficient support is one of the criteria a woman can use to divorce a man according to Islamic law, few women in these circumstances either have the resources, knowledge, or the familial support to mount a successful divorce suit; others do not even bother trying because they feel they would be in an even worse situation as divorced women.

43. The financial burden of marriage in Egypt is comparable to the priority of a college education for middle class parents in the United States today, who find themselves planning for the college education of their offspring as soon as they are born.

CHAPTER FOURTEEN

Keeping It in the Family: Gender and Conflict in Moroccan Arabic Proverbs

Elizabeth M. Bergman

Within the proverbial Moroccan family, only the multiple roles and relationships of an adult woman are described in detail. She is wife, mother, and housekeeper in the nuclear family of proverbs; in the extended family, she is at once mother-in-law, daughter-in-law, and sister-in-law. The proverbs that depict a woman's family life are remarkably consistent on one point: all describe her ability to exercise power or control in equivocal terms. Proverbs thus appear to confirm a view of a patriarchal society in which women are powerless. Close scrutiny of the content of these proverbs, however, suggests that women's power relationships within the family are neither absolute nor clear-cut. Further, by virtue of their ambiguities and contradictions, proverbs may provide women a means to negotiate for power within the circumscribed boundaries of home and family.

This article grows out of larger study of Moroccan Arabic proverbs. Early in my fieldwork in Morocco in 1988–89, proverbs about women caught my eye. When I looked closely at these proverbs, I found many of them hard to understand. Even so, these brief texts, in which a woman's family defines her life and her home is synonymous with her world, echoed conversations I was having at the same time with my Moroccan peers, women whose lives could hardly be called "traditional." I began asking about these proverbs, hoping that my lack of understanding was a matter of linguistic or cultural ignorance. But the women I spoke with found the proverbs equally cryptic. Some proverbs were ambiguous: they implied several conflicting views of a situation. In other cases, a proverb whose meaning seemed reasonably clear prompted women to cite one or more proverbs that directly contradicted the first.

And the ambiguities and contradictions of these proverbs invariably led us to talk about our own lives. They evoked comparisons of the conflicting demands our societies made of us, and discussions of the strategies we adapted or invented to cope with them.

I examine here only a few of the many Moroccan Arabic proverbs about women and family. Some of them were discussed in Morocco; others I have encountered since my return to the United States.[1] My approach is essentially that taken by Moroccans in our conversations. I focus on what the proverbs say, or seem to say, and how they may play out in women's lives. In other words, I look at the discursive possibilities proverbs offer rather than at contexts in which they have occured or might occur.

A textual emphasis naturally calls for investigation of the contextual use of these and other Moroccan Arabic proverbs about women and family. Even if the scope of this article allowed for it, however, the study of proverb context poses certain problems. The most obvious is the difficulty of recording proverbs in their natural context.[2] Proverbs, unlike other oral or folkloric genres, do not typically take place in performance or in other well-defined situations. Instead, they play an integral role in the give and take of conversation, a fact which makes it difficult to predict contexts in which proverbs might occur. In addition, because proverbs are often embedded in longer utterances, even identifying the presence of a proverb within a statement can pose a challenge.[3]

Even if we could resolve these difficulties, we would face another problem: the selection of appropriate proverb contexts for citation. It may be helpful to illustrate the meaning of a proverb with a single example, or even with several examples of its use in context, but it is ultimately misleading. The result defines the proverb in terms of that context or set of contexts. Bakhtin describes the paradox of context thus:

> There cannot be a unified (single) contextual meaning. Therefore, there can be neither a first nor a last meaning; it always exists among other meanings as a link in the chain of meaning, which in its totality is the only thing that can be real. In historical life, this chain continues infinitely, and therefore each individual link in it is renewed again and again, as though it were being reborn.[4]

In spite of the social contexts in which they occur, I would suggest, proverbs are linguistic as well as social texts. They consist of and exist within language, that slippery medium that hampers communication as often as it enables it.

The nature of language is nowhere more evident in proverbs than in proverbs about women in the family. Like other proverbs, these take the form of categorical statements, admitting of no ifs, ands or buts. They evaluate behaviors or suggest possible courses of action. Yet proverbs about women and family can be read in more than one way. That is to say, these proverbs speak to and about women with multiple voices. It is in this fashion that proverbs reveal the possibilities for negotiation in women's lives. By offering several points of view of a situation, a proverb provides alternative definitions of that situation and, thus, multiple options for working through it. Proverbs appear to be one of the resources upon which women may draw in the process of what Rosen calls "bargaining for reality."[5]

Proverbs offer women the possibility of negotiating roles and relationships in two principal areas in the family. First, they evaluate in equivocal terms a woman's ability to exert power or influence over persons and resources within the nuclear family, that is, over her children and over the household itself. Second, they present distinctly ambiguous views of her interactions with her female kin by marriage, with the women of her husband's family. The first has attracted a good deal of notice in the literature on Moroccan society and culture. Because the second has received less detailed attention from observers of the Moroccan scene, the nature of women's interactions with each other merits some discussion. Proverbs about a woman's relationships with her in-laws suggest that these relationships, which appear to be characterized by open hostility, are in fact open to negotiation.

Male and Female in the Proverbs

As portrayed in proverbs, many of a woman's roles and relationships are negotiable. Notable exceptions are her interactions with adult men, especially with her husband. Before we turn to proverbs that describe the interactions of spouses, it may be useful to look briefly at the nature of a man's social and familial relationships as depicted in proverbs.

The negotiable interactions of women stand in sharp contrast to those of men. In the family as in the outside world, hierarchical relationships of ruler to ruled, rich to poor, old to young, or skilled to less capable typify proverbial relationships between men. Proverbs of course acknowledge that all men are created equal, but more frequently they point out that all men are not equally endowed with the resources that give some men power over others.[6] In addition, they note that the lowest rung of the social ladder is not occupied by a man:

(1) /lli ghəlbu-h r-rzhal fə-z-zənḵa ta-yzhi l-ʿisha fə-ḍ-ḍaṛ/
'He over whom [other] men triumph in the street comes to Aisha at home.' (I 576)[7]

Even the most miserable, lazy, and apathetic creature, or so this proverb claims, is master over his wife in the home. In comparison with the social hierarchy of men, the mutable, negotiable interactions of women in proverbs are indeed *fitna* (chaos).[8]

It should come as no surprise, then, that a woman's proverbial relationship to the family differs from that of a man. Two very similar proverbs provide one basis for comparison:

(2) /ṛ-ṛazhəl bla wlad bhal ʿud bla ḵəyd/
'The man ['husband'] without children is like a stallion without a halter.' (W 159)

(3) /mṛa bla ṛazhəl ʿəshsh bla bṛaṭəl/
'A woman ['wife'] without a man ['husband'] is [like] a nest without sparrows.' (K 217)

Both of these proverbs use simile to describe a person who lacks an essential family tie.

The use of 'stallion' as a symbol in proverb (2) underlines a man's role in family and society. The horse may carry a heavy symbolic load in Moroccan folklore, but a non-symbolic horse must be guided and controlled to be of any use.[9] Furthermore, the parallel drawn between 'children' and 'halter' recalls that children are one of the responsibilities that harness a man's energies on the road to maturity.[10] It also suggests that a man's love for his children may act as the 'halter' that keeps him in an unsatisfactory marriage.[11]

In contrast, proverb (3) describes women in symbolic terms of definition and dependency: a woman needs a man just as a nest needs birds. The proverb does not refer to her dependency as a practical matter, but rather one of value, identity, and function. The sparrows that, for whatever reason, leave the nest abandon it to the forces of nature; if other birds do not take it over, wind and weather eventually destroy it.[12] According to this notion, a woman depends on a man to ratify and enable her existence. This idea is encountered repeatedly in proverbs that describe the lives of women without men, the lives of spinsters, divorcees, and widows.

The proverbial Moroccan woman, defined through her tie to a man, is obviously in no position to bargain with him. Proverbs portraying the interactions of women and men rarely occur in published sources. Three examples, however, describe spousal relationships in the context of public and private space.

The most important behavior shared by a woman and a man in the context of the public space of proverbs is her concealment. Man and woman both are responsible for concealing her, presumably from other men who seek to "redefine" her, or worse:

(4) /ana lli lḥəft b-izar-i w-zhəbt lə-bla l-ḍar-i/
'I am the one who wrapped up my *izar* [a sheet-like garment traditionally worn by women outside the home] and brought misfortune to my home.'
(K 260)

(5) /lli dda mṛat-u lə-zhmaʿa ta-yṭəllək-ha/
'He who brings his wife to the group divorces her.' (I 496)' [13]

As these proverbs suggest, failure to conceal a woman can only result in disaster. The fault may lie with the woman who dares to venture outside or the man foolish enough to expose her to public view.

Another unusual proverb portrays the interaction between spouses in the context of private space. Notice, however, that it draws the veil of discretion over the actual goings-on:

(6) /ḳəṛṛi wəld-ək fuḳ lə-ḥṣir w-ḳəṛṛi mṛat-ək fuḳ lə-srir/
'Teach your son on the mat, but teach your wife on the bed.' (K 167)

This proverb effectively reduces a woman to the level of a child. Wife and child differ only in the locations of their instruction. A woven mat is a floor covering that doubles as seating and sleeping space in poorer homes. In other words, the child's instruction takes place in the more public area of the home. Situating the wife's education in a specialized piece of furniture, the bed, does not mean that her education is necessarily sexual. It does, however, allude to the intimate physical and emotional bond between wife and husband. As his wife's teacher, the husband bears the responsibility for her education and its outcome as he does for that of their children. His methods of education, at least in proverbs, are as private a matter as the couple's sexual activity.

Moroccan proverbs seldom portray women and men interacting within the family; the rarity of such portrayals says something about the nature of those interactions. It suggests, of course, that cultural resources other than proverbs regulate female-male and especially spousal relationships. Moroccan law, for example, details the rights and responsibilities of women and men in the family. In the law, as in proverb (6) above, women and men do not enter a relationship from positions of equal status or power. A man is bound to support his wife financially and represent her legally; he authorizes her comings and goings and must give his permission if she is to work outside the home.[14] A woman is, then, reliant on and subordinate to her husband, much as a child is to her parents. It seems likely that relations of dominance and dependency would permeate and regulate many aspects of female-male interaction in the family, as the preceding proverbs describe.

At the same time, it should be recalled that the structure of Moroccan society limits female-male interaction even within the home and family. Much of women's unpaid and paid labor takes place in the home, while men work elsewhere, in the field, the shop, or the office.[15] If few proverbs deal with female-male interaction, this may simply reflect economic and social reality. In addition, however, men can and often do choose to spend time outside the home, even when employment does not require it.[16] The following proverb describes the result:

(7) /lə-ʿyalat w-l-ulad fə-ḍ-ḍar wə-r-rzhal fə-lalla-w-mali/ [17]
'The women and children are at home but the men are out on the town.'
(M 48) [18]

In the absence of a man, this proverb suggests, the triumvirate of home, children, and female kin represents the sum of a woman's emotional resources and potential sources of power. Each of these sources, as the following discussion illustrates, is problematic in its own way.

Ruling the Hidden Realm: The Household

The man, as breadwinner, controls the flow of money and goods into the home; he even makes most household purchases.[19] Once goods enter the home, however, it is the woman's job to oversee their distribution and use.[20] A wife is also the legal owner of most of the contents of the home: she owns her clothing and jewelry, of course, but also kitchen utensils and bedding.[21]

Her responsibility for the physical space of the home and its material resources may give a woman at least the illusion of power. Yet it is a strange sort of power:

(8) /mṛa məkfiya malika məkhfiya/
'A woman who has enough is a hidden queen.' (K 224)

Limited to the private space of the household, a woman's sovereignty accords her none of the acclaim that a publicly acknowledged ruler receives. And it is not without its costs. Raw meat and produce do not magically turn into hot meals, nor do rugs and cushions clean themselves. Housework is hard physical labor, and the energy it requires can turn a woman from ruler to ruled. Proverb (9) shows us the flip side of a woman's power over her home:

(9) /mṛa fə-ḍ-ḍaṛ khadəm ma-ʿənd-ha khbaṛ/
'A woman in the home is a servant ['slave'] without knowledge.' (K 231)

Many women would describe housekeeping as a form of servitude, but this proverb gives the old complaint a new twist. Is the woman 'without knowledge' because she believes proverb (8)'s myth of housekeeping as power? Is she just too tired to care? Do her husband and children treat her with all the affection and respect they would give a paid caregiver? Spousal relations, we have seen, are seldom portrayed in detail in proverbs. Relations between mother and child, however, are the subject of a number of proverbs.

The Power of Motherhood?

A woman's children represent the second of her sources of potential power in proverbs. Proverbs apparently take the emotional ties of mother to child for granted, and seldom mention them. They focus instead on the benefits that accrue to a woman with the birth of a child. As we might expect, the sex of the child plays an important role in determining the nature of mother-child relations.

The birth of a male child is eagerly awaited before the fact and celebrated after.[22]

(10) /huwa baḳi fə-r-ṛham w-hiya səddat-l-u s-səlham/
'He is still in the womb, but she has already woven his cloak [lit. 'she warped the loom for him (for) the cloak'].' (M 108, K 203)

The expectant mother of this proverb, hoping for a boy, puts the cart before the horse in dramatic fashion. By warping the loom for her son's cloak, she looks not to the child her fetus will soon be but to the man he will eventually become. She can expect him to be willful as a child and worse as an adolescent. But as the mother of a son, a woman reaches the zenith of her power when the time comes for his marriage. It is her responsibility to select her son's bride and, after the marriage, shape the bride into a suitable wife.[23]

The following proverb suggests several possible reactions to the son's dependency on his mother's choice of his bride:

(11) /z-zin bə-ḥruf-u ddi-h nə-mm-u-h tshuf-u/
'The beauty with its signs, bring it to his mother [so] she can see it.' (W 109)

By proposing that a potential bride be presented to the mother, this proverb acknowledges the mother's role in the selection of the bride. It also expresses a willingness to promote the speaker's own candidate (chosen for looks or disposition rather than, perhaps, practical qualities of family ties, housekeeping ability, or potential fertility). It may also indicate a desire to hurry the selection process along. But does this proverb contain a hint of irony as well? In suggesting that a man's mother inspect the 'beauty', it underlines his inability to do more than hint at his own desires. The most dutiful son might chafe at relying on his mother to make this decision for him. A mother's power over her son may thus contain the seeds of future conflict.[24]

Only after his marriage, however, does the proverbial son voice any resistance to his mother's continuing vigilance:

(12) /ḷḷah yə'ṭi-ni ma bghat-l-i mṛat-i ləhla yə'ṭi-ni ma bghat-l-i mm-i/
'May God give me what my wife imagines [lit. 'wants'] for me, may He not give me what my mother imagines ['wants'] for me.' (I 766)

The rueful wish of this proverb reflects what might be seen as a natural preference. Whether his wife's dreams are ambitious (for her husband's endeavors) or suspicious (about his extra-familial amusements), they are an improvement over his mother's dreams, which fear the worst for her beloved son. This proverb also hints at the nature of the tensions between women in the family, particularly between women who are both united and divided by a man, as will be discussed below.

Whereas the birth of a male child represents a long-term investment for his mother, the birth of a female child promises a quick fix. A woman without a daughter, according to the following proverb, may as well resign from the human race:

(13) /lli ma-ʿənd-ha bənt-ha tədfən ṛaṣ-ha fə-ḥyat-ha/
'She who has no daughters buries herself alive [lit. 'in her lifetime'].' (K
233)

The daughterless woman of this proverb is unlikely to rest peacefully in a conventional tomb: hers is an unquiet grave that lies under heaps of dirty laundry and stacks of unwashed dishes. A mother looks to her daughter for a helping hand with housework and childcare, as well as an ally and confidant. The daughter also benefits from this arrangement. She gets hands-on training in running a home and is able to cement her relationship with the woman she will count on both before and after marriage for support and comfort.[25]

The mutual dependence of mother and daughter can, however, cut both ways:

(14) /l-bənt shrikət m̄m-ha/
'The daughter is her mother's partner ['co-wife'].' (K 187, I 546)

The two printed sources that cite this proverb interpret it very differently. According to Kabbaj and Cherradi, the proverb means: "The daughter is the associate of her mother. (Everything is shared)."[26] Ishmāʿu's comment reads: "It [the proverb] means that the daughter, when she grows up, competes with her mother for clothing, ornaments and the like."[27] These two interpretations have their source in the double meaning of the word /shrika/ in Moroccan Arabic. Kabbaj and Cherradi take it in its general sense, as the feminine form of /shrik/ (Classical Arabic sharīk) 'partner'. The proverb thus refers to the fact that mother and daughter share household responsibilities and to the belief that a daughter resembles her mother in looks and personality.[28] Ishmāʿu's interpretation relies on a more specific meaning of /shrika/ in Moroccan Arabic: it is the kinship term for a wife in a polygamous marriage.[29] Calling a daughter her mother's 'co-wife' evokes the jealousy and suspicion that characterize a polygamous marriage, where women share responsibilities and compete for resources. At the same time, it recalls the closeness that may result from dependence on the same man.

Existing tensions between mother and daughter could only add to the daughter's proverbial eagerness to marry and her parents' willingness to see her do so:

(15) /ḳalət ləʿruṣa lə-mm-ha gaʿ bkaw wə-mshaw/
'The bride said to her mother, "All of you, [just] cry and leave." ' (I 530)

The new bride of this proverb begins her married life by acknowledging her mother's sorrow. She cannot prevent her mother's tears, nor would she want to. They prove that the mother worries about her daughter and will miss her constant presence at home. Even so, the daughter is ready to move on to her new home and new life.

The dilemma that a married woman faces is apparent in the proverbs. She is dependent on her husband, and he is often absent. She thus can only look to her home and her children for confirmation of her worth and for sources of power. Her work in the home demonstrates her talents at managing physical resources. Her children are living proof of her childrearing skills and her ability to influence the lives of others. Their existence also promises her lifelong support and companionship. Yet the proverbs also allude to the stresses of a woman's roles as housekeeper and parent. The home demands enormous amounts of time and energy. Her children, no less demanding, are as likely to be resentful as grateful for their mother's care. Proverbs portray a woman's relation to her children and her immediate surroundings in equivocal terms, but they are no less ambivalent about her interactions with other women.

Conflict and Negotiation in the Extended Family

If the proverbial bond between mother and daughter has built-in tensions, the same is true of other relationships between women in the family. These difficuties are especially prominent in proverbs that describe the relationships between a married woman and the other women

of her husband's family. As the following proverb suggests, marriage
changes much in a woman's life, but not everything:

(16) /l-həmm l-mənḥus khəllit-ha fə-ḍaṛ ḅḅa lkit-ha fə-ḍaṛ lə-ʿruṣ/
'The bad-luck trouble, I left it at my father's house, I found it at the
bridegroom's house.' (K 134)

This proverb can be understood in light of the Moroccan practice of
endogamous marriage. A woman who marries within the group is not
likely to see much change in her material circumstances or in the people
she encounters daily. The 'trouble' she finds in her new home, thus, may
be one that she brings with her. In addition, her marriage creates a new
set of ties to the women of her husband's family, even if she had known
them before her marriage. Proverbs appear to portray these relationships
as mutually and unrelentingly antagonistic. At the same time, the ambiguities contained in these proverbs suggest that power relationships
between women are negotiable, that they are not necessarily structured
by a static family hierarchy.

All interactions between the women of the family, even the most
distantly related, get this equivocal treatment in proverbs.

(17) /n-nuṭa ma-tḥəbb n-nuṭa ghir ʿəwṛa aw məẕluṭa/
'The wife of one brother only loves the wife of another brother [if she is]
one-eyed or flat broke.' (K 231)

The word /nuṭa/ (pl. /nwayəṭ/) is a reciprocal kinship term used by
the wives of brothers to each other.[30] The reciprocity of the term in this
proverb conveys the reciprocal animosity of the two women. It is not
simply that one woman does not care for the other; both women are
incapable of liking each other.

This proverb, although it describes the intensity of the conflict between the wives of brothers, also suggests a possible cessation of hostili-
ties. A woman's financial hardship or physical disability might move
even her most bitter enemy to sympathy, just as it could force the
afflicted woman to evince affection for her rival in order to get help.
The source of conflict is revealed by the same means by which it may
end, by the conjunction of poverty and partial blindness. A woman's
poverty may arise from a number of causes, from her husband's financial
losses, illness or death, or from divorce or abandonment. Similarly, her
blindness may result from an accident of birth, injury, or disease. But

where poverty is unfortunate, it does not have the effect on a woman that blindness does: a one-eyed woman would presumably be unattractive to her husband and handicapped in her work in the home. The linked afflictions that call a halt to the conflict between brothers' wives, thus, suggest that the conflict originates with the brothers themselves.[31] Only when one brother is removed entirely (through death or divorce) or distanced from the scene (by poverty, illness, or alienation from his wife) can their wives reach some kind of understanding.

Conflict among the women of the family is proverbial to such a degree that one proverb even compares two kinds of female conflicts:

(18) /shrayək ta-yḥəbṭu mətʿankin wə-n-nwayəṭ mətfarkin/
'Co-wives are born [lit. 'drop down'] embracing each other but brothers' wives [are born] separated.' (K 219)

Co-wives or brothers' wives, this proverb asks, which make the most bitter enemies? The 'embrace' of co-wives, women married to the same man, seems to offer the prospect of occasional peace. The 'separation' of brothers' wives, on the other hand, threatens endless conflict. Yet this 'separation' is of a particular kind, that which stops a fight or precedes divorce.[32] In light of this definition of 'separation', the 'embrace' that joins co-wives may look more like a wrestling hold than an affectionate hug. In comparing conflicts between women, this proverb also offers a possible explanation for their differences. Co-wives embrace through or because of their husband; the man they share binds them inextricably. He is the source of the affection and resources they wrangle over and, as he thrives or fails, his wives thrive or fail with him. Brothers' wives, in contrast, are separated by their husbands and, in addition, by whatever divides the brothers. Whether brothers cooperate or compete, their wives lack the family ties that bind the their husbands.

Of all conflicts between female kin, proverbs depict the hostility between a woman and her husband's mother as the most intense and long-lasting. To a wife, her mother-in-law seems perpetually ready to interfere or criticize:

(19) /lə-ʿguza ila ma-hədrat-sh thəzz ṛaṣ-ha/
'The mother-in-law, if she doesn't talk, she shakes her head.' (M 106)[33]

In the unlikely event that a mother-in-law is silent, as in this proverb, her gestures express her disapproval. The proverb testifies to the power of a mother-in-law, which is so complete that it need not rely on words. It also expresses something of the resentment of the daughter-in-law, compelled watch for her mother-in-law's merest movements.

If her mother-in-law seems endowed with absolute power, a wife has her pick of responses to that power, mapped out in the following three proverbs:

(20) /ḥəlfət lə-ʿruṣa ma-tḥəbb lə-ḥma ḥətta təbyaḍ l-fəḥma/
'The daughter-in-law swore that she would not like her mother-in-law until charcoal turns white.' (M 106, K 202)[34]

(21) /ḥmat-i lallat-i w-bənt-ha mulat-i/
'My mother-in-law is "my lady" and her daughter is "my mistress." ' (K 201)

(22) /ḥmat-i wzhəh d-dlu hiya ḥarṛa w-wəld-ha ḥlu/
'My mother-in-law, [with the] face of a leather water-bucket, she is bitter but [lit. 'and'] her son is sweet.' (K 200, M 107)

The rancor of proverb (20) is as extreme as that expressed by proverb (17) above, about brothers' wives. The conflict between a woman and her husband's mother, however, has no predictable end in this proverb. If the wife manifests her hostility openly and consistently, it disrupts the entire household and could lead to divorce for the sake of peace. To preserve her marriage, a woman may adopt a conciliatory stance toward her mother-in-law, as suggested by proverb (21). The use of /lalla/ 'my lady' here implies a certain respect: it is the term a servant uses to refer to her mistress. It also is a term of address for a grandmother, mother-in-law, or any other senior woman. Note, however, that the proverb says nothing of affection or cooperation. It describes only the outward signs of respect. In this, it recalls another Arabic proverb, one that advises kissing the hand one cannot bite.[35] If all else fails, the harassed wife can take consolation in proverb (22). The descriptive /wzhəh d-dlu/ 'face of a leather waterbucket' that makes for rhyme in this proverb allows her to let off steam at her tormentor. The proverb also suggests that the principle of complementary distribution underlies the conflict between the two women.[36] Because the mother-in-law possesses all of the hot temper in the family, her son cannot help but be sweet-tempered. And who would change that, even if she could?

In the conflict between a woman and her husband's mother, thus, neither party possesses a guaranteed advantage. Proverbs like (19) and

(21) above, convey the power of a mother-in-law without indicating the total defeat of her daughter-in-law. In some ways, the conflict appears balanced: where one woman relies on experience and status, the other can counter with youth, energy, and the stratagems of (21) and (22). For all of her apparent advantages, then, a mother-in-law may feel her age in this conflict:

(23) /rzhəʿ l-i a ṣəghṛ-i bash nnaki ʿruṣt-i/
'Return to me, my youth, so I can aggravate my daughter-in law.' (K 204)[37]

The poignant wish of this proverb expresses the older woman's sense of handicap. In her day, the proverb suggests, the older woman was more than a match for the younger one. The older woman's wish underlines the paradoxical nature of this conflict. A return to her youth would eliminate her rival by returning to childhood the son who brought this interloper into her life. But it would also return her to the position of harassed daughter-in-law. Note that the woman does not wish to return to her youth—she wants her youth to come back to her. She wants the best of both worlds: the vigor of youth *and* the status of age. She wants the fight to go on.

Proverbs portray the conflict between a wife and her mother-in-law as natural and inevitable. Like the conflict between brothers' wives, however, this war has its occasional cease-fires:

(24) /ana wə-ḥmat-i ka-nəbkiw mən ʿəyn waḥda/
'My mother-in-law and I, we cry from one eye.' (K 196)

The proverb of course depicts "une entente exemplaire."[38] The grue-some image of a single weeping eye implies that only tragedy draws the two women together. They experience their joys and even the dreams described in proverb (12) above separately, but in times of trouble they are united. The shared eye also recalls the other bond they share, a tie through birth or marriage to the same man. The symbolic linkage of eye and man, implicit in proverb (17) above, is more overt in this proverb. The word /ʿəyn/ means 'eye, organ of sight' as well as 'spring, source of water'. In idiomatic expressions, it also refers to the most sensitive part of an object (as in /ʿəyn d-lə-ḵfa/ 'base of the skull') or the most prominent part of a thing (as in /ʿəyn l-luḥ/ 'knot in a board, knot-hole').[39] A man is all of these things to his wife and his mother: he is the eye through which they view the outside world as well as the eye with which they weep; he is the source of affection, resources and of their conflict; he is the sensitive spot in their lives, and injury to him is felt by both of them. In short, he is the most salient element of their shared life.

In Moroccan Arabic proverbs individuals play multiple and, occasionally, conflicting roles. For example, the putative speaker of proverb (12) above, finds himself caught between the personae of husband and son. Further, few family relationships are as clear-cut as the concise, categorical statements of individual proverbs make them appear. A father, no less than a mother, may find his children gratifying as well as disappointing; brothers can be close friends or bitter rivals. Yet it is the relationships of women in the family that proverbs single out for attention. The ambiguous nature of these relationships as portrayed in proverbs serves to underline differences between the interactions of women and those of men in the family.

As noted throughout this paper, proverbs describe women as they negotiate for power in the family. Proverbs take a dim view, however, of any woman's ability to exercise lasting control. She can hardly influence a husband who is seldom home, housework may get the better of her, and her children are likely to resent her when they most need her. The one person she should be most capable of dominating, her son's wife, counters age and experience with youth and strength. There appears to be nothing intrinsic to a woman's status as wife, housekeeper, mother or mother-in-law to tip the balance of an interaction in her favor. Much the same is seen in her other relationships with women in the family. Nothing, for example, differentiates the brothers' wives of proverb (17) above. Neither age, nor wealth, nor ability, resolves or even affects their conflict; only when one woman is reduced to utter misery can they reach any kind of understanding. Because there are no factors to play a decisive role in Moroccan women's interactions, these relationships, at least as their proverbs depict them, are always open to negotiation.

REFERENCES

1. These include proverbs from my fieldwork and from published collections. These collections are: Ernest T. Abdel–Massih, *An Introduction to Moroccan*

Arabic, 2nd ed. (Ann Arbor, MI: University of Michigan Center for Near Eastern and North African Studies, 1982); Muḥammad Ibn ʾAḥmad Ishmāʿū *Miʾat wa-ʾalf mathal: min al-ʾamthāl al-shaʿbiyya al-maghribiyya* ([Rabat]: [Maṭbaʿat al-maʿārif al-djadīda], 1984); Moḥamed Ben Abdellatif Kabbaj, and Mohamed Cherradi El Fadili, *Bāḵa min al-ʾamthāl al-maghribiyya: Un bouquet de proverbes marocains* ([Casablanca]: N.p., 1981); Leila Messaoudi, *ʾAmthāl wa-ʾakwāl maghribiyya: Proverbes et dictons du Maroc* (N.c.: n.p., n.d.); and Edward [Alexander] Westermarck, *Wit and Wisdom in Morocco: A Study of Native Proverbs* (New York: Horace Liveright, 1931).

2. In spite of numerous calls in the literature for the investigation of proverb use in context, few researchers have surmounted the challenges it poses. One notable exception is Mathilde Hain, *Sprichwort und Volkssprache. Ein volkskundlichsoziologische Dorfuntersuchung* (Geissen: Wilhelm Schmitz, 1963).

3. The presence of a proverb in an utterance may be flagged by a phrase such as, in Moroccan Arabic, /ka-ygulu/ 'they say' or /lə–mtəl ka-ygul/ 'the proverb says'. I would suggest, however, that frames like these serve as much to validate or authorize the statement made by the proverb as to mark it as such. And, as Mahgoub notes of Egyptian proverbs, proverbs are not necessarily framed by such phrases. Fatma M. Mahgoub, *A Linguistic Study of Cairene Proverbs*, Language Science Monographs 1 (Bloomington: Indiana University Press, 1968) 1–2.

4. M[ikhail] M[ikhailovich] Bakhtin, "From Notes Made in 1970–71," *Speech Genres and Other Late Essays*, trans. Vern W. McGee, ed. Caryl Emerson and Michael Holquist, University of Texas Press Slavic Ser. 8 (Austin: University of Texas Press, 1986) 146.

5. Rosen defines the process in this way:

> "It was not only that individuals drew on the relations and concepts available to them or even that they could on occasion dicker with one another over their mutual obligations. Rather, the process of bargaining out the terms of their relations, the definition of their situation, and the implications of their attachment were at the heart of the way such ties were conceived and formed."
>
> Lawrence Rosen, *Bargaining for Reality: The Construction of Social Relations in a Muslim Community* (Chicago: University of Chicago Press, 1984) 4.

6. Rosen downplays the effect of status differences on the negotiation process. He does, however, note that one party's possession of overwhelming material or personal advantages may eliminate the possibility of negotiation. Rosen, *Bargaining for Reality* 181–82.

7. Proverb citations in the text are numbered in order of occurrence for the purpose of cross–reference. The transcription of the proverb is based on its transcription in the published source and on Harrell's *Dictionary of Moroccan Arabic*. Richard S[lade] Harrell, *A Dictionary of Moroccan Arabic: Moroccan–*

English, Richard Slade Harrell Arabic Ser. (Washington, DC: Georgetown University Press, 1966).

Proverb translations draw on the source, but are my own compromise between readability and accuracy. In the letter and number combination that follows the translation, the letter identifies the source (A = Abdel-Massih, I = Ishmāʿu, K = Kabbaj and Cherradi, M = Messaoudi, and W = Westermarck). For A, I and W proverbs, the number is that assigned to the proverb in the source; for K and M proverbs it is the page number on which the proverb appears. Page numbers for M refer to the Arabic pagination.

8. The term *fitna* is associated with a verb that means 'to agitate, incite' as well as 'to charm, seduce, bewitch'.

9. For some of the symbolic connotations of the horse in Morocco, see Edward [Alexander] Westermarck, *Ritual and Belief in Morocco*, 2 vols. (1928; New Hyde Park, NY: University Books, 1968) 1: 97.

10. Daisy Hilse Dwyer, *Images and Self-Images in Morocco: Male and Female in Morocco* (New York: Columbia University Press, 1978) 101.

11. Dwyer, *Images and Self-Images* 113.

12. Although the horse in Morocco does not appear to have phallic associations, the sparrow does. According to Westermarck, the sparrow's nest is used only in a charm for butter-churning, but the sparrow itself goes into a recipe for an aphrodisiac. Westermarck, *Ritual and Belief* 2: 298, 341.

13. The same proverb, with minor variations, also appears in Kabbaj and Cherradi, *Bāka* 26.

14. Dwyer, *Images and Self-Images* 23–26.

15. Dwyer, *Images and Self-Images* 17. Sex segregation is breaking down in urban areas, but most of the working women I encountered in urban Morocco in 1988–89 were sheltered in one way or another from contact with men. They worked with children or other women, spent their days shielded by a counter or a uniform, or worked in small offices where traffic was minimal.

16. Dwyer, *Images and Self-Images* 32.

17. /lalla–w–mali/ is an idiomatic expression that Harrell's *Dictionary* translates as 'the easy life'. Kabbaj and Cherradi, and Messaoudi, who give French paraphrases for their material, render it as 'orgies'. My inquiries among Moroccans suggest that the current meaning lies somewhere between these two extremes, hence 'on the town'.

18. The same proverb occurs, with minor variations, in Kabbaj and Cherradi, *Bāka* 121.

19. Hildred Geertz, "The Meaning of Family Ties," *Meaning and Order in Moroccan Society: Three Essays in Cultural Analysis* 315–392 (Cambridge: Cambridge University Press, 1979) 338–39.

20. For extreme examples of a woman's control of goods in the home, see Fatima Mernissi, *Beyond the Veil: Male–Female Dynamics in Modern Muslim Society*, 2nd ed. (Bloomington: Indiana University Press, 1987) 130, 131–32.

21. Dwyer, *Images and Self–Images* 26.
22. Dwyer, *Images and Self–Images* 90.
23. Mernissi, *Beyond the Veil*, 122, 126–27. Geertz points out, however, that the relative contribution of those who participate in the selection of a wife depends on who tells the story. Geertz, "The Meaning of Family Ties" 370–71.
24. Rosen, *Bargaining for Reality* 36.
25. Dwyer, *Images and Self–Images* 88–89
26. "La fille et l'associé de sa mère. (Tout se partager)." Kabbaj and Cherradi, *Bāka* 187.
27. "*yaʿnī ʾanna al-bint ʿinda-mā takbur tuẓāhim ʾumma-hā fī al-malābis wa-al-huliyy wa-ghayri–hā.*" Ishmāʿu 65.
28. Moroccan Arabic has its own version of the well–known Arabic proverb that describes the relation of mother to daughter:

    /ḳləb l-ḳədṛa ʿla fomm-ha wə-l-bənt təshbəh lə-mm-ha/
    'Turn the cook–pot over on its mouth and the daughter resembles her mother.' (I 621)

29. The more familiar Classical Arabic term for 'co–wife', *ḍarra*, is itself ambiguous, as it is derived from or homologous with the verb root meaning 'to hurt, damage'. It is not, however, listed in Harrell's *Dictionary* or Geertz's list of kinship terms. Hildred Geertz, Annex A: Moroccan kinship terms of reference, "The Meaning of Family Ties" *Meaning and Order in Moroccan Society: Three Essays in Cultural Analysis* (Cambridge: Cambridge University Press, 1979) 380–385. The word *ḍarra* (in Moroccan Arabic /ḍəṛṛa/) occurs in only one proverb in the printed sources, Kabbaj and Cherradi, *Bāka* 318.
30. Geertz, "The Meaning of Family Ties" 362.
31. The implicit connection between eye and man in this proverb and in proverb (24) below is explicit in other proverbs that describe the effect of sexual activity on eyesight. See, for example, Westermarck, *Wit and Wisdom* 83–84.
32. Harrell, *Dictionary* 165.
33. Much the same proverb appears as I 499.
34. /ʿrusa/ (Classical Arabic ʿaṛusa) means 'bride'. For years after a woman's marriage, her mother-in-law and other women of that generation may continue to use this term. Geertz, "The Meaning of Family Ties" 361.
35. The Moroccan Arabic version of this proverb is

    /l-ədd ma-təḳdəṛ təḳṭṭəʿ-ha bus-ha/
    'The hand you cannot cut off, kiss it.' (I 433)

36. Suggested by Dwyer, *Images and Self–Images* 59–60.
37. The same proverb occurs, with minor variations, as M 104.
38. Kabbaj and Cherradi, *Bāka* 196.
39. Harrell, *Dictionary* 266–267.

Suggested Readings on Gender
in the Middle East

Nabia Abbot. *Aisha: The Beloved of Mohammed* (Chicago: University of Chicago Press, 1942).

———. "Women and the State in Early Islam, I," *Journal of Near Eastern Studies* 1 (1942): 106–126.

———. "Women and the State in Early Islam, II," *Journal of Near Eastern Studies* 1 (1942): 341–361.

Lila Abu-Lughod. "Islam and the Gendered Discourses of Death," *International Journal of Middle East Studies* 25 (1993): 187–205.

———. *Veiled Sentiments: Honour and Poetry in a Bedouin Society* (Berkeley: University of California Press, 1986).

———. *Writing Women's Worlds: Bedouin Stories* (Berkeley: University of California Press, 1993).

Janet Abu-Lughod and Lucy Amin. "Egyptian Marriage Advertisements: Microcosms of a Changing Society," *Marriage and Family Living* 23 (1961): 127–136.

Evelyne Accad. *Sexuality and War: Literary Masks of the Middle East* (New York: New York University Press, 1990).

Etel Adnan. *The Arab Apocalypse* (Sausalito: Post-Apollo Press, 1989).

———. *Sitt Marie Rose* Sausalito: Post-Appollo Press, 1989).

Janet Afary. "On the Origins of Feminism in Early Twentieth Century Iran," *Journal of Women's History* 1 (1989): 65–87.

Haleh Afshar. "Behind the Veil: the Public and Private Faces of Khomeini's Policies on Iranian Women," in Bina Agarwal ed., *Structures of Patriarchy: State, Community, and Household in Modernising Asia* (London: Zed Books, 1988) pp. 228–247.

Haleh Afshar. *Women, Work and Ideology in the Third World* (New York: Routledge, 1985).

Leila Ahmed. "Arab Culture and Writing Women's Bodies." *Feminist Issues* 9 (1989): 41–55.

———. "Feminism and Feminist Movements in the Middle East, a Preliminary Exploration: Turkey, Egypt, Algeria, People's Democratic Republic of Yemen," *Women's Studies International Quarterly* 5 (1982): 153–168.

———. "Western Ethnocentrism and Perceptions of Harem" *Feminist Studies* 8 (1982): 521–534.

Leila Ahmed. "Women and the Advent of Islam," *Signs* 11 (1986): 665–691.

―――. *Women and Gender in Islam: Historical Roots of a Modern Debate* (New Haven: Yale University Press, 1992).

Salih J. Altoma. "The Emancipation of Women in Contemporary Syrian Literature," in Richard T. Antoun and Donald Quataert, eds., *Syria: Society, Culture and Polity* (Albany: SUNY Press, 1991).

Soraya Altorki. *Women in Saudi Arabia Ideology and Behavior Among the Elite* (New York: Columbia University Press, 1986).

Arab Women in the Field: Studying Your Own Society Soraya Altorki and Camilla F. El-Sohl, eds., (Syracuse: Syracuse University Press, 1988).

Yeşim Arat. "Islamic Fundamentalism and Women in Turkey" *Muslim World* 80 (1990): 17–23.

―――. *The Patriarchal Paradox: Women Politicians in Turkey* (Rutherford: Farleigh Dickinson University Press, 1989).

Margot Badran. "Dual Liberation: Feminism and Nationalism in Egypt, 1870s-1925," *Feminist Issues* 8 (1988): 15–34.

―――. "Islam, Patriarchy, and Feminism in the Middle East." *Trends in History* 4 (1985): 49–71.

―――. "Mothers, Morality, and Nationalism in Early Twentieth-century Egypt," in Rashid Khalidi, Lisa Anderson, Muhammad Muslih, and Reeva S. Simon, eds., *The Origins of Arab Nationalism* (New York: Columbia University Press, 1991).

―――. "Women and Production in the Middle East," *Trends in History* 2 (1982): 59–88.

Margot Badran and Miriam Cooke, eds., *Opening the Gates: A Century of Arab Feminist Writing*. (Bloomington: University of Indiana Press, 1990).

Lois Beck and Nikki Keddie, eds., *Women in the Muslim World* (Cambridge: Harvard University Press, 1978).

Gabriel Baer. "Women and Waqf: An Analysis of the Istanbul Tahrir of 1546," *Asian and African Studies* 17 (1983): 9–28.

Nora Benallegue. "Algerian Women in the Struggle for Independence and Reconstruction," *International Social Science Journal* 35 (1983): 703–717.

Deborah Bernstein. "The Plough Woman Who Cried into the Pots: The Position of Women in the Labor Force in Pre-State Israeli Society" *Jewish Social Studies* 45 (1983): 43–56.

―――. "The Women's Workers' Movement in Pre-State Israel, 1919–39." *Signs* 12 (1987): 454–470.

Marilyn Booth, trans. and ed., *My Grandmother's Cactus: Stories by Egyptian Women* (London: Quartet Books, 1991).

Mounira Charrad. "State and Gender in Maghrib," *Middle East Report* 163 (1990): 19–24.

Miriam Cooke. *Gendering War Talk* (Princeton: Princeton University Press, 1993).

―――. *War's Other Voices: Women Writers in the Lebanese Civil War* (Cambridge: Cambridge University Press, 1988).

Peter C. Dodd. "Youth and Women's Emancipation in the United Arab Republic," *Middle East Journal* 22 (1968): 159–172.

Alan Duden. "Understanding Muslim Households and Families in Late Ottoman Istanbul," *Journal of Family History* 15 (1990): 71–86.

Daisy Hilse Dwyer. *Images and Self-Images: Male and Female in Morocco* (Cambridge: Cambridge University Press, 1978).

Christine Eickelman. "Fertility and Social Change in Oman: Women's Perspectives," *Middle East Journal* 47 (1993): 652–666.

———. *Women and Community in Oman* (New York: New York University Press, 1984).

Giora Eliraz. "Egyptian Intellectuals and Women's Emancipation, 1919–39, " *Asian and African Studies* 16 (1982): 95–120.

Nawal El Saadawi. *The Hidden Face of Eve: Women in the Arab World* (London: Zed Books, 1980).

———. *Memoirs from the Women's Prison* (London: The Women's Press, 1983).

John L. Esposito. *Women in Muslim Family Law* (Syracuse: Syracuse University Press, 1982).

Munira Fakhro. *Women at Work in the Gulf: A Case Study of Bahrain* (New York: Routledge, 1989).

Elizabeth Fernea. *Guests of the Sheik* (Garden City: Doubleday, 1965).

Elizabeth Fernea, ed., *Women and the Family in the Middle East: New Voices of Change* (Austin: University of Texas Press, 1980).

Elizabeth Fernea and Basima Bezirgan, eds., *Middle Eastern Muslim Women Speak* (Austin: University of Texas Press, 1977).

Erika Friedl. *Women of Deh Koh, Lives in an Iranian Village* (Washington, D.C.: Smithsonian Institute Press, 1989).

Sarah Graham-Brown. *Images of Women: the Portrayal of Women in Photography of the Middle East, 1860–1950* (London: Quartet Books, 1988).

Guneli Gun. "The Women in the Darkroom: Contemporary Women Writers in Turkey," *World Literature Today* 60 (1986): 275–279.

Yvonne Haddad. *Women, Religion, and Social Change* (Albany: SUNY Press, 1985).

Sylvia G. Haim. "The Situation of Arab Women in the Mirror of Literature," *Middle Eastern Studies* 17 (1981): 510–530.

Souad Halila. "From Koranic Law to Civil Law: The Emancipation of Tunisian Women Since 1956," *Feminist Issues* 4 (1984): 23–44.

Mervat Hatem. "Economic and Political Liberation in Egypt and the Demise of State Feminism," *International Journal of Middle East Studies* 24 (1992): 231–251.

———. "The Enduring Alliance of Nationalism and Patriarchy in Muslim Personal Status Laws: The Case of Modern Egypt," *Feminist Issues* 6 (1986): 19–43.

———. "Class and Patriarchy as Competing Paradigms for the Study of Middle Eastern Women," *Comparative Studies in Society and History* (1987): 811–818.

———. "The Politics of Sexuality and Gender in Segregated Patriarchal Systems: The Case of Eighteenth- and Nineteenth-Century Egypt," *Feminist Studies* 12 (1986): 251–274.

———. "Through Each Other's Eyes: Egyptian, Levantine-Egyptian and European Women's Images of Themselves and Each Other," *Women's Studies International* Forum 12 (1989): 183–198.

Nadia Hijab. *Womanpower: The Arab Debate on Women at Work* (Cambridge: Cambridge University Press, 1988).

Valerie Hoffman-Ladd. "Polemics on the Modesty and Segregation of Women in Contemporary Egypt," *International Jounral of Middle East Studies* 19 (1987): 23–50.

Kumari Jayawardena. *Feminism and Nationalism in the Third World* (London: Zed Books, 1986).

Ronald C. Jennings. "Women in the Early Seventeenth-Century Ottoman Judicial Records: The Sharia Court of Anatoliam Kayseri," *Journal of the Economics and Social History of the Orient* 28 (1975): 53–114.

Deniz Kandiyoti. "Bargaining With Patriarchy," *Gender and Society* 2 (1988): 274–290.

————. "Emancipated but Unliberated? Reflections on the Turkish Case," *Feminist Studies* 13 (1987): 317–338.

Deniz Kandiyoti, ed., *Women, Islam and the State* (Philadelphia: Temple University Press, 1990).

Nikki Keddie. "The Past and Present of Women in the Muslim World," *Journal of World History* 1 (1990): 77–108.

Nikki Keddie and B. Baron, eds., *Women in Middle Eastern History: Shifting Boundaries in Sex and Gender* (New Haven: Yale University Press, 1991).

Sahar Khalifah. *Wild Thorns* Trevor LeGassick and Elizabeth Fernea, Trans. (London: al-Saqi Books, 1985).

Peter Knauss. *The Persistence of Patriarchy: Class, Gender and Ideology in Twentieth Centry Algeria* (New York: Praeger Press, 1987).

Marnia Lazreg. "Feminism and Difference: The Perils of Writing as a Woman on Women in Algeria," *Feminist Studies* 14 (1988): 81–107.

————. "Gender and Politics in Algeria: Unraveling the Religious Paradigm," *Signs* 15 (1990): 755–780.

Anh Nga Longva. "Kuwaiti Women at a Crossroads: Privileged Development and the Constraints of Ethnic Stratification," *International Journal of Middle Eastern Studies* 25 (1993): 443–456.

Arlene MacLeod. *Accomodating protest: Working Women, the New Veiling and Change in Cairo* (New York: Columbia University Press, 1990).

Shireen Mahdavi. "Women and Ideas in Qajar Iran," *Asian and Africa Studies* 9 (1985): 17–27.

————. "Women and the Shii Ulama in Iran," *Middle Eastern Studies* 19 (1983): 17–27.

Vanessa Maher. *Women and Property in Morocco* (New York: Cambridge University Press, 1975).

Malti-Douglas, Fedwa. *Woman's Body, Woman's Word: Gender Discourses in Arabo-Islamic Writing* (Princeton: Princeton University Press, 1991).

Abraham Marcus. "Men, Women and Property: Dealers in Real Estate in 18th Century Aleppo," *Journal of the Economic and Social History of the Orient* 26 (1983): 137–163.

Afaf Lutfi al-Sayyid Marsot. "Women and Social Change," in Georges Sabah, ed., *The Modern Economic and Social History of the Middle East in its World Context* (Cambridge: Cambridge University Press, 1989).

Billie Melman. *Women's Orients: English Women and the Middle East, 1718–1918* (Ann Arbor: University of Michigan Press, 1992).

Fatima Mernissi. *Beyond the Veil: Male-Female Dynamics in a Modern Muslim Society* revised edition. (Bloomington: Indiana University Press, 1987).

Mona Mikhail. *Images of Arab Women: Fact and Fiction* Washington, D.C.: Three Continents Press, 1978).

Farzaneh Milani. *Veils and Words: The Emerging Voices of Iranian Women Writers* (Syracuse: Syracuse University Press, 1992).

Naila Minai. *Women in Islam: Tradition and Transition in the Middle East* (New York: Seaview Press, 1981).

Chandra Mohanty. "Under Western Eyes: Feminist Scholarship and Colonial Discourses," *Feminist Review* 30 (1988): 61–88.

Chandra Mohanty, Ann Russo, and Lourdes Torres, eds., *Third World Women and the Politics of Feminism* (Bloomington: Indiana University Press, 1991).

Afsaneh Najmabadi, ed., *Women's Autobiographies in Contemporary Iran*. (Cambridge: Harvard University Press, 1990).

Guity Nashat, ed., *Women and Revolution in Iran* (Boulder, CO: Westview Press, 1983).

Cynthia Nelson. "Old Wine, New Bottles: Reflections and Projections Concerning Research on Women in Middle Eastern Studies," in E. L. Sullivan and T. Y. Ismael, eds., *The Contemporary Study of the Arab World* (Edmonton: University of Alberta Press, 1991).

——. "Public and Private Politics: Women in the Middle Eastern World," *American Ethnologist* 1 (1974): 551–563.

——. "The Voices of Doria Shafik: Feminist Consciousness in Egypt, 1940–60," *Feminist Issues* 6 (1986): 16–31.

Emelie A. Olson. "Muslim Identity and Secularism in Contemporary Turkey: 'The Headscarf Debate,' " *Anthropological Quarterly* 58 (1985): 161–169.

Aihwa Ong. "Colonialism and Modernity: Feminist Representations of Women in Non-Western Societies," *Inscriptions* 3/4 (1988): 79–93.

Ivy Papps. "Women, Work, and Well-being in the Middle East: an Outline of the Relevant Literature," *Journal of Development Studies* 28 (1992): 595–615.

Julie Peteet. *Gender in Crisis: Women and the Palestinian Resistance Movement* (New York: Columbia University Press, 1991).

Leslie P. Pierce. *The Imperial Harem: Women and Sovereignty in the Ottoman Empire* (New York: Oxford University Press, 1993).

Nesta Ramazani. "Arab Women in the Gulf," *Middle East Journal* 39 (1985): 258–276.

——. "Behind the Veil: the Status of Women in Revolutionary Iran," *Journal of South Asia and Middle Eastern Studies* 4 (1980): 27–36.

——. "Women in Iran: the Revolutionary Ebb and Flow," *Middle East Journal* 47 (1993): 409–428.

Alifaa Rifaat. *Distant View of a Minaret* , trans., Denis Johnson-Davies. (London: Quartet Books, 1983).

Elizabeth Sanasarian. *The Women's Rights Movement in Iran: Mutiny, Appeasement and Repression from 1900 to Khomeini* (New York: Praeger Press, 1982).

Bouthaina Shaaban. *Both Right and Left Handed: Arab Women Talk about Their Lives* (London: The Women's Press, 1988).

Huda Shaarawi. *Harem Years, The Memoirs of an Egyptian Feminist* (New York: The Feminist Press, the City University of New York, 1987).

Irvin Schick. "Representing Middle Eastern Women: Feminism and Colonial Discourse," *Feminist Studies* 16 (1990): 345–380.

Rokhsareh S Shoaee. "The Mujahid Women of Iran: Reconciling 'Culture' and 'Gender,' " *Middle East Journal* 41 (1987): 519–537.

Gertrude Stern. "The First Women Converts in Early Islam," *Islamic Culture* (1939): 290–305

———. *Marriage in Early Islam* (London: The Royal Asiatic Society, 1939).

Earl L. Sullivan. *Women in Egyptian Public Life* (Syracuse: Syracuse University Press, 1986).

Azar Tabari and Nahid Yeganeh, eds., *In the Shadow of Islam: The Women's Movement in Iran* (London: Zed Press, 1982).

Mary Ann Tetreault. "Civil Society in Kuwait: Protected Spaces and Women's Rights," *Middle East Journal* 47 (1993): 275–291.

James Toth. "Pride, Purdah or Paychecks: What Maintains the Gender Division of Labor in Rural Egypt?" *International Journal of Middle East Studies* 23 (1991): 213–236.

Fettouma Touati. *Desperate Spring: Lives of Algerian Women* (New York: Interlink, 1989).

Nahid Toubia, ed., *Women of the Arab World* (London: Zed Press, 1988).

Binnaz Toprak. "Religion and Turkish Women," in *Women in Turkish Society* , N. Abadan-Unat, ed., (Leiden: E. J. Brill, 1981) 281–292.

Judith Tucker. *Women in Nineteenth Century Egypt* (Cairo: American University Press, 1986).

Susan E. Waltz. "Another View of Feminine Networks: Tunisian Women and the Development of Political Efficacy," *International Journal of Middle East Studies* 22 (1990): 21–36.

Judith R. Wegner. "The Status of Women in Jewish and Islamic Marriage and Divorce Law," *Harvard Women's Law Journal* 5 (1982): 1–34.

Unni Wikan. *Behind the Veil in Arabia: Women in Oman* (Berkeley: University of California Press, 1991).

William C. Young. "The Kaba, Gender, and the Rites of Pilgrimage," *International Journal of Middle East Studies* 25 (1993): 285–300.

Sherifa Zuhur. *Revealing Reveiling: Islamist Gender Ideology in Contemporary Egypt.* (Albany: SUNY, 1992).

Index

Abortion, Turkish law, 65
Abu-Lughod, Lila, 13
Abuse: Iran, 92; Turkish campaign against, 103, 104, 107, 108; Turkish law on, 65
Accad, Evelyne, 158
Activism. *See* Protest
Adams, Mary Louise, 7
Adultery: dress "provoking," Morocco, 52; Turkish law on, 65
Ahmed, Leila, 13
Algerian culture and society: colonialism, 28; women's rights, 153–55
Algerian Revolution, 144, 152–53
American influence, gender identification, 28
Anthropology: feminist, 81–83; interaction with subject, 97–98; self-disclosure, 96, 97; women in Cairo, 174; women's issue handling dilemma, 95. *See also* Ethnography
Arabic literature: Hebrew literature and, 170; proverbs reflecting Moroccan family life, 141, 201–15; songs on Intifada, 125–28
Arabs: in Hebrew literature, 169–72; in Israel, status, 122; Jewish relations in view of conflicts, 169–72; Palestinian in Hebrew Literature, 168, 169; Palestinian in Hebrew literature, 141; prostitute metaphor, 140, 167, 168; and war, women, 140, 144–63
Arab wars, women's experience, 144–63
Arab world: studies, 10, 12; systematic war, 155; war myth, 148, 169

Arat, Yeşim, 82
Arat, Zehra F., 24–25
Army service: Jews in Israel, 117, 118, 121–22; women soldiers, 160, 161, 162
Ashrawi, Hanan, 162
Atatürk, Mustafa Kemal: on clothing, Western influence, 61; education of women, 59; education of women, administrative policy, 67–71; legal reform, 25, 28, 57–59; legal reform, policy, 62–67; legal reform, speeches, 59–62; on veiling, 61, 62
Autobiography: Behbahani, Simin, 31; Intifada, 156; Persico, Rachel, 82; voices of Middle Eastern women, 10–11
Awwad, Taufiq, 147

Babism, 37
Badran, Margot, 10, 11
Bain, Donald, 148
Bakhtin, Mikhail M., 202
Banking in collective community, Egypt, 176, 188–91
Baron, Beth, 43
Baudrillard, Jean, 151
Beauvoir, Simone de, 8
Beck, Lois, 10
Behbahani, Simin, poetry, 26, 31–39
Bergman, Elizabeth, 141
Bernstein, Debbi, 114
Bezirgan, Basima Q., 9
Bible in Jewish law, 120, 121
Boupacha, Djamila, 153

Bourdieu, Pierre, 8
Butler, Judith, 151

Capitalism, influence on Middle Eastern society, 28
Casualties from Intifada demonstrations, 130
Chedid, Andree, 158
Cherradi El Fadili, Mohamed, 209
Children: day care, Israel, 119; education, Egypt, 182–84; Intifada participation, 131, 132; kibbutz upbringing experience, 115–16; in Moroccan proverbs, 204, 205, 207–10, 215; parental responsibility, Egypt, 181
Clothing: cross-dressing in war situation, 140, 153, 167, 168; hijab and djellaba, veiling, 40–42, 47, 48, 50–55; Intifada, headscarves and masks, 129, 131, 157; nudity concept in Morocco, 52; uniform in Turkish schools, 71; Western influence, Turkey, 61–62
Cold War, 146
Colonialism in Middle Eastern society, 28
Conflict resolution: Cairo family life, 178, 179; Moroccan family, proverbs, 210–15
Cooke, Miriam, 10, 140, 141
Coppola, Francis Ford, 150

Daneshevar, Simin, 11, 12
Debeche, Djamila, 154
Deh Koh, (village) Iran, 13, 14, 82, 86–98
Demographics: Iran, 87; Turkey, 24
Divorce: Jewish law, Israel, 120; legal policy, Turkey, 63, 64, 65; Moroccan law, 52
Djebar, Assia, 144, 154
Domination: Atatürk's Turkey, 25, 63; male in Iran, 91, 92; male in Israel, 116, 122; male in Morocco, 44, 45, 55; power and, 8; proverbs, 206, 215; Western influence in Iran, 38

Downs, Laura, 7, 8
Dress. *See* Clothing
Dulaymi, Lutfiya al-, 159, 160
During, Simon, 151
Düzkan, Ayşe, 103

Economy: collective community, 185–94; collective community, business, 186; collective community, finances, 176, 188–91; collective community, goods and services, 182, 184, 193
Education of women: administration policy, Turkey, 67–71, 72; Iran village, 88; Israel, 115; Moroccan proverbs, 206; public life, Turkey, 102; vocational curriculum, Turkey, 68, 69, 70
Egyptian culture and society, 11, 12, 24; collective community, 175, 176, 178, 182; collective community, goods and services, 184, 185, 193; collective community, political economy, 185–94; familial ethos, 178, 179, 191; family, 185–86, 191; women, politics and power in Cairo, 142, 174–94
Egyptian government: curtailing freedoms, 177, 178; education policy, 182, 183, 186; manipulating policy of, 179, 180, 187
Engels, Friedrich, 3, 4
English people: travel in Middle East, 13; working class formation, 4
Enloe, Cynthia, 156
Esposito, John, 13
Ethics: Arab in Hebrew literature, 169; Cairo family life, 178, 179
Ethnography: evaluative views on women, 94; feminist, 81–83; fieldwork style, 95, 96; Middle East, 13–14; Middle Eastern societies, 180; narrative approach, 91; procedure, 86, 88, 89; traditional, 94; village women in Iran study, 85–98. *See also* Anthropology

Exile experience in Middle Eastern writings, 12, 83
Experience: Arab women and Arab wars, 144–63; fragmentation, social science approach, 86; growing up in Israel, 113–22; in occupied Palestine, Intifada, 123–34; reconstructing gender in Middle East, 1–4, 6, 14–15; women and politics in Cairo, 175; women and power in Cairo, 142

Farman-Farmaian, Sattareh, 10
Farrokhzad, Forugh, 12
Feminism: anthropology, 81–83; ethnography, 81–83; gender identity primacy, 7, 81; Iran, 37–38; patriarchal hegemony emphasis, 1; Persian literature, 37; Third-world women, 5–6; Turkey, 25; Turkey, Kemalist reforms, 58, 72, 101–2; Turkey, liberalism, 105–6; Turkey, socialist, 104; Turkey, women's movement, 25, 58, 72, 102–5; voice and experience standpoint, 3, 10, 11; women's studies, 82
Fernea, Elizabeth, 9
Foucault, Michel, 8, 43
French influence, gender identification, 28
Friedl, Erika, 13–14, 81, 82
Fussell, Paul, 146, 148, 149, 157

Gender: concepts of, 124; construction of, 93; defined, 2; studying of, 81, 82
Gender roles: Algerian revolution, 153; Cairo study, 174, 177–78; codified in Moroccan society, 40, 43–45; complementarity in Moroccan society, 42–45; education administration policy, Turkey, 67–71; engendering respect, Morocco, 53; equality, Iran, 92; equality, Turkey, 59–60, 63, 65, 104; ethnographic approach, 91–92; Ghazal, 32, 33; Gypsy (Kowli), 36, 37; in Hebrew literature, 168, 170; ideology matter,

167; inequality, Israeli jobs, 118–19; inequality, Israeli kibbutz, 114, 115; Intifada, 124, 127–28; Intifada, complementary, 125; Intifada, ritual, 128–34; legal reform policy, Turkey, 62–65; proverbs, 203–6; proverbs, cited, 204–14; separation in Morocco, 47–48; suicide, 90; village life in Iran, 85–98; in war situation, 158; in war situation, change, 156–57; in war situation, cross-dressing, 140, 153; in war situation, Israel, 117–18
Gilbert, Sandra, 154
Goods and services: distribution in Cairo, 182, 184, 193; opposition movements exploiting, 185
Gubar, Susan, 154
Gusfield, Joseph, 189
Gypsy (Kowli): gender in Persian poetry, 26; Persian literature, 36–39

Hall, Stuart, 7
Hammudi, Basim Abd al-Hamid, 147
Hanley, Lynne, 145, 149
Hanniff, Nesha, 178
Harding, Sandra, 2
Harem life, 11
Hebrew literature: Arab in, 141, 168–72; dead texts revitalized, 141, 168
Heglund, Mary, 96
Helie-Lucas, Marie-Aimée, 155
Hessini, Leila, 26, 27
Higonnet, Margaret, 152
Hijab: compared to veil, 42; and djellaba, veiling in Morocco, 40–42, 47, 48, 50–55; religious significance in contemporary context, 51–55; symbolic significance, 41–42, 47, 50, 54
Historicity and experience, 4
Honor: Intifada, 125, 126, 128, 133; in Iranian society, 90; in Moroccan society, 52, 53
hooks, bell, 156
Hudson, Leila, 82, 83

Human rights: Egypt, 178; Palestinians in occupied territories, 121
Hussein, Saddam, 159

Identity: collective, Cairo, 175, 176, 179; concepts of, 6–8, 86, 92, 93; fashioning of, 2, 24, 27, 28, 81; fashioning of, Persian poetry, 26, 37, 38; hijab and djellaba, veiling in Morocco, 40–42, 51–52, 54; national, 23, 83; reconstructing gender in the Middle East, 1–4, 7, 15; sexual, 23; social science research, 85, 86
Idil, 105
Individuation and identity, 7, 86, 92
Inner city drug wars, 152
Intifada, 82, 83; coming of age in occupied Palestine, 123–34; family participation, 128–32; literature on, 144, 156; metaphorical sense, 140, 141, 155; name origin, 156; rituals of confrontation and manhood, 128–34; songs, 125–28; war status, 155
Iranian culture and society: ethnographic study, village life, 13–14, 82, 85–98; Khomeini's influence, 28; literature, 11, 12; self-constructions of women, 28; suicide, 89–90; villagers' stance, 86; Western influence, 30, 38
Iranian literature. *See* Persian literature
Iran–Iraq War: literature, 144, 146, 147, 159–61; propaganda, 159, 160
Ishma'u, Ahmad, 209, 210
Islam: gender roles under, 91; history of women, 13; interest-free loans, Egypt, 190; marriage and family, Turkey, 63; social implications in Morocco, 49–51, 54; and veiling in Morocco, 41–42, 54; women's place, Turkey, 108, 109; women's role changes under, 24–28
Israel: growing up in, 82, 83, 113–22; myth deflation, 82, 113–14, 117
Israel history: occupied territories, 121; occupied territories, language issue,

141, 168, 169; occupied territories, Palestinian Intifada, 123–34; occupied territories, prostitute metaphor, 140, 167, 168
Israeli army: anecdote on Arab impersonation, cross-dressing, 140, 167, 168; Intifada clashes, 128–30, 131, 133; Jews in, 117, 118, 121–22; myth about, 117; women, 117
Israeli culture and society: army service, 117, 118, 121–22; Hebrew literature reflecting, 170–72; kibbutz life, 113–16; male domination, 116, 122; patriarchal democracy, 113, 121, 122; views on Intifada demonstrations, 130; women writers, 155

Jawwad, Abdul, 132
Jayawardena, Kumari, 13
Jewish law: Israel, 120–21
Jews: Arab relations in view of conflicts, 169–72; army service, Israel, 117, 118, 121–22; growing up in Israel, 113–22; kibbutz life, 113–16; oppression of, 113
Jones, Kathleen, 4
Journals of Turkish women's movement, 103–6

Kabbaj, Mohamed Ben Abdellatif, 209
Kandiyoti, Deniz, 13
Keddie, Nikki, 10, 43
Khalifa, Sahar, 144, 157
Khomeini, Ruhollah (Ayatollah), 28
Kibbutz: communal housing for children, 115; growing up in, 113–16; pioneer mythology, 114
Kinship: Cairo family life, 178; Cairo financial transaction, 188; Intifada, 125, 126, 127; Morocco, 141, 142; Morocco, conflict resolution, 210–15; Morocco, proverbs, 201–15
Koppel, Ted, 151
Kowli (gypsy): Persian literature, 36–39
Kuttab, Daoud, 131

Lakoff, George, 150
Language: metaphor, Hebrew, 168, 169, 172; military metaphor, 139–41; proverb, 203, 209–10; revitalizing of dead, 141, 168
Laquer, Thomas, 23
Latin America, 175; movements, 176
Lebanese, 158
Lebanese Civil War, 147, 157–58
Lebanon, 147, 158, 161
Legal aspects: codified roles in Moroccan society, 40, 43–45, 52, 206
Legal reform: adequacy of, Turkey, 102; and feminist writings, 82; Jewish law in Israel, 120–21; women's issues, Turkey, 25, 101–2, 105; women's movement, Turkey, 100–110; women's rights, Turkey, 57–59, 101–2; women's rights, Turkey, policy, 62–67; women's rights, Turkey, rhetoric, 59–62; working women, Israel, 119, 120
Lessing, Doris, 156
Literary characters in Hebrew literature, 170
Love poetry, Ghazal, 32–33, 35

Malti-Douglas, Fedwa, 13
Marcus, Abraham, 12
Marriage: adultery provoked by dress, Morocco, 52; Cairo customs, 181–82, 189–90; Cairo customs, financial transaction, 142, 189–90; conflict resolution, Moroccan proverbs, 210–15; co-wives, proverb, 212; divorce grounds, Morocco, 52; endogamous, proverb, 211; family, division of labor, Turkey, 60, 63, 64; family life in Morocco, 43–45, 47; gender roles, proverbs, 203–6; Jewish law, Israel, 120–21; legal policy, Turkey, 63, 64; mother-in-law role, proverbs, 208, 212–14; polygamous, proverb, 210; working outside the home, Morocco, 45–48; working women, 89

Marx, Karl, 3, 4
Media in war reality and representation, 151, 156
Meir, Golda, 122
Melman, Billie, 13
Memories: as defining factor, 89; journal writings, 105
Metaphor: Hebrew language, 168, 169; Intifada, 140, 141, 155; military, 139–41, 150, 155; occupied territories, language, 168, 169, 172; occupied territories, prostitute anecdote, 140, 167, 168
Middle Eastern culture and society: anthropology, 95; capitalism, 28; colonialism, 28; experience role in reconstructing gender, 1–4, 6, 14–15; identity, 1–4, 6–8, 15, 82; industrialization, 23, 24; multiplicity of voices, 9–14; patriarchy, 23, 54, 58, 59; population growth, 24; power, 1–4, 8, 15; reconstructing gender, 92, 93; reconstructing gender, organization of material, 14–15; tradition, 1, 3, 4, 5–6, 14; voice role in reconstructing gender, 1–3, 9–14
Middle Eastern history: Muslim, Islam, 23–25; women's role, 12–13
Migdal, Joel, 179
Milani, Farzaneh, 11, 26
Mohanty, Chandra Talpade, 5–6, 7
Moroccan culture and society, 26, 27; family life, public and private space, 43–45, 47, 205, 207; gender roles in public and private space, 42–45, 51–55, 205, 207; hijab and djellaba, veiling, 40–42, 47, 48, 50–55; honor and respect, 52, 53, 213; Islamic practice, 49–51, 54; proverbs reflecting, 141, 201–15; working outside the home, 45–48
Morris, Benny, 114
Morrison, Toni, 139–40
Motherhood: Intifada, 140; Intifada songs, 127; Israel, 115; Israel, single

Motherhood (*Continued*)
mothers, 119; marriage negotiation, proverb, 208; power of, 142; power of, Moroccan proverbs, 207–10; Turkey, 60; in war situations, 140, 156, 160, 162
Mubarak, Hosni, 180
Mudwanna, Moroccan Personal Status Code, 40, 44–45
Muslims: Shi'ite, village life in Iran, 87, 93; veiling, 26, 41–42, 48, 51, 53
My Michael, 170–72
Myth: character of, 82; deflating of, 82; equality in Israel, 114; Israeli army, 117; kibbutz institution, 113; kibbutz institution, pioneers, 114; Palestine as empty land, 113–14; war, 141, 147, 148, 149, 152, 169
Mythology, Gypsy (Kowli), 36–39

Narration: ethnographic approach, 91; Intifada songs, 127
Nasrallah, Emily, 157
National identity, 23, 83
Nationalism, Turkey, 58, 59, 60
Neotraditionalism: Algeria after revolution, 154, 155; Persian literature, 32, 35, 38

O'Donnell, Guilermo, 107
Ong, Aihwa, 5–6
Organizations of feminist activism, Turkey, 103, 104
Orientalism, 5
Oz, Amos, 170, 172

Palestine: empty land myth, 113–14; Intifada, Israel relations, 123–34
Palestinians, 83; gender roles, 124–25; human rights in occupied territories, 121; Intifada, 123–34; Intifada, rite of passage, 130–31; language, 168; male in Hebrew literature, 141; war literature by women, 155–57, 158, 161. *See also* Arabs

Palestinian uprising. *See* Intifada
Parenting: family responsibility, Egypt, 181; kibbutz life replacing, 116
Paternalism in Atatürk's Turkey, 25
Patriarchy, 23; Algeria, 153; feminism emphasis, 1; Islam, 109; Israel, 113, 122; Palestine, 124; power, 3; reinforcement issue, 82; Turkey, 58, 59, 67, 72, 102, 109, 110
Patronization of women during Iran–Iraq war, 159, 160
Peattie, Lisa, 185
Persian Gulf War, 151
Persian literature: Behbahani, Simin, 31–39; Gypsy (Kowli), 36–39; modernity, 30–31
Persico, Rachel, 82, 83
Poetics: elegy, 33; Intifada songs, 125–28; ode, Ghazal, 31–33, 35; proverbs, 204–14; proverbs, rhyme, 213; proverbs, simile, 204; war poem, 148
Political science research approach, 174, 175, 177
Polygamy: ban in Turkey, 63; Moroccan proverb, 210
Power: defined, 8; family enterprise affording, Cairo, 186; reconstructing gender in the Middle East, 1–4, 15, 93; religion in Israel, 122; symbolic, 139; women bringing up children in kibbutz, 116; women in Cairo, networking, 142, 175, 176, 178, 180, 181–85, 192–93; women in Morocco, proverbs, 142, 201, 203, 206–8, 211–15
Propaganda about Iran–Iraq War, 159, 160
Prostitute as metaphor for military occupation, 140, 157, 167, 168
Protest: Intifada, 123–34; Iran—Iraq War, 161; Jewish Israelis, 121; Lebanese Civil War, 157–58; organizations, Turkey, 103, 104; over family reproduction threats, 189; support

from goods and services provision, 185

Proverbs: conflict resolution, 210–15; meaning and definition problems, 202–3; Moroccan family life, 141, 201–15; motherhood, 207–10; ruling the household, 206–7; symbols, 204, 214

Qajar dynasty, 10–11
Qur'an: gender equality, 46, 108; veiling, 26, 48

Race relations in Hebrew literature, 170–72
Rassam, Amal, 180
Rein, Martin, 185
Religion: Israel, 122; Jewish law and, 120–21, 122
Research procedure: approach to issues dilemma, 95; ethnographer, 88, 89, 90; on gender, 91; political science approach, 174, 175, 177; social science approach, 85, 86; veiling in Morocco study, 41; women in Cairo, politics and power, 174–75, 187
Respect in Moroccan society, 53, 54, 213
Rifaat, Alifa, 12
Ritual: Intifada, 128–34; Intifada, rite of passage, 130–31; village women in Iran, 94
Rosen, Lawrence, 203
Ruddick, Sara, 158
Rules of the game in Cairo politics, 179
Rushdie, Salman, 167

Salman, Suhayla, 159, 160
Samman, Ghada, 158
Satire on gender roles in war situations, 160
Saudi Arabian culture and society, 12
Schmitter, Philippe C., 107
Schwartzkopf, Norman, 151

Scobey, David, 8
Scott, Joan, 2, 4
Self-worth, identity and, 6, 54, 86
Sexual identity, 23
Sexuality: Arab in Hebrew literature, 172; avoidance by subjects in Iran ethnographic study, 96–97; Intifada song, 128; Moroccan proverbs, 206; prostitute as metaphor for military occupation, 140, 167, 168; segregated education controlling, 71; sensitivity to, Egypt, 189; taboo, Palestinian, 131; women's dress provoking men, 52; women's dress reflecting neutrality, 62, 71
Shaarawi, Huda, 11
Shammas, Anton, 140, 141
Sharfman, Dafnah, 120
Short story: Hebrew literature, 169; Intifada, 156; voices of Middle Eastern women, 12, 13; war experience of Arab women, 145
Singerman, Diane, 142
Smith, Dorothy, 2, 3
Social science research approach, 85, 86
Songs, Intifada, 125–28
Southgate, Minoo, 12
Spivak, Gayatri, 5, 6
Stallybrass, Peter, 139
Steedman, Carolyn, 6
Storytelling: ethnographic approach, 91; folktale, 95; Persian literature, 35–36; war experience, 144, 147, 148
Suicide in Iran, 89–90

Tahir, Umm, 142, 143, 181
Taj os-Saltanah, Khatirat-i, 11
Talib, Aliya, 145, 159, 160
Tamari, Salim, 133
Teenager Intifada participation, 131
Tekeli, 66
Television and war reality and representation, 151
Theater, war as, 151, 156

Third World: feminism, 81; political exclusion, 178; public goods production, 182; reconstructing gender in Middle East, 1, 3–7, 10; tradition, 5–6
Thomas, Gareth, 147
Thompson, E.P., 4
Torun, Şule, 100, 102
Tradition: complementary gender roles, 125; ethnographic study, 94, 96; Intifada and, 124, 128, 132; male war experience, 158; Palestinian women, 133; Persian literature, 30–32; reconstructing gender in the Middle East, 1, 3, 4, 5–6, 14, 94; Turkish education, 68, 70; Turkish legal reform, 101; Turkish women, 58, 59, 72; use of term, 125; veiling in Morocco, 42, 55; villager in Iran, 86
Tucker, Judith, 24
Turkey: democratic society and women's movement, 106–8, 110; education administration policy, 67–71, 72; legal reform, 57–59; legal reform, policy framework, 62–67; legal reform, rhetorical framework, 59–62; legal reform, women's movement, 25, 100–110; myth deflation, 82; nationalism, 58, 59, 60; public administration, 66; women professionals, 57, 60; women's issues, 24–25, 28, 101–2, 105; women's rights, 57–62, 62–67, 101–2, 103, 108

Veiling: Atatürk on practice, 61, 62; ban in Turkey, 62; choice and tradition in Morocco, 40–42, 47, 50, 54–55; clarification of term, 41; in combat situation, 154; compared to hijab, 42; feminist writings, 11, 25; history and practice, 24, 26–27, 28; liberating aspect, 50, 54; symbolism, 47, 53; Western influence on practice, 24
Vietnam War, 150
Village life: Iran ethnographic study, 85–98; urban life tied to, 97

Virginity in Turkish law, 64
Virilio, Paul, 150, 156
Vocational education for women, Turkey, 68, 69, 70
Voice: Arab women on war, 162; feminist women's groups, Turkey, 105–6; reconstructing gender in Middle East, 1–3, 9–15

Wages: inequality, Israel, 114–15, 118; teachers, Egypt, 183
War: bombing reality and representation, 151; media and, 151, 156; mystic boundaries, 149–50, 151; myth, 141, 147, 148, 149, 152, 169; shifting attitudes, locus, 146; as theater, 151, 156
War experience: Arab women of Arab wars, 144–63; Israeli women, 117; Middle Eastern writings, 12, 83, 141, 144–63; military metaphor, 139–41, 150
War literature by Arab women, 144–63
War poetry, 148
Western influence: Persian literature, 30, 38; veiling practice, 24, 54
Westernization, Turkey, 58, 61–62, 101
Western views: competition in gender roles, 43; tradition in Third-World women, 5–6
White, Allon, 139
Williams, Raymond, 5
Women: acting in place of men, 153; activism, Jewish Israelis, 121; anthropological approach to issues dilemma, 95; army service, Israel, 117; bringing up children in kibbutz, 116; concealment in Moroccan proverbs, 205; conflicting policy toward, 24–28; critical of Iran—Iraq War, 159–61; education. *See* Education of women; in Egyptian economy, 176; evaluative views, 93, 94; experience, 1–4, 6, 14–15; experience, Arab wars, 144–63; experience, growing up in Israel, 113–22; experience, village life

in Iran, 89; family life in Morocco, proverbs, 201–15; financial status, Cairo, 176, 186–92; hijab and djellaba, veiling in Morocco, 40–42, 47, 48, 50–55; identity, 1, 2, 4, 6–8, 15; identity in Persian poetry, 37, 38; Intifada, 128, 132–33, 155–57; networking power and politics in Egyptian society, 175, 176, 177–80, 181–85, 192–93; power, 1–4, 8, 15; power, Cairo, 142, 174–94; power, Morocco, proverbs, 142, 201, 203, 206–8, 211–15; race relations in Hebrew literature, 170–72; relationships between, proverbs, 203, 208–15; tradition, 1, 4, 5–6, 14; village life in Iran, 87; voice, 1–3, 9–15; voice, Arab women on war, 162

Women's movement: feminism and anthropology, 81; influencing Middle Eastern women's studies, 9–10; Turkey, 25, 66, 72, 100–110; Turkey, liberalism, 105–6; Turkey, redemocratization, 106–8; Turkey, secularism, 108–10

Women's rights: Iran, 92; Israeli job equality, 116, 119–20; Turkey, 57–59; Turkey, legal reform, 59–62, 101–2, 103; Turkey, legal reform policy, 62–67

Women's studies, 15; feminism, 82; multiplicity of voices in Middle East, 9–14; politics and power in Cairo, 174–94; proverbs reflecting gender and conflict in Moroccan family, 201–2, 215; reconstructing gender in the Middle East, organization of material, 14–15; social scientific writing, 91; veiling of urban women in Morocco, 40, 41; village life in Iran, ethnographic study, 85–98; war experience, 141, 144–63; working women in Egypt, 186, 187

Women's suffrage, Turkey, 57, 66, 101

Working class, British, 4

Working women: Egypt, 180, 187, 192; Egypt, domestic labor, 187–88; Egypt, family enterprise, 186; Egypt, teachers, 183; Iran village, 88; Iran village, married, 89; Israel, 117, 118–20; Israel, wages, 114–15, 118; Israeli kibbutz, 114–15; Morocco, 45–48, 206; Palestinians, 133; Turkey, 64, 72; Turkey, legal restriction, 65–66, 72; Turkey, opportunity space, 101, 102; Turkey, organizations, 103, 104; Turkey, preparation, 68; Turkey, professional, 57, 102

World War II, 146

Yizhar, S., 169